The Films of Derek Jarman

The Films of Derek Jarman

——— WILLIAM PENCAK ———

McFarland & Company, Inc., Publishers
Jefferson, North Carolina, and London

Library of Congress Cataloguing-in-Publication Data

Pencak, William., 1951–
    The films of Derek Jarman / William Pencak.
    p.   cm.
    Includes bibliographical references and index.

    ISBN 0-7864-1430-8 (softcover : 50# alkaline paper)

    1. Jarman, Derek, 1942– — Criticism and interpretation.
I. Title
PN1998.3.J3P46   2002
791.43'023'092 — dc21   2002013831

British Library cataloguing data are available

©2002 William Pencak. All rights reserved

No part of this book may be reproduced or transmitted in any form or by any means, electronic or mechanical, including photocopying or recording, or by any information storage and retrieval system, without permission in writing from the publisher.

Cover Photography: Photospin and Eyewire

Manufactured in the United States of America

McFarland & Company, Inc., Publishers
  Box 611, Jefferson, North Carolina 28640
    www.mcfarlandpub.com

For Peter Bolte, George Boudreau, Peter Buck, Keith Graffius, Jason Kelly, Mary Miles, and David Zeeman, wonderful young people whose enthusiasm for life, art, music, and the life of the mind has preserved my own.

Contents

Preface 1
Introduction 11

1. *Akenaten*: A Queer Pharaoh? 21
2. *The Garden*: The Relevance of a Queer Jesus 29
3. *Sebastiane*: Early Christianity and the Roman Empire 44
4. *Edward II*: From the Middle Ages to the Renaissance 55
5. *Caravaggio* and the Italian Renaissance 70
6. *The Angelic Conversation*: Queer Dee and Shakespeare? . . . 85
7. *The Tempest*: From the Renaissance to the Present 100
8. *Wittgenstein*: The Grey Flame and the Early Twentieth Century 108
9. *War Requiem*: The Long Shadow of the Great War 120
10. *Jubilee* without John Dee? Modern Times 132
11. *The Last of England*: Modern Times Revisited 142
12. *Neutron* and *Sod 'Em*: Possible Futures 151
13. *Blue*: "Our Time Is the Passing of a Shadow" 157

Afterword: Imagining October 167
Appendix: Pier Paolo Pasolini, Jarman's Predecessor 171

Notes 185
Works Cited 197
Principal Films Discussed 199
Index 201

Preface

This book is neither a biography of the filmmaker, painter, diarist, poet, and queer British political activist Derek Jarman (1942–1994) nor a comprehensive guide to his work in any or all of these areas. Marvelous studies of his films have been made by Michael O'Pray and the contributors to volumes of essays edited by Roger Wollen and Chris Lippard; his own writings—including the last set of diaries, superbly edited by Keith Collins—are the best guide to his life and thought; a splendid biography by Tony Peake not only effectively summarizes the plots of all Jarman's films, but intelligently finds sources for them in the director's personal experiences.

As a historian, what can I therefore contribute? Taken collectively, Jarman's film projects, completed or existing in screenplay, offer nothing less than "reclaiming a whole history for gay people,"[1] as Jarman noted in an interview. They bring to life what it might have meant to engage in same-sex love in various eras, and the possible implications of this largely hidden love for history in general. An art and history student at King's College, London, and an avid reader,[2] Jarman wrote texts to accompany several of his films in which he scrupulously cited his sources. Many of his films show careful attention to current historical scholarship while offering creative variations on it. This book attempts to show that Jarman was indeed successful in offering an alternative, and largely plausible, vision of civilization, a philosophy of history if you will, from a homosexual point of view. Historical understanding, however, was not an end in itself for Jarman. He believed that understanding the achievements and survival of gay people under centuries of persecution could serve as an inspiration for the growing struggle of his own era.

But from a historian's perspective, Jarman's historical films do more than construct a possible gay past. Because he had to interpret the expression and repression of same-sex love in past times from the most fragmentary evidence, Jarman's films invite us to ponder how all historical stories, or "narratives" as the professionals call them, are also constructions based on fragments — supported to be sure by larger or smaller amounts of sources — but all designed by people living at a specific time to suit the interests and stylistic conventions of their age. So while on one level, Jarman is doing nothing more than any historian in constructing a useful past, on another, he is reclaiming for history a nearly vanished heritage that may shock those adhering to the heterosexist[3] conventions of the modern world.

Jarman complained that as a schoolboy he and his classmates "never heard of Caesar in make up and drag, the soldiers' moll, or for that matter Alexander, the greatest general of all screwing Hyphaestus ... that the Olympic games were conducted in the nude ... that Hadrian went mad with grief when his beautiful boyfriend Antinotous drowned in the Nile.... Ancient history was an interminable war. All violence and no sex."[4] Jarman's first full-length film, *Sebastiane*, set a pattern for his work in general; it "didn't present homosexuality as a problem and this is what made it different.... It was also homoerotic."[5]

Restoring eroticism, for the most part homoeroticism, to history, is Jarman's great achievement. As he points out, "The sexuality of so many men was not loved in the history books."[6] Much of his output expands on a point he made in an interview concerning the way homosexuality manifested itself in the past: "If you are living under psychological terror, what deals do you make with your oppressors?"[7] Throughout history, same-sex love has appeared in various guises and disguises precisely because people who ought to have been queer and proud of it in the best of all possible worlds had to make "deals" to save their lives as well as protect their sanity from the contest between their inclinations and indoctrination to the contrary. These remarks applied to Jarman's own time, the late twentieth century: "My whole life has been spent under assault," he maintained. "I was a criminal for the first twenty-five years of my life [when homosexuality was still a crime in Britain] and a second class citizen for the next twenty-five," he wrote in his fiftieth year.[8] It has been historically respectable for scholars to talk about economic, political, ideological, and geographic factors in their analyses, but they rarely touch on, let alone bring to vivid and disturbing life, such matters as the eroticism and sadomasochism Jarman found in early Christianity, Renaissance theater and court life, twentieth century warmaking and athletics, and the modern repression of homosexuality. That is why Jarman could justly claim of *Sebastiane*, and by extension much of his cinema, that it "was historically important; no feature film had ventured here."[9]

Furthermore, Jarman made *Sebastiane*, and the films which followed, "so that young men could have an option; the doors were opened into another world,"[10] one excised from standard histories. And I in turn write this book to help open those doors. All historians, including those who pretend to be objective, write with an agenda for their own times: to promote or prevent social change, to glorify or vilify particular people or societies. Jarman put his cards on the table from the beginning, thereby sidestepping the fiction of objectivity, whose principal adherents have shamelessly prostituted themselves before the altars of particular states, classes, and individuals—usually great white (sexless or sexist or heterosexist) men.

Given the scanty evidence he had to work with, Jarman's reconstructions become more plausible, at least to me, as he approaches the present and his sources become more explicit. Jarman's view of Akenaten's sexuality is his boldest, and hence most dubious interpretation, in part because many of the conclusions on which he relied have been disproven by scholarship that appeared after he wrote this unmade filmscript.[11] With *Sebastiane* and early Christianity, his theory that Christ and his apostles were an alternative same-sex community receives support from a minority of scholars, although I would make the point that if anyone who was not considered a god traveled around with twelve men and only occasional female companionship, the conclusion would be foregone.[12] The sometimes none-too-latent (homo)eroticism of the religious fervor Jarman finds in Christian mysticism, on the other hand, receives considerable scholarly support, especially from the path-breaking scholarship of Peter Brown, and indirectly from the studies of the Cistercians as presented in their journal.[13] With Edward II of England, Jarman is relying on his subject's historical reputation which may or may not be correct. Scholars have in general considered Edward predominantly homosexual because the only available sources say that he was. Yet not only did most appear three centuries or more after the fact, they mirror with almost uncanny accuracy the situation of late-sixteenth-century England and could by changing the names serve as a comment on the imminent accession to the English throne of King James I.

From the Renaissance to the present, however, Jarman is dealing with figures whose sexual orientations were definitively known or could be reasonably intuited. He can thus put aside the question of what really happened and concentrate exclusively on his far more important concern—

what is the role of same-sex love in history? But all his historical films raise interesting questions. For instance, questions such as the extent of change and continuity between Akenaten's sun worship and the increasing importance of the sun in the Egyptian pantheon during his father's reign; the relationship between Christianity and other oriental monotheistic religions in *Sebastiane*; how or whether a ruler's sexual behavior should affect the way we praise or condemn him have been discussed.

To be sure, Jarman did not labor in his vineyard alone. Scholars of same-sex love — Michel Foucault, John Boswell, John D'Emilio, Marc Stein, George Chauncey, Jonathan Ned Katz, and others — have come out, in both senses of the word, in our postmodern era to show both the extent of this love in the past and the magnitude of its repression.[14] Foucault has demonstrated diverse sexualities that lacked discourses to pigeonhole them before modern times. Boswell has shown remarkable tolerance for same-sex unions in a medieval era still stereotyped in the popular consciousness as the "dark ages." Katz has more explicitly dated the invention of heterosexuality to the late nineteenth century. Stein and Chauncey have discovered vibrant same-sex communities in Philadelphia and New York City in the years "before Stonewall" (pre–1969), and D'Emilio has uncovered a good deal of homosexual efforts at legitimation and self help beginning in the 1940s. But Jarman was ahead of his time and his compass was wider than most professional scholars who came after him. He was already scripting his films in the mid–1970s, at a time when gay studies were in their infancy. Furthermore, his historical films span much of the course of Western civilization. And his imaginative cinema makes history live with a vividness even the best writers can only approach. Jarman essentially accomplished for the grand sweep of Western civilization what groups of historians and literary critics have done for particular eras. *Queering History*, in fact, would be a possible alternative title for this book, for Jarman's work could be considered in this same vein as two other excellent scholarly collections — *Queering the Middle Ages* edited by Glenn Burger and Steven F. Kruger[15] and *Queering the Renaissance* edited by Jonathan Goldberg.[16]

This book has several purposes. First and foremost, I hope it inspires interest in Jarman's films and life. The individual chapters may serve as "program notes" to Jarman's films from a historical perspective. Although the films can be appreciated without much background, I think presenting the historical context will enhance our understanding not only of the films, but of Jarman's importance as a keen student of the limits of historical knowledge and the role of history in inspiring change or preserving inertia in the present struggle against homophobia. I explain the historical contexts of the films and offer what I consider to be plausible interpretations of Jarman's intentions, in light of the director's own historical reading and other evidence gleaned from his own writings (to a large extent) and writings about him (to a lesser degree).

I do not pretend to be comprehensive or definitive. Not only are the films simply too rich, and too problematic, but any claim to such authority would contradict both Jarman's and my own way of looking at historical writing (or cinema) as an ever-changing story about the past invented by the present to shape the future. As Jarman wrote of *The Last of England*,"The audience will tell me what I've made. I'll find out in the question and answer sessions, I'll adopt their best guesses." Jarman's scripts always differed somewhat from his films. Words were changed and scenes reordered in the process of filming. Jarman termed the scripts his "restraints" and claimed to make films "for myself with my collaborators." He viewed himself as someone who "gathers the communal threads ... what's important is the creation of the work itself, not the finished product ... the harnessing of everyone's creativity." He said the same about his paintings: "The process is a struggle, the product always annoys me. It's unnecessary."[17]

Jarman's approach to history and film appears vividly, not to mention ironically, in his argument with postmodern critic Terry Eagleton over his script for the film *Wittgenstein*, with which Jarman took great liberties. Contradicting his own postmodern literary approach, Eagleton claimed that "the film was 'full of errors.'" Jarman responded that "'error' is the weapon of the jailors of truth." "Joy," "sparkle," and people "working together" make history live on the screen, not literal adherence to facts.[18]

For Jarman's achievement to be recognized, it is important that a body of critical yet appreciative literature develop that explains just what his accomplishment was. It should explore ways of understanding elements in his films that mystified and repelled his contemporaries, most of whom thought a film ought to be a more visually spectacular version of a linear narrative, as might be presented in a play. I offer my interpretation of Jarman's films to historians, homosexuals, and potential radicals to stimulate their efforts to understand the past and to struggle for a better future.

I do not do three things in this book that I might have, and offer the following reasons besides sheer laziness. First, I do not retread the contemporary debate over the appropriate terminology for same-sex love in the past because it has been gone over so many times and probably no closure is possible. Jarman wrote: "The names — gay, queer, homosexual, are limiting. I would love to finish with them. What about 'same-sex relationships.' Maybe that's the best."[19] However, Jarman eventually settled on the term "queer" as "a liberation" and used it most of the time to refer to himself beginning in the mid–1980s after he became deeply involved in radical political activity.[20] As British politicians and a respectable bourgeois gay constituency began to court each other, repudiating the sexual freedom and political turbulence which had characterized same-sex politics in the 1960s and '70s, Jarman stated: "If this is what gay has to offer, I'm glad I'm queer." Shortly thereafter, he outlined a defiantly queer political agenda:

> Queer people should demand equality in all aspects of life: legally binding unions, the right to bring up children, adoption rights, rights of access and property, equal opportunity in employment, an end to proscription in the military, an equal age of consent, inclusion in all sex education, a bill to outlaw homophoibia in the media, an end to Church pronouncements on homosexuality, deletion of anti-queer statements in the Bible, establishment of teaching facilities in universities, a national archive.[21]

Jarman's films reiterate his great argument against the contemporary heterosexist hegemony: it is historically inaccurate, a repudiation of the very civilization upon which it parasitically rests. Jarman believed that in past times there were communities of people in which same-sex love predominated (among males in some parts of ancient Greece, for one) and others where it was an important, although perhaps not dominant factor, but nevertheless a stimulus to art and thought. He cited the paintings of Tuke, the boys' adventure books of the Edwardian era, and the Boy Scouts (who as of the year 2000 in the United States will not admit homosexuals, or at least those who are honest about it) as examples along with such medieval saints as Anselm and Aeldred who wrote explicitly of their attraction for young men. Jarman termed this sexuality "timeless," the link in a "brotherhood" that he implicitly compared to the spiritual brotherhood Christianity ought to embody by paraphrasing the liturgy saying that it "was then, is now, and will be in the future."[22] I like Judith Bennett's stipulation that "lesbian-like" behavior occurred among women in past eras and that all efforts at definition need to begin with this certitude.[23] Jarman's films make the same point for "homosexual-like" conduct.

Thus, while my ideal term for the activity Jarman depicts is "same-sex love," I sometimes use gay or homosexual as alternatives in full awareness these terms are modern constructions. "Queer" I use to identify gay people who consciously and militantly celebrate homosexuality, and sexuality in general, or campaign for gay rights. Jarman's dream was to "queer the planet." His agenda foreshadows that of Michael Warner, who has argued that gay people should stop trying to fit in and be respectable for the benefit of a heterosexist society that oppresses them. Instead, they should reject traditional family arrangements and sexual identities and pioneer a more varied, happier, and politically committed existence for both gay and straight people alike.[24] Or to appropriate Marxist terminology, queers have to become a class for themselves, aware of their true identity and fighting for their own rights unencumbered by false consciousness. But I do vary the language, if I may be excused a definition that repeats the thing to be defined, so my writing does not repeat the same words too often. Those who seek entry into the terminological debate are referred to Bennett's excellent article among many other sources.

Second, I do not engage Jarman's critics directly. Two principal groups disliked both his films and his sexual-political stance: heterosexists and a conservative gay media which found his work too celebratory of sexuality and too critical of a straight society they believed needed to be wooed rather than warred against. Like those of any great artist, Jarman's works were frequently received with indifference or hostility. To dwell on Jarman's critical reception (except where I think such discussion enhances understanding of the films) would make this book far more tendentious, not to say cranky, than it needs to be. This topic would simply get in the way of the viewer (or reader, in the case of the unmade screenplays) trying to understand what Jarman was up to. Furthermore, serious criticism, hostile as well as positive, by people with divergent perspectives is essential if art and literature are to survive as thriving, controversial enterprises. But just as it is possible to discuss musical works of the past without confronting *The Lexicon of Musical Invective* prepared by Nicholas Slonimsky to show how the most important critics of their day panned everyone from Beethoven to Berg, I think Jarman deserves comparable respect in the cinematic world.[25] My criticisms of the critics would have the effect of trivializing or satirizing their remarks, many of which are serious statements about the gay rights movement and the nature of cinema, narrative, and history. To engage in polemics here would require another, larger, and far more argumentative book that I predict would exhaust rather than enlighten the reader.

Third, I apologize to a host of queer theorists, semioticians, postmodern thinkers, and others whose work might either contribute to or distract from my discussion. My analysis occasionally turns theoretical, especially in the preface and introduction, but even here I try to tread lightly. Indisputably, Jarman's films can be brought to bear in the service of, or in opposition to, theoretical debates about postmodernism, the gay rights movement, the construction of gender, and the ideas of specific contemporary thinkers such as Michel Foucault and Deleuze and Guattari. But I had to choose. Did I want to write a book for the relatively small community of postmodern theorists, or did I want to reach reasonably well-educated yet theoretically unsophisticated people in language they understand to bring them closer to an understanding of Jarman's work? I opted for the latter course, and apologize to this potentially wider audience in advance if I have failed to be as clear as I ought. I cheerfully subject myself to the slings and arrows of theorists — especially my fellow semioticians. (In studying human societies, semioticians try to understand the hidden meanings behind the stories people and institutions invent, that is — the signs they create — to justify [or lie about] themselves and others.) For what it's worth, Jarman did not have much use for film theory either, whereas Pasolini, whom he admired, published extensively on this topic in *Semiotica* and elsewhere. "I can't see that writing about a visual medium can be much of an enlightenment," he responded to a critic. "I've never read film theory and never bought a cinema book unless I was interested in a life." He claimed, perhaps sarcastically, not to know what a genre was, and insisted that "film critics have no visual training, they are writers who make their pronouncements through a fog of English lit." Jarman read books such as Boswell's on the history of same-sex love, but comments on Foucault and other postmodern thinkers are absent from his written works.[26]

    I could not have completed this book without the support of a whole host of friends, some of whom were unaware it was even being written. But without mentioning the late Roberta Kevelson, Baruch Halpern, Lynne Koppeser, Guido Ruggiero, C. G. Royer, Terry Prewitt, Cathy Lugg, Bryce Tugwell, Lori Ginzberg, Jeff Brendle, Cathy Lugg, James Sweeney, Tramble Turner, Nan Woodruff, the late, great John Musselman, and the wonderful friends I've made among the faculty and graduate students at Penn State in the history and other departments, I would be sorely lacking in gratitude. The Irreconcilable Differences: Dan Beaver, On-cho Ng, Barry Kernfeld, Dan Letwin, Mary Ann Maslak, Charlie Yood, and Matthew Restall — my jazz/rhythm and blues band — has proven to me the truth of Jung's and Jarman's contention that mind and matter, spirit and technique, are complementary rather than contradictory. When we get together, the Age of Aquarius lives! Equal thanks go to the members of the Round Table for Law and Semiotics, the Semiotic Circle of California (especially Irmengard Rauch), and the Semiotic Society of America, which welcomed a stray historian into their midst. I thank Richard Lanigan, editor of the *American Journal of Semiotics*, for permission to reprint revised versions of articles on *Edward II* and *Caravaggio* I published in that journal in 1994, vol. 11, and 1995, vol. 12. The publisher encouraged me to write a richer book that included all of Jarman's films.

I must, as always, thank my parents, Harriett and Charles, for their moral support of my eccentric scholarly career. My father died as I was finishing this book. I can now understand how people whose loved ones die from AIDS feel. From an extremely handsome and physically active man, frequently mistaken for the actor Stewart Granger, my father suffered from lymphoma for the last three years of his life, becoming increasingly bedridden. He weighed less than a hundred pounds when he died and despite his determination to keep his mind clear and die at home, was forced to re-enter the hospital and take morphine for his pain at the very end. The symptoms of AIDS and cancer can be so similar; I hope that people who have witnessed either can sympathize with those who endure the other and work together to alleviate suffering and discover cures. My father received exemplary, humane care at Long Island Jewish Hospital. Similar care is a right all AIDS patients should have. To perform two thought experiments: suppose AIDS care and research equaled that for cancer, or cancer somehow acquired the stigma of AIDS.

I have arranged with the publisher to donate royalties from this book to OUTrage!, where the money can be used to further the causes in which Jarman believed. Kate Stanworth of the British Film Institute kindly arranged for the illustrations.

Introduction

The films, paintings, written work, and personal activism of British director Derek Jarman (1942–1994) stand as towering monuments in the struggle for gay liberation. Several of his films are imaginative efforts to reconstruct the nature of same-sex love in past times when such passions could only be expressed surreptitiously or in unusual, protected settings. *The Garden* links the persecution of homosexuals with the crucifixion of Christ. *Sebastiane* deals with the Christian saint supposedly martyred by arrows and depicted erotically in religious art, *Edward II* with a British king who may have loved his chief advisor Piers Gaveston, and *Wittgenstein* with the famous homosexual Austrian philosopher. *War Requiem* is a meditation on gay composer Benjamin Britten's work of that name set to words by Wilfred Owen, a British poet who died in World War I. *The Angelic Conversation* and *Jubilee* present Jarman's interpretation of the Elizabethan Age and juxtapose it to contemporary times. *The Tempest* connects these two eras. *The Last of England* and *Imagining October* deal with the repression of homosexuals and class-based injustice in modern times. *Blue* is a film about Jarman's own death and interweaves the AIDS epidemic with other tragedies of the late twentieth century. Several unmade filmscripts offer Jarman's further thoughts on modern historical issues while *Akenaten* is a highly speculative interpretation of this ancient Egyptian pharaoh.

Covering millennia of sexual repression and efforts to escape it, bringing to life people whose homoerotic passions had a major impact on Western civilization in religion, art, politics, philosophy, and war, Jarman has single-handedly provided a cinematic history to enhance and accompany work being done by scholars of homosexuality in the late twentieth century. As James Cary Parks has eloquently written:

> Taking apart history, especially in his films, Jarman rooted out the discrepancies of acquired learning. A subversive academic, he mocked, mauled and made use of the past. A process of reclamation is both necessary and inevitable for any cultural exponent of a subjugated group, class or race. Gay historians, theorists and artists are driven to make of us a fragmented history. Jarman did this with ease and relish. His work is filled with artifacts brought from a forgotten past to the present in order to legitimize and ornament contemporary gay culture.[1]

To present this vision, Jarman "read between the lines of history," as he put it. "The hunt was on for forebears who validated my existence." Once history was properly investigated, Jarman insisted that "civilization is queer — especially the Renaissance ... Leonardo ... Michelangelo ... Botticelli ... Rosso, Pontormo, Cellini, Caravaggio, all the main artists, Shakespeare, Marlowe, Bacon, and I suspect all the rest. To deny this is not only to betray all these artists, but civilization itself." Turning the clock back even further, Jarman noted Plato was more than an academic philosopher, he provided "a blueprint for same-sex relationships and a handing down of wisdom, from one generation to another, in each other's arms." The Romans, too, practiced same-sex marriage, and medieval clerics wrote of their love for young men.[2] Jarman thought it essential that "history is not left in the hands of" scholars and religious apologists "who can hide these ugly-minded men"— that is, Christian thinkers such as St. Augustine and their successors who subordinated body to mind, and condemned sexuality in general and homosexuality in particular. "Their legacy allowed us to be sent to the gas chambers without a murmur."[3] To borrow the apt words of thinker Walter Benjamin, himself a victim of Nazi tyranny, Jarman insisted that "only that historian will have the gift of spanning the spark of hope in the past who is firmly convinced that even the dead will not be safe from the kidnappers unless he wins."[4]

Jarman explained that the oppressed and dissatisfied must write their own history because "all establishments rewrite history" to obliterate or vilify their enemies. He made this remark when the media hailed the Oscar-winning film *Chariots of Fire* as actor Ian Charleson's supposed first screen appearance, ignoring his earlier role in Jarman's *Jubilee*. By this erasure, the radical, the homosexual, and his work are swept away or co-opted in favor of the "official story"— in this case a film openly touted as influencing public opinion to support Britain's war against Argentina for the Malvinas (or Falkland) Islands in 1982.[5]

In the long run, Jarman was ambivalent about which "history" would win. "As the Establishment always writes the history," he wondered about his own reputation. Plagued not only by homophobic critics, but by assimilationist gays who believed their best tactic was to conform as much as possible to the greater society that persecuted them, Jarman feared that he might be considered "a bitter man who resented life? Took it out on those nearest? Put the clock back for homosexual reform?" Upset that a 1991 television special on gay life in Britain left out not only himself, but the whole art scene, he lamented: "Who holds the keys of history and why were we not asked? They connived with the straight media which had already turned me, quite falsely, into a dangerous producer of video nasties."[6]

Yet at other times Jarman expressed confidence that his version of history would win out. And if the history of historiography is any guide, this confidence is probably correct. Today we side with the nineteenth-century labor movement against the capitalists, the civil rights protesters against the bigots, the Jews against the Nazis. Speaking to a tabloid reporter who lied about AIDS as a disease spread primarily by uncaring homosexuals, Jarman remarked: "I'm writing a diary which I'm publishing .... When all is said and done what I choose to write, I expect, will be the only trace of your life. Your memory is in my hands."[7] If the twentieth century is true to form, Jarman and other outsiders will shape the way the future remembers history, while the memoirs and biographies of the so-called statesmen will come to resemble a post–Christian hagiography.

Jarman not only scavenged the past for historical evidence, he literally scavenged it for historical relics, in junkshops, in the remaining vestiges of the "green and pleasant" England one of his heroes, William Blake (see Afterword) was already mourning in the late eighteenth century. "I scrabble in the rubbish, an archaeologist who stumbles across a buried film," he described his method of constructing sets and designing costumes.[8] The sets for *Caravaggio* came from "rubbish and old discarded [theater] sets in London's Limehouse district."[9] Jarman searched a long time before he found "a good vegetable garden" for the *War Requiem*, as "the supermarkets have wiped them out."[10] His garden at Dungeness incorporated the detritus of shipwrecks with flowers that could survive amid a beach of shingles. Biographer Tony Peake astutely notes that Jarman's interest in alchemy — the metaphorical conversion of earth into gold — followed from the way he created beauty out of what others had discarded.[11]

Jarman's low-budget cinema made a virtue of necessity. He filmed at times with a home-movie camera and recycled his family's home movies into his own. Such economies "reflected the flawed situation I worked in.... Perhaps that's their strength." By 1987, he had yet to spend a million pounds on all his films combined: "I'm proud of that, also filled with fury for those who deal out the cash."[12] He made *Sebastiane* for £30,000,

Jubilee for £50,000, *The Tempest* for £150,000, *The Last of England* for £240,000.[13] He complained that the British Film Institute allocated a mere £200,000 and ten days to shoot *Wittgenstein*, which meant no sets (hence the black cloth backdrop) and one lighting set-up.[14] Another advantage to Jarman's enforced poverty was that his "rent-a-crowd cheaply" actors were "sympathetic people, people who really wanted" to be in the films. Most spectacularly, he inserted into *Edward II* the radical gay "OUTrage! boys who came along and did it, for the love of it, [while] a number of others ... just went on and on about the union rates."[15]

To those accustomed to the millions of dollars invested in films and made by major contributors, Jarman's poverty will astonish. Upon receiving royalties of £700 for *The Angelic Conversation*, he noted, "That film is making more money than any of the others." On a trip to France in May 1993, he ran out of money; that July, in debt to his landlord, he declared himself terminally ill to receive £70 per week. In his final years, he spent what money he had on refurbishing his cottage at Dungeness and assisting friends.[16]

Jarman took his history seriously. He realized that the concerns of the present shape the past we construct, rather than discover. People who lack historical knowledge — much of which he provided in his published books and screenplays — may find his films puzzling. Many of his writings demonstrate how his own biography and the perils and promises of gay life in his own time related to comparable situations in the past. As he wrote of the appearance of OUTrage! in *Edward II*: "The whole central relationship between Edward and Piers Gaveston is mirrored by what is happening right now."[17] Comparing deaths from AIDS to the slaughter of men in World War I, a struggle blessed by the established churches of all the powers, he dedicated the *War Requiem* "to all those cast out, like myself, from Christendom. To my friends who are dying in a moral climate created by a church with no compassion."[18] If anything, AIDS was in general a worse fate than death in battle: "A bullet in the back of the head would be easier, just a moment of terror.... With this illness you can take longer than the Second World War to get to the grave, ending your days looking like the tympanum of the damned at Autun."[19]

One of Jarman's most effective means of presenting these historical similarities was to insert obvious anachronisms into his films. He explained that he could do so without worrying because of his "very heavy academic upbringing." This left him "free to make all of those leaps" and "dispense with certain concerns" such as a spurious effort to achieve objectivity or authenticity. (In other words, he knew enough historiography and theory not to be a slave to the inauthentic authenticity and meaningless minutiae cherished by history "buffs" who are comic relief to real historians.) Historical films which had such goals were "awful ... you knew perfectly well the eighteenth century wasn't like that, or the Middle Ages." The popular directors of his own time he disliked included Kenneth Branagh, Peter Greenaway, and Francis Ford Coppola. He found their work "dull" and "trivial." Why were they so famous? "The pea-brained critics deserve to be shot ... don't say it too loud: they're all paid off."[20] Instead, as in his *Caravaggio*, he planned that viewers would not think that something "is out of sync" unless "I deliberately made it funny"— such as Ranuccio's motorcycle or Baglione's typewriter. These bits of humor, in fact, encourage us to think more deeply about the past than we otherwise would have. The homophobia that plagues the world today, we can only hope, will strike future ages as an absurd prejudice much as we view the racialist "science" of the late-nineteenth century. What Jarman might have presented literally and innocuously in *Caravaggio*— a man riding a horse or writing a critique — becomes more meaningful to modern audiences when they realize that they too encounter youthful punks like Ranuccio and finicky pedants like Baglione.[21]

Several of Jarman's films take the study of a gay past to yet another level (a meta-level, the theorists would say) by commenting on the work of artists, writers, philosophers, and musicians who today would be considered homosexual. Jarman's films about the painter Caravaggio, the composer Benjamin Britten's *War Requiem*, the philosopher Wittgenstein, and the Elizabethan dramatist Christopher Marlowe's play *Edward II*, comprise a major part of a lifelong crusade to demonstrate the contributions of gays to civilization and their triumphs over obstacles placed in their way by the dominant society. "Most of the work on our Queer lives underestimates the effect of art in favor of political action," he wrote. "I know that my world at eighteen wasn't the gift of politicians" but of "homosexuals such as [Jean] Cocteau, [Jean] Genet, [William S.] Burroughs, and [Alan] Ginsberg," all of them writers. Later in the 1960s, artists David Hockney and Andy Warhol and dancer Rudolf Nureyev joined them.[22] Jarman recounts his lifelong struggle to come to terms with his sexuality and then to express it artistically in *At Your Own Risk: A Saint's Testament* (1993). The second half of the title summarizes the major thrust of his career: turning the critical gaze of heterosexuals back upon themselves, thus reversing the "Other" and revalorizing the persecuted practitioner of alternative sexuality as both a martyr and a driving force in history.

Jarman through film vividly fulfilled the requirements of postmodern theorists for constructing "effective" History. He accomplished what Michel Foucault has said of Nietzsche's writings: "history becomes effective to the degree that it introduces discontinuity into our very being — as it divides our emotions, dramatizes our instincts."[23] Jarman deconstructed, took apart, the so-called moral justification for a dominant heterosexist society which has sometimes stigmatized but usually silenced a healthy alternative. To dramatize his position, Jarman outrageously declared that "Nature is Queer" and that "all men are homosexual, some turn straight."[24] Far from being "natural," Jarman argued — perhaps with tongue in cheek to give heterosexists a taste of their own medicine — that "heterosexuality is an abnormal psychopathic state composed of unhappy men and women whose arrested emotions, finding no natural outlet, condemned them to each other and lives lacking warmth and human compassion."[25] He had no doubt that open acceptance of homosexuality would free the straight world as well as homosexuals themselves: "Subservience to Family and State remains the pattern from here to China — homosexuality can cut across this sad world."[26]

In any case, modern notions of sexuality emerged only recently, in the late nineteenth-century Western world. Earlier, condemnations of "sodomy" by the Christian Church coexisted with considerable latitude for sexual experimentation and same-sex affection. Once heterosexuality was defined as the only acceptable behavior, as Jonathan Ned Katz has shown, it became necessary for those who denied it, again to quote Foucault, to find "points of insubordination [which] open a void, a moment of silence, a question without an answer, [to] provoke a breach without reconciliation where the world is forced to question itself."[27] Jarman did for homosexuals what W. E. B. DuBois did for people of color.[28] He constructed a new history of the sort Lynn Hunt has described, as "a search for a truth [which] is not an objective one in the sense of a truth standing outside the practices and concerns of the historian," but a history "better defined as an ongoing tension between stories that have been told and that might be told."[29] Or, to borrow from Deleuze and Guattari, Jarman refuted that "history [which] is always written from a sedentary point of view, and in the name of a unitary State apparatus." He has written what they call a "Nomadology, the opposite of a history ... which multiplies the narrative accounts like so many plateaus with variable dimensions."[30]

Jarman was a nomad roaming the centuries in search of the same-sex discourse which has occasionally erupted from a community of nomads that civilization has usually stigmatized as outlaws. He experienced the same stigmatization throughout his life. The inequities from which he suffered still exist in many places, such as the state of Pennsylvania when this book was written and in many others where it will be read. Jarman said, "no right to adopt children.... Illegal in the military ... no right of inheritance; no right of access to a loved one; no right to public affection; no right to an unbiased education; no legal sanction of my relationships and no right to marry.... These restrictions subtly deprived me of my freedom."[31] Queer communities and their celebration by Jarman therefore may be viewed analogously to the heroic outlaws praised in folk ballads as described by the late philosopher Roberta Kevelson:

> The dramatizations of outlawry in the Robin Hood Ballads [and of homosexuality in the films of Jarman] are thematized by a reordering of the usual structures of power, and law, and logic; consequential time is subordinated to the mythic.... The balladeer [or film-maker] translates the legendary and mythic conventions of an almost forgotten age into situational language which points inwardly to the past, and by extension, to the contemporary order of ... Law that threatens to flatten the past by transitivizing it into quasi-mechanical signs of cause and effect. The specificity and immediacy of individual contestants in the Ballads [or Jarman's homosexual rebels] opposes the abstractly over-coded rhetoric of a simulated universality that the legal system attempts to effect.[32]

Like the outlaws of Sherwood Forest or the pirates on the high seas, Jarman spent most of his life escaping from an oppressive world. In *The Last of England*, barbed wire is everywhere as a sign of the "great confinement" Foucault has talked about as the legacy of the Enlightenment "project" in which ideas and institutions would "normalize" the inquiring and creative people who brought vitality to the world.[33] Jarman "talked of the barbed wire that had hemmed me in, quite literally, in the RAF camps [where his father served] — the fenced-in boarding school, the proscribed sexuality, the virus" as a symbol for the constraints of the English society in which he grew up.[34] Barbed wire is everywhere in the Western Front scenes of *War Requiem* and is a recurring motif in other films. Jarman thus spent his life escaping into "spaces of freedom," Kevelson's outlaw forests and Foucault's heterotopias.[35] Like Foucault, Jarman "distrust[ed] all figures of authority," especially those "with blueprints for our salvation."[36]

For Jarman, spaces for creativity, contemplation, and copulation included men's rooms, where sex and graffiti — "the scratchy attempts by the sexually imprisoned to liberate themselves ... pathetic remains of the lost language of love ... stammerings ... always man to man" — could be found in the back rooms of gay bars, where "sex can be the sweetest and most transient, the imagination runs riot, and the anonymity is a treasure."[37] Combining art and horticulture, two of the great loves of his youth, he considered painting "my secret garden ... an escape out of Heterosoc," the socially dominant world of heterosexuality.[38] The art studio was in fact physically separate from the main building of his school. For most of his life, Jarman lived in out-of-the way places, "derelict warehouses" at first, and ultimately, Prospect Cottage in Dungeness, "the last of a long line of 'escape houses' I started building as a child at the end of the garden."³⁹

Jarman's fear was that queers would stop being rebels and escape artists and become pillars of the establishment, much as the most prominent figures in the worlds of contemporary music and art sold out and accepted subsidies and publicity from those they criticized. For instance, Jarman criticized the "King's Road fashion anarchists who call themselves punks." While ostensibly the rebellious youth of the 1970s, they were in fact "boys and girls who have the music business behind them to give them a real high with its coke-rolled banknotes of international finance … the same old middle-class bourgeois art students … who've read a little art history and adopted Dadaist typography and bad manners."⁴⁰ Observing London two decades later, in the 1990s, he mourned: "The young are so conventional now, not a surprise in sight — tight-arse boys, aping a fictional '50s."⁴¹

"All art is dead," Jarman proclaimed, "especially modern art," exaggerating as was his wont to compel people to face the truth. "Only when art is demoted to the ranks again, treated as nothing remarkable, will our culture start to breathe." Since the Renaissance, the art "establishment" has preached a spurious individualism funded by the very people it attacks: it "began by collaborating with the banks of the Medici [and] ends in bankruptcy on Wall Street."⁴² Much as he sought to preserve and remember landscapes of an older England, Jarman urged that young artists abandon modernist fads: "We did not study the Old Masters, they were closed off from us; we were Modern then — we learnt the inventions of the century without understanding … isms ruled the fifties school and were neatly stored in the postcard drawer. What isms might I become?"⁴³

Jarman believed homosexuals were in special danger of being co-opted by their oppressors. He argued that the "AIDS charities' tie-up with the art world" and its glamorous names were "in no-one's interest," producing a mere "drop in the ocean" of what was needed, only serving up "the illusion that a caring society is caring."⁴⁴ On a Cruisaid (raises funds for HIV and AIDS research and education) benefit gala in 1991, he said that in health care, there was "one rule for the rich, another for the poor. Until schools and hospitals are integrated into a state system with no private bolt-holes, they will always be in crisis. The rich don't experience, do nothing to help them, while Madonna sings for them." By contrast, Jarman told of a friend who went to a public hospital, "waited an age at the outpatients' department," and "they sent him away with indigestion pills." In St. Bartholomew's hospital where Jarman himself underwent treatment, a pitifully inadequate AIDS ward had eighteen beds: "get ready to die in a corridor" (AIDS patients are particularly susceptible to contagion). "Private charity," he concluded, "is an affront to all of us ... there is no morality in charity when it lets others duck their responsibilities." Nothing short of adequate health care for all could be acceptable in a world in which the AIDS epidemic has struck primarily the poor, children, and people of color, not gay men as the heterosexist media implies.[45]

Jarman found sell-outs everywhere: "The queers of the sixties, like those since, have connived with their repression under a veneer of respectability."[46] "They are the enemy who attempt to put our clock back ... they are my generation." Jarman singled out the actor Ian McKellen, who accepted a knighthood from the homophobic Thatcher government, as "shocking," representing his "integration into the worst form of British hetero politic — the closed room, the gentleman's club — where decisions are made undemocratically for an ignorant population which enjoys its emasculation." Claiming to be "a much better role model," Jarman insisted that "if a gay man of my generation didn't strike out for the horizon then he performed a small betrayal. It was a duty for those of us marked as 'different' to lead adventurous lives.... It's not us who hold things back, we are doing things — books, poetry, radio, TV — it is the assimilationists who are the enemy." Far from trying to win the good will of straight society, Jarman proclaimed: "The onus is on heterosexuals to explain themselves.... It's they who have warped sexuality, who have murdered and driven innocents to suicide, they who should ask for forgiveness."[47]

Jarman was equally critical of Tony Blair's "New" Labor Party, which he thought stood "far to the right of [never married] Edward Heath's old [early 1970s] Tory party." "Labour has been driven far off course," Jarman noted in 1991, "they would do anything to win the ghoulish public vote.... We have only the frying pan and the fire to choose from ... the loons of Right and Left."[48] Among the latter he placed the band Pink Floyd and their movie *The Wall*, which "ignored the glaring truth that [they were] themselves the Wall that had to be torn down." Schoolteachers "who might just be telling their students to think for themselves," rather than mindlessly parroting some official line, "were painted as monsters of conformity [in a film that] had the power-mad glamour of a Nazi rally."[49]

"Gay liberation is no liberation," Jarman approvingly quoted writer William S. Burroughs. Like their superficial straight contemporaries, Jarman found many gays to be victims of a herd mentality, dependent on changing, superficial signs — "rings on fingers and limp wrists are replaced by running shorts and vests, work-out muscles and moustaches." Jeans, leather jackets, and white T-shirts have become for gay culture the equivalents of suits and ties. Many gays simply bought into the materialism that stigmatized them. In a manner similar to W. E. B. DuBois writing of the "double consciousness" that burdens black people in the United States, Jarman noted that homosexuals have a comparable "struggle to define themselves against the order of things, an equivocal process involving the desire to be both 'inside' the dominant yet oppressive society, and yet 'outside' of it as members of an alternative and more humane culture."[50] But Jarman never doubted that the dilemma was to be solved by repudiating its conformist, assimilationist horn.

Jarman believed that one way queer, that is, militant gays, could liberate themselves, and the rest of society, was to launch a worldwide crusade against AIDS, dramatizing the lie spread by heterosexists that it was a "gay disease." Queers need to show that most of the afflicted are women and children, either in poor countries or among the poor in wealthy countries. If queers took this approach, heterosexist scapegoating of gay people for spreading the disease could be a blessing in disguise. "We have been turned into the people who have to bear all of the responsibility ... for the epidemic. Then we have to act responsibly while they do nothing.... We live in a situation where few speak up.... I don't think we can expect any solutions or resolutions.... But when people talk we return to sanity."[51]

Jarman concluded *At Your Own Risk* with the quotation in full of the Montreal Charter, a declaration against AIDS, which only briefly mentioned gay men and lesbians (to call for legalized relationships), but focused attention instead on the special vulnerability of women, prisoners, and people in underdeveloped countries. Rather than being seduced by dreams of bourgeois assimilation, Jarman suggested gay activists side with the wretched of the earth. The Montreal Charter, and Jarman's book, ends: "It must be recognized that in most parts of the world, poverty is a critical co-factor in HIV disease. Therefore, conversion of military spending world wide to medical health and basic social services is necessary."[52] By taking the charge leveled at the gay community by homophobes on account of AIDS, reversing it to expose the absurdity and the evil motives underlying it, queers have a chance to put themselves at the head of a movement for social justice based on international solidarity. For the fate of people with AIDS in First World countries — their life expectancy reduced, scapegoated for their sufferings, and offered inadequate health care — has created the basis for such a solidarity with the poor and suffering throughout the globe, and in a perverse way demonstrated that all humanity is created equal.

1
Akenaten:
A Queer Pharaoh?

Although Derek Jarman never turned his mid–1970s screenplay *Akenaten* into a film, he believed it "could be made into a film," which he doubted for "*Sebastiane* or *Jubilee*, which were." He described it as "poetic-operatic," and suggested it be "made very simply, against sand floors and whitewashed walls," somewhat in the manner of *Wittgenstein*.[1] *Akenaten* illustrates the major themes of Jarman's finished work: historical scholarship, creative but careful use of anachronism, and the effort to reconstruct a possible past for practitioners of same-sex love. Jarman relates that "in the early seventies" he developed "a passion for Ancient Egypt.... I spent hours tracking down books in second-hand bookshops until I had over a hundred, from Victorian travel books to an obscure little pamphlet on the construction of a wig."[2] Chronologically, in both his own collected works and in historical time, *Akenaten* marks the beginning of Jarman's speculative construction of a gay past.

Yet *Akenaten* differs from Jarman's completed films in a significant way. Unlike his other works, *Akenaten* is based on a such slender thread of evidence that its thesis would probably be repudiated by every respectable Egyptologist today.[3] The archaeological excavations into the tombs of Akenaten and his era — largely the work of Donald Redford, who is a colleague of mine at Penn State — now clearly show Akenaten's love for Nefertiti, their children, and the idealistic basis of his monotheism, all of which were disputed in the 1970s when Jarman wrote his script. Christopher Marlowe, Benjamin Britten, and Wittgenstein were all known to practice same-sex love, but Jarman is grasping at straws in dealing with the Egyptian pharaoh. Still, as with the films he actually made, Jarman is constructing a past which might, improbably but possibly, have happened. We can hardly fault him for doing the most he could with the best, yet sharply divided and highly speculative, serious scholarship of his time.

The story of Akenaten has fascinated Egyptologists and scholars of religion and philosophy since early nineteenth century archaeologists began to decipher the hieroglyphs. Pharaoh from 1358 to 1340 BCE, Akenaten tried to eliminate the pantheon of Egyptian gods and institute monotheistic worship of the sun. One of the most controversial figures of ancient history, he has been regarded as "a religious reformer, a witness to the truth [and] a forerunner of Moses" on the one hand and "dismissed as a voluptuary, an intellectual lightweight, an atheist [and] ultimately a maniac" on the other.[4]

Worship of the sun itself and monotheism are linked with same-sex love in both Jarman's works and ancient history. In *The Garden*, he identifies early Christianity with the supposedly alternative, gay community of Jesus and his disciples, while *Sebastiane* brings out the homoeroticism some Christian mystics may have experienced with respect to "penetration" by the Holy Spirit and the piercing rays of the Sun/Son God. More generally, cults of the Sun-God tended to monotheism. A single, male, sky God replaced a pantheon in which goddesses — of the night or the moon, of fertility and the earth — held a prominent place.

This degradation of the feminine was new to Egypt. During the fifteenth and fourteenth centuries BCE, prior to Akenaten's ascendancy, the role of the pharaoh's principal consort as "God's Wife" was passed on much as the kingship itself, with powerful queens such as Hatshepsut, Tiye, and Nefertiti holding this office.[5] The sky–God linked to this female line was Amun. During the reign of Akenaten's father, Amenhotep III (1384–1346 BCE), "statuary on a really enormous scale made its appearance in great quantities," including over seven hundred statues of Sekhmet, "the goddess of war and pestilence." The Egyptian cult of the dead also reached a peak, with increasing numbers of courtiers and leading officials reposing in tombs alongside those of the royal family.[6]

Jarman handles the transition from father to son in ingenious, symbolic fashion. His work reveals a sophisticated understanding of Egyptian historiography as of the early 1970s. In fact, it attempts to synthesize and comment on it. For example, although the evidence shows that Akenaten either served as co-regent with his father — a practice many pharaohs adopted to ensure peaceful succession — for a period of twelve years, or else succeeded to the throne without incident after his death, Jarman turns Akenaten into a child cast out by his parents. An oracle told them he would bring destruction to Egypt and its traditional gods. Jarman thus has the youthful Akenaten appear suddenly out of the desert, accompanied by his followers, the "wild boys," who are usually naked — indicating the homosexual passion Jarman attributes to Akenaten — and painted blue, the color of the sky. Jarman bases these episodes on symbolic interpretation of historical fact: Aldred writes "the cult of the nude reached its apogee in the reign of Akenaten"[7]; frequently both men and women were depicted unclothed in art at that time. Similarly, Akenaten's religion appeared suddenly, if not literally out of the desert, as an unprecedented abandonment of the Egyptian pantheon for the exclusive worship of the Sun God, an example of the monotheism that appeared among the Hebrews and other Middle Eastern peoples at the time.

In Jarman's text, Amenhotep III welcomes his son as his successor despite his advisors' warnings. Jarman here is faithful to the scholarship although he dramatically personalizes the continuity between the two men: assuming they served as pharaohs together, Akenaten — known as Amenhotep IV until his father died — began building his first temple to Aten immediately upon joining his father on the throne. But even if the older man kept his son waiting, Jarman is still in step with the historical sources. Recent scholars have emphasized that the gods Amun and Sekhmet, whom Amenhotep III favored, were also sky gods, a preference probably due to the increasing migration of Middle Easterners into the Nile Valley. As Aldred writes: "In many respects, the rule of Akhenaten was an extension of his father's reign."[8] Father and son were striving for a similar revitalization of a culture, formerly insular, whose supremacy was questioned by an increasing influx of foreigners.

To portray at the same time the continuity and discontinuity of the two reigns, Jarman finds ways of depicting Amenhotep III's historically proven concern with growing old. Rejuvenation was the purpose of three huge jubilees he held in years thirty, thirty-four, and thirty-seven of his reign. Jarman has the older pharaoh "made up to look as young as possible by a group of child beauticians"; he swims in a pool with children while his adult wives sit "bored and disconsolate"; he kisses both male and female children on the mouth as if he hoped their youth could pass to him that way. He also walks around under an enormous umbrella held by three naked youths, symbolically protecting himself from the Sun and its God for which he simultaneously yearns while revealing the homoerotic aspects of his sexuality.[9] Jarman is suggesting that the old order harbors the same desire for love and life as Akenaten, but these desires are perverted into pederasty and an old man ridiculously attempting to keep his youth. (Current scholarship has Amenhotep III dying in his mid-forties, but Egyptologists formerly believed he was older.)

The realm Akenaten ascends to, as Jarman presents it, is thus waiting for an injection of life: Amenhotep III anticipates his son's revolution by ordering "a very great monument without equal since the beginning of time" dedicated to the Sun God — but as a feature of his tomb.[10] The incorporation of the sun into the cult of death signifies the complex and complementary relationship of life and death, night and day, and sun and darkness, in traditional Egypt. Jarman plays with these ambiguities: he associates Akenaten at various times in the script with both "life" (for his adherents) and "death" (for his adversaries), a serpent (symbol of both death and fecundity), and burning fire (either as the life-giving sun or the destructive element).

Thus, when Jarman has Amenhotep meet Akenaten, the elder pharaoh regards his son as having "returned from the dead,"[11] welcomes him and his "wild boys" to the court, and forbids his hostile generals Ay and Horemheb from acting against them. Again, Jarman is historically accurate, insofar as is possible given the fragmentary evidence. In replacing incumbent officials with younger men, Akenaten was not so much conducting a purge as effecting a typical pharaonic transition in which the new ruler installs his own men.[12] And while there is no evidence that the generals — future pharaohs who will undo Akenaten's changes, attempt to obliterate his name, and in fact restore the old gods — personally opposed Akenaten this early on, Jarman has them stand symbolically for the old religious order. We can never know whether they opposed the new order from the beginning, or only turned against it when war, plagues, and administrative nonchalance began to characterize Akenaten's reign.

Akenaten's revolution centered on ideas rather than personnel. Jarman has him say: "In the desert I am at home, Pharaoh of the sun. Living in truth.... I shall renew Egypt, breathe fire into her, recreate her for the wildest joys of life. All creation shall rejoice in my return." Later Akenaten remarks that Thebes, Egypt's traditional capital before he builds the new city of Aketaten, "was oppressive. Every moment of the day was ordered.... Day followed day in endless monotony." Once again, Jarman's historical research comes through. He has Akenaten speak translations or approximations of the poetic lines the pharaoh either wrote or caused to have written, words of a naturalistic, lyric bent previously absent from Egyptian inscriptions. "Withered flowers from the oldest tombs had more beauty to the people of Thebes than the blossoms of jasmine on their own doorsteps," is how the pharaoh condemns the old Egyptian religion with its emphasis on the cult of the dead. He intones the Great Hymn to Aten: "Great sun of the desert, Aten/ When you arise the world lives,/ When you set, the world dies/ .... I, Akenaten, your son, will create the world for you/ As you created me. Your beauty holds my heart captive."[13]

Another beauty who held Akenaten's heart captive was his Queen Nefertiti, or so the available evidence dictates. Jarman does not dismiss this love, for he reconstructs a love poem in which the pharaoh mourns his dead queen: "How sweet was our love,/ sweeter than wine or the fragrance/ of spice, like a locked garden planted/ with the rarest flowers, nard and saffron, calamus and cinnamon.... Bright bird flying through the blue sky,/ Beating the light air with your wings/ You have gone, leaving no trace/ Of your journey."[14] Furthermore, affectionate paintings, again unprecedented for Egypt, of Akenaten, Nefertiti, and their six daughters survive. But once more Jarman seizes on historical ambiguity. When he was doing his research in the 1970s, most Egyptologists believed that Nefertiti had been displaced at court, perhaps banished in disgrace, several years before she died. They also considered Smenkhare and Tutenaten to be Akenaten's sons.[15] Modern scholars disagree. New evidence shows that the queen continued to appear in Akenaten's art and inscriptions after her death. Also, recent researchers explain why Akenaten's supposed sons did not appear in these artworks along with the rest of his children. Their ages at death and the evidence of their bones (both bodies survive, Tutanaten being the famous "King Tut") suggest they were almost certainly Akenaten's younger brothers.[16]

But Jarman could not have known that Nefertiti did not die disgraced or that Akenaten was succeeded by his brothers. So he tweaked the available evidence to show that the pharaoh may have taken his own sons as lovers to replace his wife. Jarman interprets the fact that Smenkhare took the name of Nefertiti when he became co-regent to mean that he replaced the queen in the pharaoh's affections. Instead of his new name paying tribute to the queen—a plausible interpretation—Smenkhare therefore replaced her as Akenaten's spouse, a ceremony Jarman was planning to film.[17] Jarman drives the spousal relationship home by having Akenaten recite a love poem to Smenkhare incorporating words that will later appear in the pharaoh's funeral lament for Nefertiti: "You ravished my heart with a glance of your eyes." Jarman has the queen killing herself upon learning of Akenaten's same-sex wedding with their own child. Jarman could cite the fact to support his thesis that upon assuming co-regency, Smenkhare appeared in inscriptions as the "beloved of Akenaten."

Jarman's interpretation explains why he believed Smenkare to be Akenaten's son although none of the younger pharaoh's texts make that claim. Upon becoming Akenaten's spouse, he was no longer his son. Jarman reinforces this interpretation when he introduces Akenaten's master sculptor, Bek, who identified himself in stone as "the apprentice whom His Majesty [Akenaten] taught," and turning him into Smenkhare's lover. What did His Majesty teach Bek? The art of sculpture or, Jarman suggests, how to love Smenkhare?[18]

When it comes to the struggle that took place in Egypt between Akenaten and traditional religion, Jarman is on far firmer ground, although for dramatic effect he condenses the conflict in time and highly personalizes it, all the while keeping everyone on the historically correct side. He situates Akenaten and Smenkhare against Tutanaten to symbolize the new and old religions' struggle for supremacy. Jarman has their followers brawl in the streets and Tutanaten kills his brother Smenkhare in single-handed combat. Jarman remains neutral in the struggle. He does not so much strike a mean between competing schools of historiography as to whether Akenaten tried to redeem a moribund order or ruin a healthy one as to preserve paradox and ambiguity concerning the merits and inadequacies of the two sides.

Although a champion of homosexual rights, Jarman never descended to the historical nonsense which unambiguously pits a good, persecuted minority against their evil oppressors. On the one hand, he does full justice to those who have praised Akenaten as a religious visionary attempting to restore life and love to a stagnant social order, while on the other, incorporating evidence used by those who have denounced him as a religious fanatic unconcerned with administration, the welfare of his people, or anything save his luxurious court and its intellectual and artistic life. One way to look at Jarman's analysis is to suggest that he intended to show such questions were unanswerable if not irrelevant, anachronistic labels pinned by people in modern times — seeking to recreate an ancient civilization about which they know precious little — according to their own special agendas. Jarman seems to be simply taking the evidence, dramatizing it, and letting people draw whatever, if any, moral or historiographical conclusions they may. That is why Jarman's attribution of homosexuality to Akenaten is so fascinating: he is going further — but not that much further — with the fragmentary evidence that survives than professional scholars of Egypt.

Jarman's presentation of the equivalence, or ambiguity, or irrelevance (take your pick) of the respective moral merits of Akenaten and his religious opponents appear in two sets of parallel scenes. First, early in the screenplay, one of Amenhotep's daughters condemns her brother and his "wild boys" as "savages" when they are allowed to feast at the palace. An orgy follows and they swim naked in the Nile. Later on, it is Smenkhare who uses the term "savage" to denounce his brother Tutanaten ("he spends all his time hunting in the marshes"). In a reversal of Akenaten's own change of name, Tutanaten becomes Tutankhamun at the end of the screenplay. Then he ascends the throne and announces the restoration of the old gods favored by Amun. Jarman is symbolically right on target. He also dramatizes the historically established fact that Akenaten did not wage war either directly or support the efforts of client states like his predecessors and successors. Nor did he travel throughout his kingdom as they did: he remained for the most part in his new city, not the hunter or soldier, but the priest and artist. No wonder the generals detested him.[19]

Yet, while Jarman may seem to be calling attention to the feminine or artistic aspects of Akenaten's reign as opposed to those of traditional rulers, in reality he is pointing up the difficulty of proving the case. Some scholars have considered Akenaten's portraits as effeminate, and at least one image of Nefertiti wore a beard, which suggests some kind of gender confusion. But it certainly makes no sense to impose modern notions of gender on people who lived several thousand years ago. We can also recall that for Jarman it is Akenaten who came out of the desert with his wild boys, whereas Amenhotep built the most and largest statues in Egyptian history thus far and painted himself up to simulate a young man. Jarman seems to be telling us that the winners write history, and evidence exists for a variety of interpretations for those who carefully study the Egyptian sources. What we have are two styles of art and civilization, two styles of savagery and religion, each condemning the other, each asserting its supremacy through fragmentary archaeological evidence that can only be tentatively interpreted across millennia.

Jarman also constructs the deaths of Nefertiti and Smenkhare to parallel each other. After Nefertiti's suicide, Jarman has Akenaten cremate her body after he silences a mourner with the words, "The dead are comforted by silence. Prayers offend them." The destruction of the corpse horrifies the boy prophet Amenhotep kissed — that is, the priest of the old Egyptian gods — for in accordance with traditional Egyptian religion the boy exclaims: "He has destroyed my lady. He has murdered her soul." Similarly, after Tutankhamun slays Smenkhare, Akenaten stabs his own mother, Queen Tiye, through the heart for taking the side of her grandson who murdered his elder brother Smenkhare — that is, Akenaten's lover, according to Jarman. With her dying breath, Tiye curses Akenaten (or is it Smenkhare? or is it both of them? Jarman is ambiguous here) with the same threat of oblivion to which she believes the cremation of Nefertiti has condemned that queen: "You shall have no soul. Nor spirit, nor body, nor shade. You shall have no house, no shelter, no tomb, no light. Burning be on you to eternity."[20]

Paradoxes abound in Jarman's treatment, which, same-sex love aside, points to the difficulty of interpreting Egyptian sources. Akenaten's religion did indeed favor the outdoors and the brilliant desert sun, thus, the eternal burning to which Tiye condemns him is the very unity with the Sun-God he claimed. Artistic images frequently show Akenaten (and Nefertiti, appropriately considering the fate Jarman reserves for her remains) irradiated by beams of descending sunlight. And the efforts of both Akenaten and his adversaries to efface each other failed. Today, we remember Nefertiti, and Akenaten, and also the effort to obliterate his reign and religion, not to mention the boy king "Tut" as leading figures in one of the most interesting episodes in ancient, if not human, history.

The conclusion of Jarman's screenplay leaves us debating Akenaten's two historical reputations and debating whether we indeed ought to be debating them at all. On the one hand, the pharaoh is dethroned and returns to the desert, or in terms of the old order sentenced to death real or symbolic, for Tiye and Amenhotep consider the desert the place of death rather than the source of life Akenaten claims it to be.[21] On the other hand, as Akenaten sits alone, going blind, cradling the body of his son and lover Smenkhare, staring into the sun, he speaks not of death, but of eternal life and resurrection:

> My desire is to hear your voice every day, like the sigh of the north wind. Love will renew my limbs. Give me the hands that hold your soul. I will embrace you. Call me by name again and again, for ever, and never will you call without response.[22]

Is Akenaten calling to Smenkhare (same-sex love) or to the sun (his God)? Or is he addressing the audience, referring to his own immortality in the annals of human history? Is he, or Jarman, urging us to espouse his love, his religion, or both? Or does his worship of the sun blind him to the realities of human experience, and we are simply witnessing the ravings of a lunatic? After all, the film would have ended with night descending.

If Akenaten is indeed addressing the audience, the screenplay's final scene takes us back to the very first, the only scene which occurs in the present, where tourists with cameras snap pictures of the Sphinx. The Sphinx is the narrator of the story, but let us remember the Sphinx speaks in riddles, although Jarman has Akenaten claim to have solved "the" riddle.[23] But there is sufficient ambiguity in the screenplay, reflecting Jarman's complex rendering of the theories of Egyptologists, that we are left in the end with the riddle and with the historians and tourists who can only capture imperfect versions of the riddle rather than accurate versions of the past. "The Sphinx at Giza stares into the sun" is how the screenplay begins. At the end, a blind Akenaten "stares motionless into the sun," the image of the Sphinx itself, a riddle.

2
The Garden: The Relevance of a Queer Jesus

All his life, Derek Jarman loved gardens. He has said "flowers sparkled in my childhood as they did in a medieval manuscript." The first "grown-up" book he read was *Beautiful Flowers and How to Grown Them*. Lawns were the "enemy," which he associated with the sterile middle-class suburbs and his authoritarian father, who insisted on neatly mowed grounds. They "are against nature, barren and often threadbare.... For the same trouble as mowing you could have a year's vegetables ... mixed with pinks and peonies, shirley poppies and delphiniums; wouldn't that beautify the land and save us from the garden terrorism that prevails?" Jarman told his readers to try to grow their own "wild garden.... It will bring you much happiness."[1] Many of his written works and films evoke and juxtapose the beauty of flowers and the outdoors with the sterility and environmental destruction of his age. In addition to everything else, he was a radical ecologist.

Jarman's last garden, where he filmed his motion picture of that name, was set in Dungeness' remarkable landscape around his final home, small, wooden Prospect Cottage. It was located in the shadow of a nuclear power plant, but this monstrosity could only hide so much from the discerning eye. "We have the strongest sunlight, the lowest rainfall and two weeks less of frost than the rest of the U.K."[2] At the same time, "the wind blows

Jarman is seen here sitting in his garden at Prospect Cottage in Dungeness, where much of *The Garden* was filmed. *(British Film Institute, Posters and Designs.)*

here without ceasing." Jarman compared the scene to "a premonition of the far North, a landscape Southerners might think dreary and monotonous [but] which sings like the birch woods in Sibelius' music."[3]

As in his films and life in general, Jarman sought in his garden to wrest beauty from the ruins of civilization. Nearby were wrecks of vessels and

2. ~ The Garden

mine craters from the Second World War, placed at Dungeness to meet a possible German invasion.[4] The first paragraphs of the book *derek jarman's garden* explain how he scoured flea markets and thrift shops for antique gardening tools. His garden became a sculpture garden, in which flowers were intermingled with both the shingles and fabulous shapes he constructed of the detritus he found on the beach.

Like Jarman's films, his garden required only a minimal investment of cash but a great deal of loving work. He "was not put off by being told that gardening at Dungeness was 'impossible,'" wrote correspondent Christopher Lloyd. To make a hole for his seeds, Jarman would "excavate" a shingle, only to have half of it roll back. Then he would take rotted manure, scavenged from a neighboring farm, put stones in the hole, and "dribble" in the seeds between the cracks in the stones to protect them and prevent them from blowing away.[5] Jarman's garden became a symbol and monument to his life's work.

Much the same can be said about the 1990 film set in and named after his creation. *The Garden* is a meditation on the meaning of the birth and death — there is no resurrection — of Jesus, and Jarman himself appears frequently in the film. He is seen writing, surrounded by Christian symbols. By turning himself into a character in the film, Jarman links his own struggle and anticipated martyrdom from AIDS to both the life of Christ and the fate of gay people in his own society.

Jarman openly espouses the plausible theory that Jesus and his disciples were an alternative, persecuted gay community themselves. He thereby followed in the footsteps of none other than England's King James I, who, when criticized for his affair with the Duke of Buckingham, responded: "Christ had his John" and he had his George.[6] But even if this interpretation goes too far, the film powerfully compares Jesus' persecution with the treatment of homosexuals in pseudo–Christian contemporary society. The historical Jesus is juxtaposed with his modern incarnation, represented by two persecuted gay lovers. Not only have many died from AIDS — Jarman himself succumbed four years after directing *The Garden* — but thanks to a cruel and bigoted society, they go to their deaths with curses in their ears, adding psychological agony to physical pain.

Jarman thus turns this film into an inquiry as to why contemporary society is so homophobic. The third of four original poems he reads in its course provides the explanation. He first writes of global warming as "the sky, pierced and torn/No longer sheltered the naked earth." "Criminal rulers," prevailed, people who "burrowed deep to hide their shameful poisons," which would contaminate the earth for "a million years, thirty thousand generations." Scenes in *The Garden* show this nightmare world being born before our eyes. The polluters — capitalists in collusion with government — are the real villains, not the homosexuals whom they scapegoat to divert attention from their "shameful poisons."

But there are even more "shameful poisons." Jarman suggests that "straight" society is a psychological as well as physical hell. The body of a person with AIDS — via Jarman's own appearance in the film — is a sign of what modern society has done to its members and to the world, expressing its passions through greed, voyeurism, violence, sadism, and homophobia rather than appreciating natural beauty or exhibiting tenderness and joy. Jarman puts this all on the screen by continually juxtaposing opposites. He contrasts brief and occasional moments of happiness and natural beauty, which must be snatched on the sly and sometimes struggled for against nearly impossible odds, as in the Dungeness garden itself, with the nightmares of postmodern physical and spiritual blight.

Beginning with the film's opening, Jarman boldly invites comparison of his own plight with that of Jesus. In the first of four poems, he states his purpose: to share "emptiness ... silence ... the void, this wilderness of failure." Unlike those who have built "a highway [with] fast lanes" — the architects of material progress — Jarman promises "a journey without direction [leading to] many paths and destinations." The price of freedom is uncertainty and possibly unhappiness, but the price of progress is inevitable destruction — the fast lane to perdition.

As he speaks these lines, Jarman sits dejectedly at a table in his small cottage. Water drips from the ceiling; he puts it on his face, using it to refresh himself, recalling the water for which the crucified Christ thirsted. Jarman is framed by a painting and a sculpture of Christ in agony on the cross. Close-ups in the film frequently focus on the stigmata — on the historical Jesus, on his dual modern representation, and on the sacred images in Jarman's cottage. A globe sits on his table, resting on what appears to be a crown of thorns. Later, in a fetal position, Jarman writhes on the same bed surrounded by the identical torchbearers celebrating the modern dual Jesus making love. The image suggests the impossibility that Jarman could ever fulfill his vision or mission in the hostile world in which he was dying even as the film was being made. We see him working in his garden too, in the progressively fading light of which his first poem speaks, as the film proceeds. This is no Garden of Eden, but a Garden of Gethsemenae or even a Golgotha, suggested by the skull-like rocks which the Magdalen, played by Tilda Swinton, later gathers. Crosses are not only suggested by the stark sculptures in the garden, but by the towers supporting the power lines to and from the reactor. These are among the crosses we bear in our times.

2. ✥ The Garden 33

Placing Jarman's first poem in the setting in which he reads it, it becomes clear that he regards Jesus not as a god, but as a "failure," although a heart-wrenching one who attempted to present "a journey with many directions." Jarman cannot believe in the conventional Jesus misrepresented by his putative followers with "false notes" and the illusion that he was a god. The director proposes that now that the light has faded, and conventional Christianity demonstrated its bankruptcy, we may go in search of both a better world and a truer Jesus. This involves acceptance of homosexuality as one of these "many directions."

Jarman cinematically compares the enemies faced by contemporary queers with those Jesus encountered. Near the film's opening, a nearly-naked policeman, dressed in black sado-masochistic leather gear, a scowl on his face, crawls toward a historical representation of Jesus, who wears a white robe and looks like the typical nineteenth-century image of a young man with a brown beard and long hair. This conventional Christ insures that he is instantly recognizable. The policeman is carrying either a large dildo or a nightstick. His appearance is the first of many indications Jarman offers that much homophobia and violence are perverse manifestations of deeply repressed homosexuality.

Shortly thereafter, two nude young men try to approach this Jesus. But one is restrained by a third, also naked. When the two finally draw near, they are afraid to touch Jesus or talk to him, and finally run away. This scene is set amid flames and fumes on a desolate landscape. It symbolizes the fact that the true audience for Jesus' message is inhibited by a social environment in which he only appears surrounded by noise, chaos, and smoke — Jarman's interpretation of the world forged by contemporary "Christians." Jarman thus portrays Christ as a model for contemporary homosexuals, who nevertheless are unable to reach him because of interference from the malevolent religious establishment which misinterprets his true nature.

Jesus himself is juxtaposed with Judas as well as Jarman. (A modern Judas-figure lurks around Jarman's cottage, twisting a hangman's noose for himself after betraying one of the two modern Jesuses with a kiss.) Having hung himself — he is a young, probably gay man who lusted in vain after Jesus, as symbolized by both his clothing and his huge black tongue sticking out — Judas is the prototype of the Anti-Christ. He enjoys his own resurrection in the film as Christmas is transformed into "Credit Card Day." The twentieth century has resurrected the betrayer of Christ instead of Christ himself. "Judas is beautiful, with beautiful cards," sings a sleazy entertainer using a voice resembling actor Peter Lorre's, a macabre hymn of thanks as he licks the cards to indicate how shopping and spending have become substitutes for both religiosity and eroticism, and in the process turned into unnatural sources of lust in themselves. The cards can bring about "all of your dreams," Judas sings, and the very next line illustrates one such dream. It is "I am your wish," suggesting that the Ferraris and similar items these magic cards can purchase are tokens to impress others and gain sexual access to them on the one hand and the signs of a pact with the devil on the other. Contemporary Christmas itself is presented as a diabolic light show, with neon signs of "Santa" (Satan?) and "Merry Christmas" blinking amid people rushing about in a pitch-black, urban landscape which then turns into a depressingly blue image of the Dungeness nuclear reactor.

Within this shopping saturnalia, a single flower stands as testimony amid the devastation to the world we have lost, recalling that the whole Christmas sequence is prefaced by images of flowers. But far from being beautiful, they are unsettling: too large, too bright, too phony, like enormous photographs in a homes and gardens magazine. Modernity corrupts even vestiges of a beautiful past as flowers become as plastic as the credit cards and people that purchase them. Only amid the ruins, as in Jarman's Dungeness garden where plants grow amid rocky soil and rubble, can beauty and nature be perceived. Consciously selecting an old cabin in the shadow of England's largest nuclear reactor, Jarman transformed it, and the film he set there, into a parable of how real beauty can shine forth more brightly and be appreciated even more profoundly in the midst of a world that seeks to obliterate it. A similar heart-wrenching effect appears in Act III of Hans-Jürgen Syberberg's film of Wagner's *Parsifal*, where the radiant spring meadow of the Good Friday Spell is replaced by a handful of flowers in a barren landscape watered by rusting pipes.

After Jarman's Anti-Christ and Christmas scenes are finished, children sing a round: "London's burning/ Fire, fire/ Get the engines/ Pour the water." What was once a children's game has become the symbol of a terrible reality as both city and country are depicted throughout the film in various stages of devastation. Much of London indeed burned in the eighties. A burning chair atop a pile of rubbish appears; it signifies some of the film's most poignant moments. Then, after the round, a boy bathes one of the two young men who together represent the contemporary Jesus throughout the film, as prelude to both Jesuses taking a bath and making love. Here for the first time people and scenery appear in a realistic, pleasant setting on the beach. This is a taste of the salvation we need, Jarman implies, and yet cannot find.

Another particularly striking episode, reinforcing the resurrection of Judas, is a singer's rendition of a fifties song "Think Pink." It is introduced by the same menacing flowers as the Christmas sequence. A woman all in pink urges us to "banish the black" as she removes her gloves in what appears to be the beginning of a striptease. This silly song about fashion, addressed "to the women of America" and "the women of the world," becomes a scathing commentary on prejudice, for the song also kills off "red" and "brown" among various other colors. A gay pride parade is the background for most of a song that tells us "you've got to switch" [to pink]. Thus, since the song is addressed only to women, Jarman choreographs it to castigate sexual as well as racial prejudice, for the parade appears indistinctly in the background as Jarman scathingly mocks those who would glorify women as sex objects and fashionable shoppers. Genuine alternative sexualities are banished, burned, buried, and drowned, as are other colors in this song, while the woman as consumer who lives to serve and attract men is foregrounded.

Pink, of course, has another meaning: the pink triangle the Nazis made homosexual prisoners wear, which has become the symbol of the gay liberation movement. Modern queers have modeled themselves on the early Christians in that they also have adopted the principal symbol of their persecution — the pink triangle rather than the cross — as the sign of resistance and triumph. Thus, the passage in which the pink lady urges us to "Think pink on the long, long road ahead/ And the world is rosy red," has a double meaning. The color that stands for the oppression of women also symbolizes freedom for homosexuals, an interpretation which is eclipsed in heterosexist society much like the pride parade is almost completely masked by the garish singer. "Rosy red" also has more than one meaning: it stands for more than the false "rosy" dream of bland happiness reflected by the woman's song and the too-red flowers and lipstick. For the most part, Jarman uses red to indicate fire and destruction. The second of his two poems praises the "scarlet" poppy, a flower of the "wasteland." It can flavor "bread, the staff of life," memorialize the dead, or bring dreams of forgetfulness if smoked as opium. Poppies can feed, console, or obliterate misery in the wasteland. Not coincidentally, poppies are most usually associated in modern history with the vast graveyards of those who died on the Western Front in World War I. Jarman here implicitly refers to his film *War Requiem*, completed the year before *The Garden*, which sets Benjamin Britten's musical tribute to the fallen soldier-poet Wilfred Owen.

Throughout the film, Jarman juxtaposes the queer and authentic life of Jesus with modern horrors which destroy human beings. Near the beginning of the film, the Virgin Mary appears holding her baby. Both are smiling, wearing crowns, exemplifying the great medieval paintings of the

Madonna as Queen of Heaven with her infant son. The crowns then come off, revealing Mary's beautiful red hair and a cuddly little child. As in later styles of art, exuberance turns to introspection, ceremony to naturalism. But reverence and beauty are maintained, and Mary has become, if anything, more meaningful to mothers and others in search of a tender guardian and intercessor. However, several men with cameras, wearing ski masks, paparazzi as terrorists, keep closing in, making Mary more and more uncomfortable. They begin to tear her robes, one attempts to rape her, and two others fight over who gets the next turn. Baby Jesus is abandoned to play in a barren stone garden with the scepter he once held now degraded into a cheap toy.

In this fragment which lasts less than five minutes, Jarman has given us a quick history of how Western attitudes toward women and art, modes of communication, and the nature of religion and spirituality have changed in the modern world. Mary today would be interesting as a mere celebrity, notable only if she had a sleazy sex life. She would be prevented from bringing up her child by inquiring reporters and photographers, her womanhood and sacrality exploited to titillate the masses. The Christ child becomes associated with the cheap playthings we buy in wastelands of stone with the soon-to-appear credit cards and their patron Saint Judas.

After Mary leaves, Jarman retells the story of the Nativity. A scribe narrates the journey of the three Wise Men, their search for Jesus, and their need to avoid Herod, who has all the male babies in the kingdom slain. Instead of the wise men, however, we only see several clergymen, headed by what appears to be the Pope in a huge miter, followed by cardinals and priests, hauling a great rock with huge effort. "Upon this rock I shall build my church," Jesus referred to the disciple Peter: this statement became the justification used by the Roman Catholic Church — the world's leading homophobic association — to claim divine authority for its decisions.

This scene recalls Albert Camus' *The Myth of Sisyphus*, in which life is compared to an effort to push to the top of a hill a rock that always rolls back down to the bottom. There is no joy in history and conventional religion, only the painful yet varied construction of oppression. The distortion of the Adoration of the Magi during the age of the clergy gives way to the age of the capitalist: the rock is next set in place by laborers dressed in the nineteenth century garb of the Industrial Revolution. Only the two gay men who symbolize Jesus find the missing crown worn by the Madonna. For all the miseries of history Jarman has flashed before us in a few minutes, the recovery of the crown implies that our own times offer us hope that has previously been missing. Acceptance of genuine sexuality (which straight society paradoxically terms perversion) and understanding and overcoming the real perversions which have propelled what has passed for Western, "Christian" civilization are now possible. However, the message of the rest of the film, in which the reborn Jesus will again be crucified, is that these hopes are again being dashed.

The only people who receive Jesus in this film are a boy (before his teachers get to him), the Magdalen, a poor woman who gathers in a basket stones that miraculously become bread in a post-modern memorial service for Jesus, and two nude young men who crawl before him. Other sorts of people reveal their true selves. A rich capitalist snidely observes as three women in evening gowns chase, throw stones at, and strip a transvestite attired exactly as themselves. Another well-to-do man out jogging in a fancy outfit blows a rape whistle when he encounters the historical Jesus. Jesus, of course, was a homeless vagrant, and Jarman drives home the fact he would thus be treated as a deviant to be policed in the modern world. As the founder of a gay community, he would also be viewed according to heterosexist stereotyping as ever-prone to raping straight men.

The portrayal of how modern education leads to homophobia and sterile lives are among the most powerful scenes in the film. A boy is first shown having mixed impulses. On the one hand he bathes the modern Jesus — in effect, sanitizing him while exhibiting the uncomprehending adoration of the established religions — but on the other he stabs an insect with a stick and plays at whipping an imaginary object. A pillow fight the boy joins is not only a playful sublimation of aggression, but a preview of the mocking of Jesus by the police who cover him with down feathers. The boy is applauded by a crowd as he dances with an exuberant flamenco artist, but the audience soon grows tired of her art and his performance, and they are abandoned. Art is degraded into entertainment.

The victory of the boy's evil impulses over the good is accomplished through his formal schooling. Aged teachers in professorial robes first turn hour glasses and then some books of the Bible upside down, oblivious to the apocalypse Jarman has occurring in the background behind them. Numbers and Leviticus, whose texts are traditionally misinterpreted to condemn homosexuality, rather than the lack of hospitality, as "the sin of Sodom," are the most prominent of their distortions.[7] Officially sanctioned learning is irrelevant and downright wrong, an excuse to discipline and punish people, as Foucault has taught us. The teachers' most powerful signifiers are the long rods they pound, loudly and what seems interminably, in perfect rhythm. The content of learning is subordinated to the mind-numbing reiteration of the same ugly, standardized message through which society destroys its children and perpetuates its injustices. The rods signify the traditional punishment for pupils who fail to learn their lessons. The masters sit at the long table where the boy has just danced the flamenco. Symbolically, Jarman is observing that formal education does not perfect and nurture our creative impulses, but destroys them. The same table at which the teachers sit is also the site of a reinterpreted Last Supper, where women dressed for mourning, almost all of them old, rather than the young apostles, make eerie music on empty wine glasses while eating nothing. The life-giving Eucharist is turned into a somber meditation that religious sincerity in our society is frequently the preserve of old women trying to deal with impending death. Such women live on as young men are persecuted and die in an epidemic.

Once the masters have (apparently) socialized the boy, he spins a black globe faster and faster on the table. Jarman thus criticizes the (mindless) operation of modern knowledge in hurtling the earth on a course of destruction. The boy's learning of history is symbolized by the Roman helmet he dons, with which he marches around, and a cord he wields as though it were a whip. History as conventionally taught in schools and through the media, especially military history emphasizing the accomplishments of great men and empires, masks whatever alternative history may exist and perpetuates a status quo continuous with such gruesome past achievements. That we really worship the Romans and seek to emulate their imperialism rather than the Christianity we pretend to profess appears in our preferred architectural styles for government and office buildings.

Jarman signifies the horror of official history by having the flagellation of the dual, modern Christ — a prolonged, bloody, yet intensely erotic scene — set to the rapping of the teachers' rulers. He thereby points out that a critical yet unspeakable aspect of modern education is the lust of instructors for students' bodies, which expresses itself in sadistic rituals such as forced memorization of trivia, idiotic assignments, and grading.

No sooner has the flogging been concluded — mercifully, at last, we think — than it is repeated with renewed vigor. In the interim, a church bell has rung out; the Jesus figures look toward the Heavens as though expecting relief. But the institutionalized church is the last place homosexuals suffering persecution can find sympathy. The policemen administering the whipping are dressed in the Santa Claus outfits they had earlier worn to harass the sleeping Jesuses (the two men in each others' arms) with a sarcastic, off-key, fortissimo rendition of "God Rest Ye Merry, Gentlemen." Jarman is driving home the point that the sort of people who celibrate the contemporary Christmas are exactly the sort who are persecuting those who would follow in Jesus' footsteps by practicing genuine and same-sex love. The refrain to this carol, wishing the auditors "Glad tidings of comfort and joy," is especially ironic as the policemen Santas lead the Jesuses off to Pilate in a cruel parody of the "glad tidings" the savior himself brought to humanity.

At any rate, these policemen, like the teachers, are homophobes with hidden homoerotic desires. Jarman depicts the mocking of Christ as taking place at the sort of late-night, cheesy restaurants where policemen in cities sometimes eat. The crown of thorns is symbolically smeared with jam and worn by the two Jesuses who have been beaten if not tortured. The smearing starts somewhat playfully, one policeman laughing and proceeding rather slowly, but he soon begins to sticking out and wiggle his tongue and make mocking erotic gestures. At this point, all four join in, tearing apart their uniforms and, using the jam as glue, sticking the downy material on their inside sleeves all over the victims' bodies. The police are thus undressing themselves to some extent — the Jesus characters are also partially stripped — to signify urges they themselves share but cannot consciously or openly express. This brutal bodily contact, as with sports as well, is the sort of homoerotic release allowed in homophobic society.

Part of the mockery of the Christs is the police singing the tune of "La Donna è Mobile" to nonsense Italian syllables. "Women are fickle" is how this tune from Verdi's *Rigoletto* may be translated. The promiscuity of gay men is here degraded by being feminized; ironically, the tune in the opera is sung by the unfaithful and uncaring Duke of Mantua. Straight male stereotyping of gays and women proceeds on the assumption that heterosexuals are somehow the normal and the natural rulers, and that others basically exist for and at their pleasure. Yet another subtext of this use of "La Donna è Mobile" is to show how gays' love of art, especially opera, is one more excuse for insult by the envious "real men" who have been denied cultural as well as sexual pleasure.

Joining the police, the educational establishment, and the media as repressive of both their own and others' sexuality are the politicians. Jarman has Pontius Pilate surrounded by fat and elderly elite Jews and Romans, the people who send Jesus to his death, sitting in a Roman bath. Two attractive yet unhappy young men are being massaged by these hypocrites who at the same time deny the homosexual Christ. The Jewish high priest, Caiaphas, wears a paper crown (such as children are given at fast food restaurants) with a dollar sign and various mathematical symbols written on it; Jarman is again depicting the use of establishment learning as the pathetic facade behind which a corrupt elite hides money-making, the quest for power, and sexual lusts.

Pontius Pilate, wearing sunglasses, is laughing hysterically as the dignified, silent Jesus is brought before him (Jesus says nothing in the film), his two personae gently, sadly leaning on each other. As Pilate washes his hands, he sings, mocking the very words he utters: "I'm going down to the River Jordan." Note he is not saying he will cross into the Promised Land, to which the passage over the Jordan served as prelude. Perhaps he thinks he is going to paradise, but the only promised land Jarman foresees is the apocalypse which the crucifixion initiates. Black skies whirl across the screen, the sun and moon turn red (as foretold in the Book of Revelations) then black. As terrifying skies and seas rush backward, time itself seems to be ending and the nature of existence changing. Jarman articulates this catastrophe in his poem predicting that a million years of miserable, truncated existence will result from contemporary ecological negligence. He gave this figure some thought, as he also expresses the same length of time as thirty thousand generations. By fighting through his art and life against this seemingly inevitable apocalypse and the sexual and political repression accompanying it, Jarman joins Canute in what appears to be a futile effort to stop the waves, only the tides he seeks to turn back are those of history. Jarman is hoping against hope that the world will not destroy itself and its most creative and loving people, who in fact fulfill in their art and lives the very ideals the establishment hypocritically proclaims.

We do not see the crucifixion itself. The dual Jesus, who had made love covered by white sheets on a white bed by the seashore as beautiful, half-naked men and women celebrated by circling with torches, now stands exhausted, dejected, wearing black. Two fearsome figures in black robes, reminiscent of either the Inquisition or of contemporary Klansmen, are the escort to the crucifixion. Only a transvestite approaches Jesus, and in appreciation for a fellow sufferer kisses his bleeding feet.

Jarman's Jesus is not resurrected. As though peacefully resting, his dual incarnation remains asleep as the three Marys mentioned in the Bible visit. The two Jesus figures do appear again, but to signify how we should interpret the film rather than to indicate that Jesus was indeed a god who would bring salvation to humanity. Still in black, the two youths carry a flame before a number of old men who are now seated at the Last Supper table. They seem to be a panel of British judges, but they are wearing white handkerchiefs on their heads rather the black coverings justices would don before sentencing criminals to death. Just before Jarman reads his final poem, these figures are identified not as the wicked, corrupt establishment which sentences queers to death and infamy, but as people with AIDS who grew old and died before their time. Memorial candles appear on their heads, lit by tapers the dual Jesus has in turn lit from the flame. Jesus can bring hope to the dying and the damned, if they do not sentence him to death, as black handkerchiefs would have symbolized, but instead permit him to light candles rather than to remain in darkness. Humanity's real judges in the late-twentieth century are people with AIDS. Our treatment of them is the standard against which our Christianity has been tested, and for the most part found wanting.

Jarman's last poem, which he reads in the next-to-last scene of the film, is a moving lament accompanied by a magnificent threnody for strings composed by Simon Fisher Turner, who wrote the largely elegiac original score. Jarman, who knew he was dying, here expresses solidarity with the dead as he changes the poem's refrain in successive verses from "They died so silently," to "You died so silently," to "We died so silently," and, ultimately to "I died so silently." Jarman thus assumes the mantle of the dual Jesus, completing the parallel between the ancient Christians and contemporary homosexuals. Like the old men at the Last Supper, "old age came quickly" for his "frosted" and "forgotten" generation. He laments that they "died so silently." But what did this silence mean? Acquiescence or fatalism for some, but Jarman himself is so furious, he writes, that he cannot even scream: he is shaking with rage. Saying goodnight to his deceased friends, he insists that Jesus' disciples "fucked" each other, validating their love. Praying that "his sweet garden of vanished pleasures" might return next year, he nevertheless includes the words "cold, cold, cold" in each of the stanzas, all of which end in silent death. The global warming and ecological nightmare of the film's beginning have become an ineradicable frost.

In this final poem, Jarman explicitly articulates at last the underlying premise of his film: that Jesus and his disciples were probably homosexuals and that at least some of their persecution may have been attributable to that fact. He debates the value of silence in the face of contemporary homophobia. On the one hand, Silence Equals Death, the motto of the gay rights movement, yet on the other, no words can do justice to the persecution and its effects on straight and gay alike. Like the holocaust, which denied Jews the right to exist, the horror inflicted by a society which persecutes homosexuals is unspeakable. Yet we must try to remember and counteract this erasure and persecution through whatever imperfect approximations our art, intellect, and political skills permit.

Claude Lantzman's *Shoah* is an appropriate counterpart to Jarman's work which can help us understand what he was trying to do. Both men's films are very difficult to understand for people who cannot comprehend the urgency that if the memory of the unspeakable is lost, then a terrible history is effectively denied and the doorway to its repetition is left open. That holocaust deniers exist at all should make us realize the ineradicability of anti–Semitism; that the community of civilized people looks upon them as kooks or closet Nazis is only possible because Jews and their allies will not let the memory die. But those who deny the legitimacy of same-sex love constitute the world's most powerful churches and governments rather than what holocaust studies and remembrances have marginalized — permanently, one hopes — as a lunatic fringe. For a gay person who hides out is no more a gay person than a Jew who denies her identity is a Jew. Perhaps bodies of closeted Jews would have remained alive had the Nazis won, but not as Jews. Jarman is fighting against a world that would transform gays from the outlaws they are now into silent accomplices in their own annihilation. The Jewish example is both a powerful model for gays, and yet a sobering example of how far many homosexuals are from realizing the urgency of their cause.

So Jarman made his films, which speak with a power that texts such as the book you are reading can only hint at. Yet even such a book has a purpose, as Jarman needs to be interpreted and remembered as one of the principal voices attempting to reverse heterosexist efforts to erase the critical role of same-sex love in the shaping of human history. Historical and literary exegesis is crucial as the late-twentieth century milieu of Margaret Thatcher's England, in which he did most of his work, and the historical and literary allusions with which Jarman filled his work, become more distant. Future miseducation must be countered by reviving a meaningful past of struggles against injustice and hypocrisy. Knowledge that personal autonomy and beauty can flourish under the least auspicious circumstances must be preserved. The works of art, film, and the garden Jarman created amidst the rocks of Dungeness while dying from AIDS, like the music and art produced by inmates of the concentration camp at Terezin, stand as monuments to this indomitable human spirit. *The Garden*'s final poem's final words, which Jarman speaks ever so sadly, are both a farewell to whatever good nights he may or might possibly have enjoyed, and a final "good night" preceding the thirty thousand generations of grief he predicts the world is condemned to endure if it does not heed his message at the eleventh hour.

The film could have ended with Jarman's last poem, as impotent rage mingles with utter despair. But a final scene provides a measure of hope if not a vision of a still unimaginable society where homophobia would be as rare as prejudice against people with brown eyes. The Magdalen, the boy, an old man, and the dual Jesus are sitting at a table. It is not the stern, ceremonial table of the Last Supper and Last Judgment which has dominated the film, but a small table around which the five sit intimately. Here is no hierarchical table in which victims face judges or inferiors perform before or attempt to please superiors, but a round table which implies the equality of those seated around it. The Magadalen has always accepted Jesus, the boy moved from acceptance to rejection, the old men (or gays) from rejection to acceptance. Jarman is signifying here the possibility of reconciliation and love. The stones the Magdalen has taken from Jarman's garden have become bread. Jarman is feeding us the bread of life and love, his flesh, his example, at a Eucharist modeled on Christ's. For the first time in the film, the modern dual Jesus smiles and laughs, as if to counter the fact that shortly before, the historical Jesus had turned his back and hidden his face in the midst of the apocalyptic imagery.

Jarman concludes his film, which among many marvelous things perpetuates the memory and symbolism of his own garden, with a moral miracle. His garden is a commentary that although the modern world has destroyed much that is good and beautiful, we can grow flowers among the stones. A comfortable old cottage may be brought back to life in the shadow of a nuclear reactor on the shores of a sea and under the cope of a sky that even modernity cannot eradicate. Artists may construct eloquent sculpture gardens, turning the flotsam of a wasteful world into memorials to real heroes and signs of a true history, thereby encouraging deep meditation on what we can still do to redeem our world and our future. Yet for it all to work, a miracle comparable to the Last Supper, the first Eucharist which brought salvation to humanity, is required.

Following the communion, the celebrants begin to toss dried flowers from the garden into the air. They laugh and enjoy their fellowship as the petals float elegantly to the ground. Modern nature, to cite the title of one of Jarman's book, is dead, and must be carefully recreated and protected even to exist as a simulacrum. Jarman, and many who loved too well, are no longer with us. But the beauty they created and their example may sustain us, enabling us to steal moments of happiness in the face of environmental catastrophe and official repression that show few signs of abating. If "the sweet garden of vanished pleasures" which Jarman filmed no longer comforts us, its bittersweet memory may perhaps sustain our long night's journey into an imagined day.

3

Sebastiane:
Early Christianity and the Roman Empire

———————— ☯ ————————

At the very beginning of Derek Jarman's *Sebastiane,* the Roman Coliseum appears as a modern cardboard cutout. This image signifies Jarman's belief that we have only a one-dimensional, superficial image of the Roman Empire, particularly of the third century in which the film's action occurs. We have viewed it with either Christian eyes or through lenses provided by Edward Gibbon of a "decline and fall" from the glorious era of the "Five Good Emperors" (96–180 CE). The cartoon serves as a theatrical curtain that when opened reveals a past in which sexuality is shown to be a major factor in Roman, if not all, history, with homoeroticism a largely underground, uncharted, component thereof. Jarman makes the claim that sexual expression, repression, and aggression fueled both the rise of Christianity and the persecution which paradoxically facilitated its growth.

Jarman rewrites the traditional story of Sebastian, the handsome young Christian martyr whose image, naked or nearly so and shot full of arrows on a stake, has been a staple of religious iconography through the centuries. Instead of exalting the steadfast saint, Jarman wrote that "Sebastian, the doolally Christian who refuses a good fuck, gets the arrows he deserved. Can one feel sorry for this Latin closet case? Stigmata Seb who sports his wounds on a thousand altars like a debutante."[1] Jarman entitles his film *Sebastiane,* the feminine form of the name, to indicate the

One of the earliest films to treat same-sex love as a natural expression of human emotion rather than a sex act reserved for people who were somehow perverted, *Sebastiane* featured explicit scenes of love-making and sadomasochism. (*British Film Institute Posters and Designs.*)

passive nature of the protagonist. Similarly, the director sometimes refers to the more gentle of two soldiers in a same-sex relationship, Adrian, as Adriana.

Jarman reconstructs history by refusing to accept the Christians' view of their spiritual purity and renunciation of the world at face value. Instead, he presents a *somewhat* sympathetic case for the Romans so offended by Christianity. Sebastian, like the Christians in general, rejected "a plural sexuality. He prays to a solar conquering god Apollo, Mithras, Christ, who demands his 'whole' attention."[2] The qualifier "somewhat" is essential. As with the characters in Federico Fellini's homoerotic masterpiece *Satyricon*, to which *Sebastiane* refers in passing, Jarman's Romans are obsessed with the pleasures of the senses. Whether courtiers of the Emperor Diocletian or soldiers at a barren outpost—Jarman filmed these scenes, nearly the entire film, on the beaches of Sardinia—the Romans of the late empire live and breathe sexuality. They persecute the Christians, who not only refuse to enjoy the world like normal folks but relegate to Hell those who do so. We of the late twentieth century, although many of us claim to be Christians, similarly stigmatize eccentric alternative communities. Although we no longer throw them to the lions, we blow them up (MOVE in Philadelphia or the Branch Davidians in Waco), ostracize them (Communist Cuba), or blame them for AIDS (homosexuals).

Jarman neither hides nor excuses the Romans' hedonism and brutality. Unlike the Athenians, the Romans failed to grant same-sex love full legitimacy, sublimating much of it though mockery, athletics, and sadism. The world which emerged in the late empire thus consisted of the complicated interaction of competing repressed homosexualites — the asexual saint versus the virile warrior. By channeling a common sexual desire into two unfulfilling alternatives, church and state in the formative era of the Christian world conspired to shape the history we have yet to escape two millennia later.

Sebastiane consists of a series of scenes with consistent symbolism running through them. The sun is the most important image, and is identified with Christ and Apollo, in both cases representing a single God in contrast to the Roman pantheon, signifying masculine beauty and its worship. The four traditional elements — earth, air, water, and fire — also appear to show how the entire universe offers opportunities for the celebration of sexuality. Jarman thereby implies that both Christian self-denial and Roman self-indulgence are rooted in the same, largely homosexual, impulses.

As the film begins, superimposed on the cardboard Coliseum is a caption which announces that on December 25 the Emperor Diocletian — who undertook the last great persecution of the Christians and under whose reign Saint Sebastian was traditionally thought to be martyred — celebrated the birthday of the Sun. Christ's birthday has become the heir of the old pagan mid-winter feast, with his greatest enemy hosting the festivities. The celebration takes the form of gaudily painted dancers riding giant mock phalluses, circling and then ejaculating on an unnaturally white, painted man who is decorated with equally exaggerated red make-up. Meanwhile, the women present engage in lesbian sex. Amidst the dance, Diocletian, a lover of young boys, has two of them murdered by a large African who bites their necks. The pretext is that they started the fires which were set mysteriously in Rome. The emperor then arbitrarily accuses Sebastian, a Christian, of setting fire to the palace, and exiles him to a barren military outpost. The slaughter of the Christians is equated, or confused, with the murder of these erstwhile royal favorites, for the burning of Rome is the most famous crime of which ancient Christians were accused. Jarman thus considers homosexuals and ancient Christians from the start as comparable scapegoats, a theme which reappears in *The Garden*.

3. ❧ Sebastiane

Max, or Maximus, narrates the first scene. At first he seems like a bizarre but apparently likable regular fellow. His sarcastic account provides the tone appropriate to the decadent carryings-on. Max himself participates in the party, accompanied by an androgynous golden figure who is probably a woman dressed up as a man. He too will be sent away along with Sebastian. Max is the leader of the six soldiers who accompany himself, Sebastian, and their commander Severus into exile. Max initiates their horseplay, which includes mock love-making, wrestling, female impersonation, and numerous sexual jokes, most of which are homophobic. Max can legitimately engage in such actions despite their homosexual undertones much like modern athletes and fraternity boys engage in similar antics. Jarman's father, a career air force officer, in fact found the soldiers' behavior quite realistic for men on remote outposts deprived of female companionship.[3]

Although Max states that "boys are OK for a quick one," especially if no women are around, he longs for a whore and wistfully pines for the old Rome. There, he tells us, Cecilli Milli, the director from Silva Screna, staged glorious pageants featuring hundreds of dancing girls. But by Diocletian's reign, instead of serving as the site where Christians were thrown to the lions, the Coliseum has fallen into disrepair and is hardly ever used. The past year, an old lion even fell asleep in the middle of a show. Max especially remembers Stephanon Paidon the great chariot racer, Claudia Frigida, and the huge Mammea Morgana, whom he claims could spread her great legs and admit a regiment. In the present decadent age, Max mourns that shows with pretty boys, such as Fellini's *Satyricon*, "Greek faggots with nets" and "clapped out Syrian archers " who shoot at easy-to-hit tamed elephants have replaced the old Roman circuses. In former days, says Max, there were "real orgies" and "men were men."

In Max's speech, Jarman employs a device that appears in many of his films: the occasional, yet significant use of anachronism to draw parallels between the past and the present. For the most part, Jarman goes out of his way to film events which could possibly have happened. In the case of *Sebastiane*, he even hired a classicist to translate his script into the rough colloquial Latin of the age, which the cast speaks as English subtitles appear. On the rare occasions when he deviates from his quest for verisimilitude, then, Jarman has a telling point to make. Cecilli Milli is Cecil B. DeMille, producer of filmed biblical extravaganzas, and Claudia Frigida is the great Italian actress Claudia Cardinale. That such a sultry siren should be called "frigid" is Jarman's way of contrasting the chaste, implied sexuality of the epics with the blatant, naked escapades he films in *Sebastiane* and which occur in real life. Mammea Morgana is a word-play on Fata Morgana, the seductive sorceress of Arthurian legend, who could be any number of large-breasted film stars. Jarman is slyly suggesting that under this old, apparently wholesome and superficially heterosexual regime, a woman's destiny was in her breasts—"mammea" replacing "fata"—for men chiefly valued women for their appearance. Fellini, of course, is the famous gay film-maker who influenced Jarman. Stephanon Paidon is Stephen Boyd, the charioteer who is Ben-Hur's nemesis in the film of that name. (Phaeton was a famous ancient chariot driver.)

By mentioning a chariot driver named Stephen, Jarman added yet another layer of meaning to his discussion of repressed homosexuality. The unrequited lust of Boyd's character, Messala, for Ben-Hur, played by Charlton Heston, was in fact a part of the script about which the writers refused to tell the straight and straitlaced Heston, or make explicit to the late 1950s audience.[4] By including the handsome Stephanon among those Max admires, Jarman is showing the homosexual subtext in many of those biblical epics—all those gorgeous galley slaves sweating under the lash and gladiators straining every exposed muscle. Jarman undermines the legitimacy of supposedly straight society by showing how it substitutes women as sex objects, masculine athleticism, and sadism for genuine homosexual love. Max's comment that both the orgies and men were "real" in those days is undercut by the fact that he is referring to filmed events (on the "Silva Screna") which were anything but.

The commander Severus is aware that Max's bravado covers his real desires, and tells Max to "shut up" since he and Sebastian "are just the same." The context for Severus' remark is that Sebastian has just won a wrestling match—he is an outstanding fighter who easily disposes of opponents here and in a sword fight—and Max mocks him as a "fucking show off." Sebastian can neither abstain from his comrades' sports or participate in them without drawing censure, much like gay athletes and soldiers in the late-twentieth century. He is, after all, a "faggot" and a "whore," according to Max.

Once the soldiers are in exile, Jarman puts them through scenes in which Sebastian's introspection is contrasted with his fellows' hearty horseplay. The commander Severus, whose name stands not only for severity but for "severe us"—to refer to hidden same-sex proclivities of those who persecute gays the most—is the first voice we hear in the desert. He lusts after the beautiful, naked Sebastian who bathes himself in an intensely autoerotic manner. It is dawn: Severus tells us that the young God rises while mankind sleeps, the scarlet cock struts (the rooster wakes or a penis grows erect), and "the world is united in peace."

3. ⋈ Sebastiane 49

Three sorts of imagery constitute "this united world." The rising young God can be the sun or its pagan representative, Phoebus Apollo; Christ (the crowing cock recalls Peter's denial in the Garden of Gethsemenae); or Sebastian himself. Jarman's boldest stroke is to have Severus suggest that these three are psychologically one, an alternative, more genuine holy trinity. Christian self-denial (that is, self-estrangement from a hedonistic Roman society); narcissistic, homoerotic, and sadomasochistic sexuality; and worship of the "Apollonian" sun are manifestations of the same impulse.

Jarman plays on this imagery throughout the film. Old Diocletian, Sebastian's former lover and the emperor for whom he fought, worships the sun and wears huge earrings representing it. As Sebastian regards his own image in a pond much like Narcissus, he intones: "Hail God of the golden sun; The heavens and the earth are united in gold; Your body, your naked body, initiated into the mysteries step forth in the world.... Your beauty holds my heart captive." Sebastian is not looking at the sky or the sun, but at himself, in whom he sees a mirror of Christ's naked body which he identifies with the Sun God he formerly worshipped.

As Sebastian lies staked out in the sun for refusing one of Severus' advances, he also assumes the position of one crucified with arms outstretched and takes on Christ's torments as well. He refuses to allow Justin ("just in?") who is his closest friend and who also loves him sexually, to free him, saying: "He is as beautiful as the sun; the sun which caresses me is his burning desire; He is Phoebus Apollo, the sun is his burning kiss.... His punishments are like Christ's promises. He holds me in his arms and caresses my bleeding body. I want to be with him; I love him." Shortly before Sebastian's death, Max forces him to wear a robe and places a crown of thorns on his head in imitation of the Christ with whom he identifies. The crown recalls a laurel wreath Sebastian wins earlier for his wrestling prowess, another symbolic link of the erotic joy he finds in both physical exertion and suffering. Max then holds Sebastian's exhausted body on his lap in the manner Mary cradles Jesus in the traditional "Pietà." Only through this mockery can Max finally caress Sebastian consistently with his homophobic bravado.

Christianity, for Sebastian, is devoid of spiritual or intellectual content. He is lost in ecstatic contemplation of self and sun, both of which he narcissistically believes to be personified in his own body. Although he will no longer fight, he still performs the dance of the sun on the waters that he did at Diocletian's court. Nor does he make any effort to convert or be reasonably friendly with his fellow soldiers, with the exception of Justin, who shares his isolation in the vain hope Sebastian will make love to him. In fact, after Severus declares his own love and begs Sebastian to return it, Sebastian savagely mocks him: "Poor Severus....You're so drunk you're impotent. Haha. You impotent fool. You'll never have me." These words provoke Sebastian's execution.

Furthermore, Sebastian is also excited by the tortures Severus inflicts on him: besides the stake-out, he is flogged, hung from his wrists, and burned with a candle before sand is rubbed in his wounds. He refuses to run away and when Justin tries to comfort him, he quietly states that Severus "can do as he likes. The truth is beautiful." Max, referring to these tortures, remarks that Severus "understands" Sebastian. Sebastian goes meekly to his death as well. He is executed by his fellow soldiers, the Cupids who shoot arrows into him after their efforts to persuade him to love them have failed. They resort to real arrows, with even Justin, who has replaced Sebastian as the new scapegoat and wears the robe and crown of thorns with which his friend had been adorned prior to execution, permitting Max to hold his hand and bow. Justin too, has been spurned even though he emulated Sebastian. The average Christian is no martyr, and will conform to the general social milieu.

A strong wind blows as Sebastian dies, ominously seconded by music signifying the soldiers' reluctance at having been driven to this extreme by the young man's stand-offishness. The wind joined to the arrows represent air, the last of the four traditional elements of the material universe against which the Christian Sebastian has set himself. He had previously been tortured with fire and earth (when Severus burned his flesh with a candle and then rubbed sand on the wounds) and with water when his comrades nearly drown him when he tries to interrupt their horseplay.[5] In his single-minded worship of self, sun, and Christ, Sebastian symbolizes traditional Christianity's unnatural rejection of a diverse, pleasurable world in favor of absorption with personal salvation and the penchant to mock, pity, or relegate to Hell those who failed to share their asceticism. To his credit, Jarman has also exposed the gross indecency of the Romans in both court and barracks, providing yet another complicating layer that interprets Christianity as a plausible if exaggerated response to Roman excess.

Yet Jarman also intuits that beneath the martyr's surface self-denial lies a perverse and intense sado-masochistic sensuality. Peter Brown, perhaps the foremost late-twentieth century scholar of late antiquity, has written at length of the psychology of the desert saints. Like their contemporary Sebastian, they gloried in their penance and persecutions. In their obsession with sexuality, they mirrored the very society they denied.[6]

For each scene in which Sebastian is off by himself, or is tortured, this social mirror is provided by accompanying scenes of the soldiers training or playing. Just after Sebastian takes the erotic bath that Severus interprets for us, the near-naked soldiers vigorously train with swords as Severus urges them to fight harder. The commander greatly enjoys watching the beautiful dueling bodies of his men. Jarman is pointing here to the erotic element in military training and physical competition that its straight-world, traditional champions have masked as "character and body building."

Sebastian next refuses first to fight, and then even to clean the men's weapons, the latter also fraught with phallic significance. He throws the swords defiantly at Severus' feet where they land in the form of the three crosses on Calvary. Sebastian then refuses to take part in a ball game the men play in the water. As they wrestle and joke, Max calls Adrian "Adriana" and urges Anthony to "screw him, that's what you want." Implicit sexuality becomes explicit as the men touch each other's bodies directly rather than symbolically with swords. Unlike the other soldiers, for whom water signifies sexual freedom, for Sebastian water represents denial, the image of his own body in which he also sees the Sun God's and Christ's reflection.

As Sebastian is flogged, the other men look at a pornographic picture of a woman. Max, as is his wont, imitates a woman and begins to kiss and fondle the other men, supposedly in jest. "Don't you want to lose your virginity or do you have piles," he taunts Adrian, the most feminine of the men. As each lash falls on Sebastian's back Max states that this "one is for Jupiter, Bacchus, Juno" and other gods in the Roman pantheon. The Roman gods are taking revenge on those who deny them. Finally, Adrian and Anthony make love, inspired either by Max or the thought of the nude Sebastian being whipped.

Justin's tender washing of Sebastian's bloody back is then contrasted next with Max's awakening of the troops the next morning. He puts on a dildo which he pretends to stick in their mouths and backsides, while he grabs their penises. Although taking the form of horseplay, once again the homoerotic content is obvious. The juxtaposition of these two scenes, like Sebastian's harsh punishment for refusing to fight or clean swords, complicates Jarman's message. He is siding neither with Rome nor with Sebastian, but rather showing how men behave when they must suppress their real nature.

Sebastian is next staked out in the sun as the men playfully toss a frisbee. This anachronism, one of the few Jarman uses, suggests that the games boys play today have erotic implications. At this time, a young man wearing a leopard skin and carrying a small branch appears for the second of three times. His branch cannot even begin to shade Sebastian's sight, let alone his body. The allusion that this mute, mysterious boy brings to mind is from the opening of Dante's *Divine Comedy*. The branch is a shadow of the "dark wood" where the poet finds himself midway on his journey of life, and the leopard skin symbolizes the leopard that often forced him to turn back before he encounters Virgil and begins his descent to Hell. It is hard to say whether the leopard-boy stands for Sebastian's own imminent salvation following his death or is the atheist Jarman's ironic comment on such hopes. It is clear that the boy's appearance is linked to the very real earthly Hell the men force Sebastian to undergo.

Near the end of the film, Sebastian and Justin sit naked on a rock, admiring and listening to the sounds in sea shells. Sebastian hears "the old gods sighing" as he believes they will soon disappear. Indeed, paganism was gradually rooted out in Europe, to survive in folk remedies, curses, lore, and the representation of pre–Christian deities as particular saints. The one God will rule the world and others will only survive underground or in disguise. But even the monotheist Sebastian hears "a song as wonderful as a nightingale" from the hidden gods, and recalls memories of a "half-forgotten" childhood. Fanatical self-denial is required to ignore the elements of life represented by the pagan gods and concentrate all attention on a single deity.[7] But the men's dreamy reverie as they intimately examine the shell is interrupted by the others wrestling in the water. When challenged—"Who will fight?"—Justin eagerly leaves Sebastian, who is nearly drowned as he tries to break up Justin and his opponents. The saint tries to deflect the normal urges even of someone who worships him.

Jarman here presents two visions of what to do with water. One can cavort in it as do unthinking, healthy, normal young people. Or in a foreshadowing of romantic sensibility, one can seek symbolic meaning through careful examination of shells and ripples. Justin is an interesting case. He loves Sebastian, and tries to woo him with tenderness, yet his heart is in the fighting and horseplay, and he is torn between two loyalties.

Jarman also introduces animals to serve as symbols of the human condition. The men prod insects with reeds to force them to fight just as Severus forces them to train endlessly to little purpose. They give the bugs the names of women from Rome's glory days—the Vestal Virgins, Messalina, Agrippina—and those who resisted the empire—Dido, "the kamikaze of Carthage," the Sabine women, and Bodicea, Queen of Britain, whom Max crushes and devours much as Rome ingested the island kingdom. Other insects are compared to Sappho, the lesbian poet, as they copulate. (One bug is named Maria Domus Alba, after Mary Whitehouse,

3. ∞ Sebastiane 53

Britain's most famous advocate of moral censorship and a strong opponent of Jarman's work.)[8] The soldiers then begin to dance and wrestle in imitation of the insects. Comparing the bugs' activities to the soldiers', Jarman is suggesting that in the long run our moments on this earth, and even the glorious history we pride ourselves upon, endures little longer than the fights of insects, perhaps the next species to take over.

Another meaning of the insect episode, however, when read in conjunction with Max's speech praising the old days of Rome when Christian torches lit up the sky and Nero played his lyre, is that Romans in the late empire have lost a sense of history. What they remember are the spectacles, the pseudo-events. Real history, the heroic efforts of women as well as men that shaped the ancient Mediterranean world, is trivialized by an age that can barely keep the barbarians at bay.

Pigs also figure prominently in the film. Sebastian is flogged and imprisoned in a pit where the pigs are kept. His murder is anticipated by a scene where the men chase and torment a small pig instead of killing it outright for food. Max comments sarcastically that "pork always keeps the Jews away" as he reveals yet another prejudice. Max pretends to chase a pig as a surrogate for Sebastian after imitating his dance of the sun on the waters. He then coos "You are a darling" to the pig while the other men laugh and yell "Stone her, Christian pig!" as they toss corn meal at the animal.

Not stoning, but the receipt of surrogate penises for those he refused to allow into his body becomes the means of Sebastian's death. As he dies, the men who executed him slowly and reverently bow down to the beautiful corpse on the stake, much as we have admired the young martyr's body in art ever since. By forcing us to think what sort of a person this Sebastian — whom history only records as a highly placed soldier who converted to Christianity and suffered a gruesome martyrdom — might have been, Jarman summons us to look deeply into ourselves and our culture, and to confront honestly the sexual underpinnings of art, literature, religion, power, and day-to-day social relations.[9]

Moreover, *Sebastiane* was both a historical phenomenon in itself and the first manifestation of a new sort of history which would become Jarman's major achievement. Jarman's first film on a gay theme, *Sebastiane* was "a milestone in the history of gay cinema," according to *Gay News*, in autumn, 1976, Britain's only gay newspaper. In Jarman's own words, "nothing like this had been seen.... Sebastian didn't present homosexuality as a problem and this was what made it different from all the British films that had preceded it." Although he later found *Sebastiane* "flawed" because it lacks any of the finesse of professional film-making, Jarman had already developed the cinematic techniques and revisionist approach to history which would characterize his output for the rest of his life. Occasional although blatant anachronisms signal the relevance of the past for the present. Jarman employs the merest scraps of evidence to point to a homosexuality omnipresent but only secretly or indirectly articulated throughout much of history. And he chooses early Christianity, a religion held sacred and emptied of overt sexuality by much of his culture, to do it. Joyous, explicit love-making, along with sexual perversity, that had previously been branded as pornography appeared in film as instances of historical and philosophical interpretation. (In the United States, *Sebastiane* was rated "X" for sexual content and "was buried in porn houses where it pleased nobody.")[10] Events and movements which most historians explain using economic, social, or intellectual factors Jarman attributes to socially constructed outlets for repressed homosexuality. In short, *Sebastiane* showed how film could powerfully advocate the open expression of same-sex love by demonstrating the contortions and consequences it has to undergo where it is suppressed. Jarman had begun his cinematic journey toward retrospectively outing the skeletons buried deep in the closet of Western civilization.

4
Edward II:
From the Middle Ages to the Renaissance

———————— ☙ ————————

In *Edward II*, a film of 1991 based on Christopher Marlowe's play of 1592, Jarman is not only inquiring into the nature of history, but also into the accuracy of that history's representation in a work of art produced in an intermediate era. Marlowe himself was reflecting on the downfall of a fourteenth century gay king from the perspective of a late-sixteenth century world of the theater, political intrigue, and sexual ambiguity which resonates powerfully with that of Jarman's late-twentieth century. Edward and his reign thus demonstrate remarkable, if depressing, historical continuity concerning the problem of expressing same-sex love over more than six hundred years.

Jarman, like Marlowe, uses his art to explore philosophical issues linking sexuality and political power. He shows how people criticize what the dominant social discourse has designated as homosexual behavior traits — love of art and culture, frivolity, and weakness — so as not to seem opposed to same-sex love for its own sake. Ulterior justifications must be found for homophobia — at least among people who pretend to be open-minded and liberal — for such people sometimes harbor many of the same desires as those they persecute and project them onto a scapegoated "Other." Simultaneously, given this context, homosexuals have had to present themselves indirectly, coded through art and artifice. Sexual discrimination, in other words, leads to a world of dishonesty and subterfuge in which neither persecutor nor persecuted can express genuine emotions. Jarman argues that gays are valuable members of society, fit to enjoy their lifestyle and to hold politically responsible positions. Those who would deny them such rights must create and represent an oppressive social order, and repress within themselves the sexual freedom they resent gays for expressing openly.

How same-sex love should distinguish a good society appears in both Marlowe's and Jarman's works: Jarman called the Elizabethan playwright "my 399-year-old collaborator, Kit the unreconstructed."[1] They share the same plot, although Jarman dresses his characters in twentieth century garb. Watching performers in modern attire speaking sixteenth century English while they wander about a medieval castle powerfully connects common features associated with homosexual and homophobic behavior over time.

To begin, King Edward II, on ascending the throne of England in 1307, recalled his male lover Piers Gaveston from the exile into which his father, Edward I, had sent him. English historical thought has usually praised Edward I and vilified his son. Jarman reverses this. In visiting the tomb of Edward I, "credited with being one of our greatest kings," Jarman noted that the guide omitted to mention that "he killed the entire population of Berwick in an afternoon, expelled the Jews, and ruined the nation in his wars."[2] But Edward II has borne the brunt of history's attacks, the standard charges being that he neglected his duties, while he showered Gaveston with titles, grants of land, and control of patronage and the treasury. This favoritism incensed the English nobility, which forced Edward to exile his companion. After Edward surrendered much of his power to secure his friend's return, the nobles murdered Gaveston, which provoked a bitter civil war. Edward won the first round and slaughtered many of his opponents. This cruelty, accomplished with the aid of a new favorite, Spencer, set off a second rebellion led by the neglected Queen Isabella and her lover Mortimer. (No first names are given for these men; Marlowe has two Mortimers, Younger and Elder, whom Jarman conflates.) The queen and her lover forced Edward's abdication in 1326 and engineered his murder — in Marlowe's play and Jarman's script although he is saved in Jarman's film — the next year. Isabella and Mortimer reign only three years, however, when sixteen-year-old Edward III and his supporters overthrow them and begin restoring stability to the troubled kingdom.

Before discussing *Edward II*'s message according to Jarman, we must first examine the meaning Marlowe seems to assign to the reign of the unfortunate king to understand how Jarman seizes on its ambiguity to

4. ✤ Edward II

Jarman cast members of OUTrage! to appear as Edward's supporters to call attention to persistent difficulties for same-sex expression from the Middle Ages to the present. (*British Film Institute, Posters and Designs.*)

make his key points. For while changing very little dialogue — although he omits a good deal, mostly connected with the coming and going of secondary characters — Jarman claims to have uncovered Marlowe's real message: that homophobia, and not Edward's own faults, accounted for both his overthrow and his abysmal historical reputation. To be sure, Marlowe uses the most famous and eloquent lines in the entire play explicitly to deny this very point. The Younger Mortimer here insists he is *not* rebelling against Edward and Gaveston because they are lovers, but because their misrule is destroying the kingdom. Were the favorite's influence not such a calamity, Mortimer would gladly:

> Let him [the king] without controulment have his will:
> The mightiest kings have had their minions —
> Great Alexander lov'd Hephaestion;
> The conquering Hector for Hylas wept;
> And for Patroclus stern Achilles droop'd.
> And not kings only, but the wisest men —
> The Roman Tully lov'd Octavius;

> Grave Socrates, wild Alcibiades.
> Then let His Grace, whose youth is flexible
> And promiseth as much as we can wish,
> Freely enjoy that vain, light-headed earl,
> For riper years will wean him from such toys.³

Marlowe has the rebellion's leader deny that Edward's sexual preference has anything to do with the revolt. He even uses the word "toy" to describe Gaveston — which apparently in Elizabethan as in modern usage meant one of two lovers dependent on the largesse of the other. But Jarman makes sure Mortimer never says any such thing. In the film, Kent, Edward's brother, makes this speech. For Marlowe, Kent is the Greek chorus, or public opinion, turning from supporting the nobles at the beginning of the play in his anguish at Edward's misuse of power to favoring his brother when the nobles prove even crueler. (Mortimer ultimately kills Kent.) For Jarman, Kent — public opinion — sides unequivocally with Edward, for the director has Kent make what he calls this "great outing speech, the classic closet opened."⁴ In fact, Kent excuses his brother's sexual orientation while he himself is being massaged in a sauna by a handsome young man. By associating this voice of public opinion with homosexuality, Jarman is signifying another major theme of the film: that many if not most people have repressed gay traits.

How is Jarman able to claim that Mortimer did not mean what Marlowe has him say about the rebellion's cause? The director brings to the screen a fact already noted by scholars. *Edward II* is not considered a great play. Too many characters shuffle on and off in too many scenes, as though Marlowe were trying to pack in just about everything from Raphaell Holinshed's *Chronicles of England* (1586) which concerns Edward's reign.⁵ (Interestingly, Holinshed himself seizes on the one of the several narratives of Edward's reign, by Jean Froissart, which makes the strongest objection to his sexual preferences. To add a layer of complexity to the historical use made of Edward, Froissart himself was worried about his own king, Richard II's, fondness for attractive young men.⁶) Marlowe dismisses and omits much of Holinshed, and the only parts of Marlowe's *Edward II* which convey passionate conviction or limn flesh-and-blood characters concern Gaveston's and Edward's relationship, and the plight of Queen Isabella, a tender, jilted woman turned Machiavellian harpy, whose predicament in turn results from her husband's neglect.

Marlowe thus treats much of Holinshed's dry chronicle perfunctorily, as though he were determined to parade the dullness of official history which stressed names, dates, and giving everyone's noble ancestor more than his due. Instead, he emphasizes, and explicitly glamorizes with his most beautiful language, the theme of Edward's homosexuality, which Holinshed (1586: 2:547) implies but never actually articulates:

> For having revoked againe into England his old mate the said Peers de Gaveston, he received him into most high favour ... through whose companie and societie he was suddenly so corrupted, that he burst out into most heinous vices ... he gave himselfe wantonnes, passing his time in voluptuous pleasure, and riotous excesse.... [Gaveston] furnished his court with companies of iesters, ruffians, flattering parasites, musicians, and other vile and naughtie ribalds, that the king might spend both daies and nights in iesting, plaieing, blanketing, and in such other filthie and dishonorable exercises.[7]

Marlowe's treatment of Holinshed suggests the playwright is presenting the official Elizabethan version of events as boring and the "Other's" version as seductive. This alternative story could suddenly if briefly be articulated with homosexual James I as heir to the throne of England when the play was produced, and those who criticized James too sharply or openly could find themselves in jail or exile.[8] In other words, Jarman sees Marlowe performing the same historical reconstruction as himself. Both are rehabilitating a king believed to be wanton and incompetent by revalorizing a life whose story had only been told, and condemned, through his enemy's narratives.

Jarman's brilliant reading of Marlowe seizes on the fact that the denials of the rebellious Mortimer to the contrary, the king's love for Gaveston *is* the real reason for the revolt, for only that love brings even the other characters in the play to life. As Jarman explains in *Queer Edward II*, a book which accompanied the film's release and contains a somewhat rearranged screenplay and commentary[9]:

> How to make a film of a gay love affair and get it commissioned?
> Find a dusty old play and violate it.
> It is difficult enough to be queer, but to be a queer in the cinema is almost completely impossible. Heterosexuals have fucked up the screen so completely that there's hardly room for us to kiss there. Marlowe outs the past — why don't we out the present? That's really the only message this play has.... The best lines in Marlowe sound like pop songs and the worst, well, we've tried to spare you them.

Jarman's own remarks articulate the paradox of his film: does he "violate" the play or has he revealed what is "really the only message the play has" by insisting it is about homosexuality first and incompetent kingship second? No problem would exist if Jarman simply said he was shifting focus from Marlowe's apparent concern with a weak, favorite-dominated king to the persecution of gays: no intelligent person has a problem with a play that is adapted to another medium such as film or opera as long as the new work is moving and interesting. But Jarman has given himself a greater task, one he pulls off successfully. He reveals a powerful gay subtext in Marlowe's own play, a quasi-hidden meaning he can bring out by juxtaposing appropriate contemporary images with Marlowe's words. We *see* Edward's masques and amusements, and the nobles' disgust at what appear to be innocuous, if not attractive, performances of music and dance, sports and exercise, and love-making. At least some of these characteristics were considered "effeminate" in late-seventeenth century England much as some homophobes regard them today.[10] We do not learn of Edward's incompetent kingship except through his opponents' discourse. By visually revealing the homosexual style of life vividly described by Marlowe, Jarman makes the telling point that for much of Western history, gays could not defend themselves directly. They had to make their case through signs which an audience could decode. Jarman's film shots thus mirror Marlowe's language: gay activities are rendered beautiful, the straight political order appears as repressive and its representatives spouters of mere verbiage even they do not believe.

Another powerful example exists in which Jarman exposes Marlowe's "true" intention. Jarman argues that implicitly, criticism of Gaveston's financial extravagance, like that of Edward's policies, was also a poorly disguised pretence for gay bashing despite their opponents' protests to the contrary in Marlowe's lines. Jarman includes a speech by the Elder Mortimer just preceding the great "outing" speech by his son. The father also states that Edward's "wanton humor [homosexual affair] grieves me not." He pretends that the real problem is that Gaveston, "so basely born, should by his sovereign's favor grow so pert, and riot it with the treasures of the realm, while soldiers mutiny for want of pay." A legitimately incensed aristocrat appears to be defending social order, fiscal integrity, and the very survival of England. So it seems. But Mortimer shows his true colors by describing, at greater length, with far more eloquence, and barely disguised envy, how Gaveston "wears a Lord's revenue on his back, and Midas-like he jets it in the court, with base outlandish cullions at his heels, whose proud fantastic liveries make such show, as if Proteus, god of shapes appeared; while others walk below, the King and he, from out a window laugh at such as we." Mortimer then turns on Edward himself: "The idle triumphs, masques, lascivious shows, and prodigal gifts bestowed on Gaveston have drawn thy treasure dry, and made thee weak."[11]

There is much to unpack here. Elizabethan Puritans criticized the frequently ribald and very physical theater in which Marlowe flourished—

in which men and boys played all the roles — for sexual perversity as well as extravagance and dependence on the patronage of a corrupt crown and aristocracy.[12] Demanding war with Spain and insisting court folly rather their own bellicosity and moralizing were responsible for England's woes, the Puritans' attack on the Elizabethan theater was echoed by Mortimer's diatribe against Gaveston. Men became rich and obtained prestige through the stage which the county elite that governed the countryside and came to dominate Parliament and the press found obnoxious: Edward's critics are thus barely disguised signifiers of Marlowe's own, as they are of Jarman's, those who identified their own good fortune under Prime Minister Margaret Thatcher's policies with the well-being of England as a whole.

In Marlowe's time, ironically, it was the homophobes who had to watch their tongues when it came to homosexuality. The heir to the throne of an aging Elizabeth (born 1533) was King James VI of Scotland (1566–1625), who had already shown a suspicious tendency to live the same life as Edward II, and thus provide a parallel opportunity for at least some open defense of their mutual sexual proclivities. (Although sodomy was a capital crime in Marlowe's day, it was rarely punished, except when force was involved with an upper-class youth as the victim.) In fact, it can sensibly be argued that since there is little or no evidence for Edward's homosexuality before Holinshed, the chronicler may have deliberately fabricated his account to attack James indirectly. Falling in love as a youth with his French cousin Esmé Stuart, for whom Gaveston was the surrogate in the play, James made him Duke of Lennox. The Scottish peers then forced James, much as Edward had been by the English nobility, to send his lover into exile. James, following in Edward's footsteps again, led a counterrevolution after being temporarily imprisoned before enjoying a succession of favorites, signified in Marlowe's drama by Spencer. James's life so resembled Edward's that Marlowe was able to give homophobes a taste of their own medicine and get away with it — at least temporarily and on stage before his mysterious death in 1594. Marlowe's detractors could prevent gay people from openly defending their sexuality, but they could not criticize a play about Edward without attacking by implication the heir to the throne.[13]

Overtly, Marlowe is having his Edwardian rebellious aristocrats say that a ruler's personal life is unimportant if he rules well. Indeed, this is the secondary point Marlowe himself is trying to make: a ruler, gay or not, should defend the realm — not be "weak," as Mortimer accuses Edward — rule with the consent of the people, and preserve the treasury. Marlowe and his audience were quite aware of two contemporary negative examples. In 1589, only three years before *Edward II* opened, the weak and effeminate King Henri III of France was assassinated after a turbulent, favorite-ridden reign in which Catholics and Protestants fought a civil war. And the great Elizabeth herself had proven susceptible to manipulation by handsome young men in her old age: first Sir Walter Raleigh — a good friend of Marlowe's — and then Robert Devereux, whom she met when he was twenty and she fifty-five in 1588. She created him Earl of Essex and permitted him to lead her army with disastrous results, another eerie contemporary echo of the Edward-Gaveston story.[14]

In the 1590s, the English feared for the stability of the realm given the expected death of Elizabeth — she survived until 1603 — and the way she and James both depended on young, politically inexperienced favorites. England was threatened by civil war as well, another possibility foreshadowed by Edward's reign. The Established Church of England was opposed by both Puritans — who ultimately did launch a civil war and behead King Charles I in 1649 — and Catholics — who attempted to blow up the King and Parliament in 1605. James's mother, the Catholic Mary Stuart, had been executed for plotting treason in 1587. Royal authority was challenged by the House of Commons, which contained increasing numbers of Puritans who leveled the same charges of weakness and frivolity at the royal court that the nobles had in Edward's time. James's accession to the throne boded the return of internal anarchy resembling the Wars of the Roses which Henry VII, founder of the Tudor dynasty, had ended in 1485. Like Shakespeare's great "king" plays which developed the same theme, Marlowe's *Edward II* on one level warned the populace of the dire consequences of a foolish monarch led astray by a sexual favorite, and on another level warned of a rebellious populace that failed to respect authority.[15]

But Marlowe's play has another point as well: that much of the criticism of James and the theater was not motivated by concern for the realm, but poorly hid a latent homophobia. As *Edward II* progresses, Marlowe's sympathies shift from the king's critics to the monarch himself. Edward is deposed, imprisoned, and hideously murdered by having a red-hot spit inserted in his posterior, which was simulated on stage. The manner chosen for Edward's execution is one hint that homophobia may have motivated the rebellion after all.

There are other hints. In both Marlowe's play and Jarman's film, we *see* Edward and Gaveston showing affection, frolicking, and talking of their love of theater. The last of these should clinch the case that Marlowe and Holinshed were really writing about the contemporary situation and fabricating history, as there was no theater in the early-fourteenth century. We only *hear* of Edward's and Gaveston's neglect of the realm through their opponents' voices. One key accusation — that Gaveston has made the king "weak" — is clearly belied in both the play and by history. Edward II fought three wars, including two civil wars, and won the first. He then lost to Robert Bruce, King of Scotland, at Bannockburn in 1314, and to his queen and Mortimer thanks to the foreign intervention of Phillipe of Hainault. Edward's love affair with Gaveston pales in comparison with the treason of his subjects and the call for foreign invasion from the French, who were detested in Marlowe's England if not in the fourteenth century when most of the English aristocracy maintained close ties with their ethnic motherland. And Gaveston himself quelled a rebellion as the viceroy of Ireland. Late-twentieth century historians now challenge the traditional image of Edward as weak, as a tale perpetrated by Holinshed and almost automatically associated with gays by their detractors. If anything, the king was as cruel, self-willed, and warlike as those he fought, and would have enjoyed a different historical reputation if he had won the last of his wars.[16]

Jarman is true to his word of "violating" Marlowe's play to reveal its true meaning. He condenses numerous accusations of the king's irresponsibility in Marlowe to a single dialogue between Isabella and Mortimer which occurs just after the nobles — sternly dressed in business suits — have interrupted the king and Gaveston at a workout in a gym. They thus incongruously accuse Edward of weakness even as he is improving his strength and developing a youthful and muscular physique. Isabella and Mortimer then go on to divide the speech Marlowe had given to the Elder Mortimer linking the king's love of theater with lewdness and extravagance. To state the obvious, they make such statements to an audience attending the theater. To drive home the irony, Jarman has Isabella wearing an absurdly gaudy pearl necklace when she criticizes Gaveston for "wearing a Lord's revenue on his back." Homophobia shares with racism the projection of the bigot's own characteristics — extravagance and weakness in the former case, sloth and disorder in the latter — onto the "Other" as flaws.

Jarman's reading of Marlowe also makes the point that rather than attacking homosexuality outright, educated and otherwise liberal people disguise their prejudice by condemning behavior associated with gays instead: love of art and theater, playfulness, wit, colorful clothes — and weakness. Teun Van Dijk[17] and Philomena Essed[18] have called attention to similar tactics used by racists. Outright racist discourse had become offensive to educated whites in Europe and America by the late-twentieth century. So they substituted related negative stereotypes to demean people of color. Instead of calling blacks the "n" word, closet racists condemn "people" who speak in an "incorrect" or "offensive" manner, listen to loud music, wear a distinctive style of clothing, or who are held collectively responsible for the calamities the dominant society has inflicted on them. Jarman eloquently applies the same analysis to a poorly masked homophobia and suggests Marlowe understood this sort of gay-bashing as well.

In fact, Jarman pushes his analysis further. He implies that Renaissance critics of homosexuality, the court, and the theater in fact yearned to practice the very behavior they condemned, yet envied, among those who enjoyed a freer existence. Jarman has Mortimer wear a dog collar as high-heeled prostitutes trample on his naked body and force him to lick their shoes. The Master would enjoy slavery, liberation from his restrictive, drab, uniform, and being placed in a position of abject weakness himself. The archbishop who excommunicates Gaveston ogles two altar boys. In one of the few passages of Marlowe's dialogue Jarman modernizes — as opposed to the many he cuts — Gaveston calls the archbishop a "fucking" priest when he returns to take his revenge, a double-entendre which criticizes his pederasty and hypocrisy simultaneously. Edward and his critics thus share what the dominant discourse would consider a perverse sexuality, but which is generally repressed with disastrous effects on personal happiness.

Similarly, Jarman dresses Edward's noblemen as conservative twentieth century business types. Even the women wear the stern outfits favored by former Prime Minister Thatcher. Their troops appear as special forces commandos. Establishment garb contrasts vividly with the loose apparel of Edward and his followers who appear in T-shirts and jeans, athletic wear, flowing robes, or nude. Supposedly straight women appear masculine while Edward's robes suggest characteristics heterosexists stereotype as feminine. Here again, Jarman points to a common yet diverse innate sexuality which Western civilization has vastly, oppressively simplified.

Like Marlowe four centuries before him, Jarman uses the reign of Edward II to signify a contemporary clash of philosophies and cultures. He argues powerfully that gays not only ought to exercise their sexual preferences freely, but that their way of life benefits society and is a healthier alternative to the "straight" world. Jarman exposes homophobes as seriously disturbed people with secret sexual lusts, trying to inflict the repression that has stunted their own lives onto others while exhibiting sadomasochistic tendencies themselves. Jarman shows Edward and Gaveston listening to a string quartet, watching a ballet, and enjoying a poetry reading. Much of culture comes from gays. So does much aesthetic flair and passion for health and physical beauty — the king and Gaveston work out a lot and participate in a naked rugby match which exposes the latent eroticism of athletic activity. Jarman pits Edward and Gaveston's patronage of the arts against the stern, formal family photograph of Isabella, Mortimer, Kent, and the future Edward III — bourgeois "art." The future king ultimately spurns the special forces uniform and gun Mortimer gives him — the toys which subtly indoctrinate many children — and dons high heels, make-up, and earrings to symbolize his triumph over his mother and her lover, who are symbolically imprisoned in a cage as he dances a ballet on top of them to signify his newly won freedom.

Most tellingly, Jarman shows how a society that represses homosexuals must deny the very principles of liberalism and democracy it trumpets. By denying a voice to a legitimate discourse and a yearning of the human soul, the establishment reveals the hypocrisy of its pretended espousal of openness and equality. For if Gaveston and Edward "squander" the kingdom's resources on art and pleasure, Mortimer and Isabella spend the treasury on guns, soldiers, prisons, and luxuries of their own. The similarity of the military-industrial complex and "law and order" mentality approved by many fundamentalist Christians in Jarman's age corresponds to the politics and ideology of the crusading Puritans of Marlowe's age. Many of the latter favored war with France and Spain and crusaded against public immorality, meanwhile making substantial fortunes in new forms of commerce which threw peasants off their land, much as the Thatcher-Reagan capitalism deindustrialized the cities of Britain and America. Both eras featured a growing number of poor people whom the moralizing elite branded as idle, responsible for their own suffering, and thus deserving of the homelessness, imprisonment, and repression that increasingly became their lot. Jarman once again demonstrates the persistence of human behavior patterns in which people and events of one era can signify those of another.

Yet Jarman and Marlowe are both too intelligent to make a simple-minded argument that gay is good and straight is bad. Modern queers, who for demographic reasons if nothing else will probably always be a minority, must persuade a straight majority to practice tolerance. The criticisms that gays are socially irresponsible, principally concerned with aesthetically satisfying experiences only a well-to-do elite can enjoy, or preoccupied with what are sometimes considered gay-specific problems such as AIDS, can indeed make sense if homosexuals do not demonstrate concern for and make alliances with other victims of injustice. Marlowe stresses Edward's and Gaveston's neglect of their duties more than Jarman to suggest that while the rebellious nobles primarily resent the king's sexuality, they would not have been able to overthrow him if their accusations of misrule did not have some basis in fact. For instance, Jarman omits Edward's cruel reply to the Younger Mortimer, when he asks for a ransom to free his uncle, who has been captured in a war with Scotland. The king sardonically offers him a license to beg for the money.[19]

But Jarman joins Marlowe in his initial sympathy for a lonely, and in the film, stunningly beautiful Queen Isabella, whose long auburn hair falls luxuriously on her silken gown — a stark contrast to her subsequently confining dresses — as she gently tries to seduce an unresponsive husband. Edward is temporarily sufficiently ashamed of his impotence to bang his head against a wall. But Gaveston later makes taunting advances to both her and Mortimer. "Not all gay men are attractive," Jarman comments in his book. "I am not going to make this an easy ride. Marlowe didn't."[20] In fact, just as Jarman exposes the straight characters' repressed sexuality, he has Edward reveal a hidden sadism as he toys with a young soldier, captured in the war with Mortimer, he has suspended from a meathook.

Edward II's opening scene implicitly warns gays that there is no "easy ride." They must fulfill their social obligations if they hope to expect anything in return. In both the film and the play, Gaveston, recently returned from France, rejoices that the king has recalled him from exile "to share the kingdom with thy dearest friend." Edward is everything to him: "Upon whose bosom let me die, and with the world be still at enmity! What need the arctic people love starlight, to whom the sun shines both day and night?" Gaveston knows that being a royal favorite will cause "lesser lights" to resent him, but he has convinced himself (falsely) that only the king's will matters. He discourses arrogantly on the insignificance of England's complex and balanced political system: "Farewell base stooping to the lordly peers, my knee shall bow to none but the king. As for the multitude that are but sparks rak'd up in embers of their poverty, *Tanti* [So much for them!]: I'll fawn first on the wind that glanceth at my lips, and flieth away." The gay lover oblivious to all except his beloved, Gaveston is advancing a theory of political power, absolute monarchy, which the play will prove false and which Englishmen abhorred as the sort of despotism found on the Continent.

However, Gaveston's ostensible desire to be rid of both nobles and commoners — symbolically, the yearning of some gays to deal primarily with each other — is immediately contradicted by his next act. He in fact "fawns" on three poor men who approach him and ask to join his entourage. He at first only accepts the "traveler"— who "would'st do well to wait at my trencher and tell me lies at dinner-time"— for this man is something of a bard, which appeals to the gay Gaveston. He then rejects a man who can ride a horse, and then a soldier. But the soldier curses Gaveston — "Farewell, and perish by a soldier's hand, that would'st reward them with an hospital" — who has dismissed him, stating "there are hospitals for such as you." Gaveston is shocked, or perhaps scared, but in any case promises to entertain all three if the king does well by him. In an aside, Gaveston remarks that although he is unmoved by their plight, "yet [as] it is no pain to speak men fair, I'll flatter these and make them live in hope."

Both Gaveston's speech about the multitude and his behavior with the poor men are highly ambiguous, a point confounded even further when he tells the traveler that "I like your discourse" — that is, lying. A man who enjoys deceit will not hesitate to employ it himself, so there is no way to know what Gaveston really plans for the three men. Is he insensitive, saying what he has to in order to shut them up? Or is he charitably keeping them around after the soldier's curse has touched him, even though he prefers, as his next speech stresses, "wanton poets, pleasant wits, musicians that with the touching of a string may draw the pliant king which way I please?" Is Gaveston's response to the three harsh, or would Elizabethan audiences that enforced poor laws — which returned vagrants to their places of birth or put them in workhouses — identify with a man who wanted to be rid of these nuisances and get on with their amusements? After all, like theater-goers in our cities today, they probably also had to run a gauntlet of the homeless before settling down to be entertained. And is Gaveston's "Tanti" — so much for them — a curt rejection or a pledge of something to come later, especially when he has promised to fawn even on the wind "that glanceth at my lips?" This last statement could signify a kiss, that Gaveston will only reward the men if their lips meet his. In any event, Marlowe's opening scene is fraught with uncertainty and open to multiple interpretations as it appears on the printed page, although the tone of Gaveston's performance in the theater may have stressed the character's indifference or sympathy. Marlowe is posing alternative behaviors for homosexuals, only one of which is attractive.

Jarman brings this moral choice of irresponsibility or social commitment up to date. In the film, Gaveston engages in the same dialogue not with three beggars, but with two sailors to whom he has just made love. The ambiguous "Tanti" is replaced by the modern double-entendre "Fuck them," which Gaveston utters in as neutral, hence ambiguous, tone as possible. The audience can interpret the obscenity to mean either "Who cares about the people in general?" or "The people in general should enjoy gay sex." The second meaning has at least equal weight with the first because that is exactly what he and the sailors have been doing. And

Jarman omits the curse placed on Gaveston after he utters the words "are there no hospitals" — while omitting the condescending "for such as you." Instead, Gaveston inquires about "hospitals" for two handsome and apparently healthy young men before he gives them a large sum of money. Jarman thus calls attention to the fact that these young sailors may have been stricken with AIDS. Only then does Gaveston go on to state that regardless of his good time with the sailors, he and Edward prefer artistic types. By having Gaveston deliver Marlowe's opening lines in the context of gay men making love, Jarman has come out in favor of the scene's possible meaning that Gaveston is more than a lout fixated on the king and the power and wealth he anticipates. Jarman thereby also intensifies Marlowe's point that to attract sympathy from the audience or the dominant society, gays must be sensitive to the sufferings of others.

Jarman, like Marlowe, also looks to an enlightened ruler and court — executive and central government, in modern parlance — to combat the homophobia of the military, church, local communities, and economic elite. In the film, as the play implies, Edward is supported by commoners who detest the nobility's misrule, a side of the story missing from Holinshed's official story. They include a prominent Welshman, representing a land recently conquered by England in Edward's time. In Jarman's scenario, Edward's grass-roots support comes from real British gay rights activists, including the most radical of these, OUTrage!, which provided many of the film's extras. They pit their placards reading "Fightin' Fags" and "Pansy Power" — negations of the weakness stereotype — against the shields and sticks of the riot police (who do not carry guns in Britain) and later against the weapons of the armed forces, who are brought in when it looks like Edward might win. Gays need to make alliances with others oppressed by the same powers if they hope to enjoy equality.

Jarman here develops another subtext from Marlowe's play. "Liberty" was not what the Puritans or the House of Commons really wanted in their struggle with the crown: that bogus liberty really meant the power of bigoted members of Parliament and local elites to stifle collectively the creative, individualistic, and sometimes homosexual forces at work in the theater and intellectual life of the metropolis in the name of a dour and intolerant popular sovereignty. James was notable for his efforts to keep peace, an "effeminate" trait that enraged the militant members of Parliament.[21] Only an enlightened executive, supported by militant gays themselves, Jarman implies, can compel the straight upper and middle classes to allow real liberty. An instructive parallel is the American civil rights movement. Racists termed efforts to achieve equal rights for blacks through a combination of central government pressure and black activism as "arbitrary executive interference" with "states" or "community" rights. Racists, like homophobes, smugly assume that they are the only legitimate community, and that community is synonymous with its most conservative elements and based primarily on geographic contiguity. Such localism has been rendered obsolete by modern systems of education and enterprise, in which people across the world may be more essential to someone's well being than the unknown neighbors in the next apartment.

Is Jarman hopeful that a grass-roots movement combined with enlightened leadership can succeed against entrenched homophobia? Despite the defeat of Edward II's forces, there are two signs Jarman has not despaired. First, he offers us two endings: the script concludes with night falling and no salvation, but in the film Edward is not executed as in Marlowe's play. The jailer, Lightborn — a role played by Jarman's real-life lover Kevin Collins, an attentive companion and much younger man who made the director's final years far more pleasant — throws away the red-hot poker, makes love to the imprisoned king, and arranges his escape. Homosexuality expressed rather than repressed brings salvation rather than death; Lightborn becomes a real rather than a perverse Satanic reversal of the Savior to whom his name obviously alludes. An audience that responds in horror rather than with satisfaction to Edward's anticipated death — which emotion Marlowe seems to be contriving as well by placing a simulation of the death on stage for his audience's contemplation — will be prepared to think about what society is doing to the Edwards, Gavestons, Marlowes, and Jarmans of our own time. Second, although Jarman knew he was dying, he kept making films and fighting for his cause until his death in 1994. As he wrote in June 1990 in the midst of making *Edward*: "I'm up and off the oxygen, though still breathless. I spent the morning working on the script for *Edward II*. It's becoming increasingly Jacobean, sexy, and violent. We have brought the classical references to life.... I don't want to die yet."[22]

If *Edward II* teaches us that homosexuals will have no easier, and perhaps a harder path, to equality than other oppressed groups, Jarman's work and life demonstrate that struggling against a bigoted, culturally impoverished society is not just the only hope for gay equality, but a necessity to achieve freedom for heterosexists obsessed with their surface straightness and gays alike. At least we can now openly decode the signs of sexual liberation and repression, and uncover a history previously not only condemned, but largely concealed. Films can juxtapose sets from one era against dialogue from another and dress from a third. They can play with historical characters and symbols across the centuries, and can thus reveal a common humanity through persistent signs of a love which, thanks to Jarman and others, may finally speak its name.

5
Caravaggio and the Italian Renaissance

> *No painter ever painted his own mind so forcibly as Michael Angelo Amerigi, surnamed Il Caravaggio. ... Darkness gave him light; into his melancholy cell light stole only with a pale reluctant ray, or broke on it, as flashes on a stormy night. The most vulgar forms he recommended by ideal light and shade, and a tremendous breadth of manner.*[1]

In undertaking to film the life of Renaissance painter Michelangelo Merisi (1573–1610), known as Caravaggio after his place of birth, Jarman faced a challenge in that the printed sources were not only scanty, but "a jumble of highly partisan and often antagonistic records."[2] No writing by the artist survives. He only signed one painting in his entire life: "I, Caravaggio did this" appears in the blood dripping from the severed head in *The Beheading of St. John the Baptist*, which Jarman interprets as a confession to the murder the painter probably committed.[3] Aside from his apprenticeship contract, some painting commissions, and admission to and subsequent expulsion from the Knights of Malta, the important primary source documents for studying Caravaggio are police reports of his brawling and drunkenness. For the most part, we only know of Caravaggio from his paintings and commentaries on his work and life by contemporaries and critics who lived within a generation of his death. They

5. & Caravaggio 71

Nigel Terry, whom Jarman cast as Caravaggio, bore a considerable resemblance to the only known portrait of the artist and to the way the mature Caravaggio painted himself into several of his paintings. Jarman had his Caravaggio — as some contemporaries claimed was true of the artist himself — construct his works from scenes in his life. (*British Film Institute, Poster and Designs.*)

delighted, sometimes savagely, in analyzing his controversial art and recorded stories of his notorious behavior circulating around Rome.[4]

It is impossible to imagine a better vehicle for studying the problem of "realism," the ability of an interpreter to represent faithfully an "objective" world, than a film about Caravaggio's life. It seems Jarman reveled in tackling this difficult epistemological task through imagery in film rather than writing an academic exegesis. First, he brings to life scenes and people who may only survive as names in a police report. Then he argues with the very scholars upon whom he relies to assert that Caravaggio was not a Christian, but probably a pagan or an atheist. Jarman presents his case through his own art much as Caravaggio signified his dissent not in words but through images of himself in his paintings — depicted as Medusa, Saint Francis, and Goliath, not merely to represent, but anticipate and instigate the life itself."[5] And finally, at the center of both Caravaggio's output and the scholarly debate surrounding it is the issue of whether or not he was a "realistic" or "naturalistic" painter. Caravaggio's masterpieces thus become case studies of the general debate over to what extent we can faithfully know and represent reality.

Caravaggio not only painted far fewer works than almost any other great master, but he specialized in works of a single type. Depending on whether canvasses of dubious authenticity, altarpieces with several parts, and nearly identical versions of the same work are counted more than once, about sixty works survive. Taken together, they resemble the corpus of no other major artist. Not only was Caravaggio's output sparse — in 1604, a contemporary, Carel Van Mander, wrote that "after two weeks of work he will sally forth for two months together with his rapier at his side ... always ready to argue or fight"[6] — but he basically only painted people as individuals, indoors, and in groups. There are no sculptures, landscapes, and very few works set in open spaces.

Even there, the figures seem to crowd out a much smaller background. Nearly all of Caravaggio's mature work is very dark. Very few props denote a specific setting. In short, Caravaggio only cared about his figures and their expressions. As Giovanni Bellori wrote in 1672: "He never showed any of his figures in open daylight, but instead found a way to place them in the darkness of a closed room, placing a lamp so high that the light would fall straight down, revealing the principal part of the body and leaving the rest in shadow so as to produce a powerful contrast of light and dark."[7] This technique anticipates that of many Rembrandt portraits.

Jarman carefully studied the two standard works on Caravaggio by Walter Friedlaender and Howard Hibbard — the latter published as the film neared completion — which reprint the relevant contemporary

5. ∞ Caravaggio 73

sources. The director quotes from them frequently in the screenplay to provide the equivalent of scholarly footnotes for much of the film. Jarman even puts on the screen Caravaggio's severest contemporary critic, the painter Baglione, and shows him at work writing. Jarman may have incorporated this unpleasant character, and permitted us to understand why his point of view deserves serious consideration, to pre-empt criticism of the film that he might be stretching the truth or using sources uncritically. We thus learn that conservative art critics who deplored Caravaggio's naturalism — in both his paintings and his earthy, plebeian life — not only provided most of the contemporaneous documents, but recognized the seductiveness and latent subversiveness of the painter's works. Jarman also implicitly compares his own contemporary reputation, and the effects of his art, to those of Caravaggio. The words he has Baglione use, "unbearable, a fingernail scratched along a blackboard," were the ones *New York Times* critic Vincent Canby had used to pan Jarman's version of *The Tempest* in 1980.[8] Great art is controversial, and must evoke the wrath of conservative commentators.

Baglione also appears so that Jarman can start us thinking about the paradoxes and ambiguities inherent in doing queer history. Like any other topic, it ought not to descend to mere worship of heroic figures. Jarman is thus instructing us in how evidence must be critically weighed from both hostile and favorable historiographical treatments of homosexual activity in the past to construct sympathetic yet critical interpretations. What Jarman takes from Baglione and those who wrote from hearsay and oral tradition is consistent with and fleshes out what the police and contemporary observers noted about Caravaggio. Jarman is bringing to life a past that could have occurred, and is exemplifying the work of historical thinkers such as Carl Becker who argue that any historical narrative creates facts to support an interpretation.[9]

For Jarman, verisimilitude is not a function of a misplaced search for literal truth, but an elusive empathy between the hearts and minds of people who left behind traces of their existence and the hearts and minds of historians who try to reach out to them across the centuries. Jarman invents scenes and characters, deliberately drops in anachronisms, to show how all history is present-minded. The film "has to take place in the present" so "the paintings will not be seen as an anachronism but in their true perspective ... only by making Caravaggio a contemporary will we see how revolutionary a painter he was."[10]

Only one original likeness of Caravaggio survives by another hand, a black-and-white sketch by Ottavio Leoni.[11] It fits the 1672 description of Bellori, who remarks that his style of painting "corresponded to his physiognomy and appearance; he had a dark complexion and dark eyes, and his eyebrows and hair were black"[12] Leoni's sketch also enables us to identify how Caravaggio viewed himself and his own life, for he painted himself into at least four paintings. As a bearded adult, his is the severed head of Goliath in *David with the Head of Goliath*. He is also King Hirtacus of Ethiopia, who ordered *The Martyrdom of St. Matthew* and looks over the shoulder of the executioner. As a young man, Caravaggio's self-portrait appears both as the *Medusa* and as the *Boy with Fruit* or *Sick Bacchus*.[13] He thus depicts himself as either a pagan god or an enemy of the true religion, consistent with the sole surviving signature where he symbolically confesses to murdering the messenger of Christ, John the Baptist. In constructing a death scene for Caravaggio, Jarman has the painter force a cross offered by a priest out of his hands as he demands the substitution of his dagger, inscribed with the words "No hope, no fear." Only a dead Caravaggio holds a cross.[14]

And a dead Caravaggio is a misinterpreted Caravaggio. Jarman seizes upon a possible paganism or atheism which Caravaggio could never have put into words to take issue with the historians upon whom he otherwise relies. Friedlaender finds in Caravaggio a "sincere and perhaps ... revolutionary ... religious expression" which sought "a direct communication between the human being and the divine through faith."[15] Hibbard notes "his blind faith in divine salvation."[16] Maurizio Calvesi similarly sees Caravaggio's pagan subjects such as the "Boy with a Basket of Fruit" and the "Sick Bacchus" as symbols of Christ.[17] Ironically, Caravaggio's enemies during his life may have understood him far better than modern scholars who hope to rehabilitate him as a somewhat respectable believer. His contemporaries' most frequently reiterated criticism was that Caravaggio was a naturalistic artist. "Some people thought that he had destroyed the art of painting," Baglione wrote.[18] His work was "mere copying" according to Guilio Mancini. Francesco Scanelli commented in 1657 that Caravaggio produced "faulty creations without completely achieving a beautiful conception, gracefulness, decorum, architecture, perspective, or other similar and significant elements that together render sufficiently worthy the true principles of the great masters."[19]

Others, however, admired Caravaggio's art for its very verisimilitude. Van Mander considered his style "very delightful and ... exceptionally beautiful."[20] Bellori noted that Caravaggio:

> Advanced the art of painting, for he lived at a time when realism was not much in vogue ... he claimed that he imitated his models so closely that he never made a single brushstroke that he called his own.... Repudiat-

ing all other rules, he considered the highest achievement not to be bound to art. For this innovation he was greatly acclaimed, and many talented and educated artists seemed compelled to follow him.[21]

Scanelli's ambivalence appears when he speaks of a "terrible naturalism," of a nude painting of St. John "which could not reveal truer flesh if he had been alive."[22] But even into the twentieth century, most critics condemned Caravaggio's "vulgarity," in part based on the misattribution of dark, naturalistic Renaissance paintings that he did not even paint.[23] In short, by recognizing that Caravaggio excised traditional Christian spirituality from what purported to be religious art, interpreters intuited but did not articulate that he was not really glorifying but undermining God. Caravaggio was, rather, glorifying the male body and the artistic milieu of Renaissance Rome which permitted its quasi-legitimate enjoyment.

Neither of his two great modern interpreters considers Caravaggio realistic at all. Friedlaender writes that "nothing could be less true. 'Realism' in Caravaggio's works means not so much detailed accuracy in rendering the natural object, as a bringing of the object — the supernatural included — near to the spectator, almost to the degree of physical tangibility."[24] For Hibbard, "Caravaggio's paintings speak to us more personally and more poignantly that any others of the time.... We see him as the first Western artist to express a number of attitudes that we identify, for better or worse, as our own. Ambivalent sexuality [and] violent death ... pervade his works."[25] Jarman agrees that his paintings "are lit with a spiritual light, whatever claims have been made for 'realism' by art historians. The progress in his works is away from reality."[26]

Yet if Jarman finds profound currents at work beneath Caravaggio's deceptively lifelike figures, he supports the painter's past critics rather than his present admirers in denying that Caravaggio's spirituality was traditionally Christian. Aware of just how subversive Caravaggio was, Jarman has the painter state: "I've trapped pure spirit in matter, and what should grow like lilies of the field is placed high on the altars of Rome in mockery." Then he points to the camera, gives the evil eye, and shouts: "God curse you! You!" Immediately the tired image of his aged patron and (according to Jarman) lover, Renaissance humanist and homosexual Cardinal Del Monte, appears.[27]

Jarman renders the object of Caravaggio's curse ambiguous. It follows after he mourns the death of his female lover, Lena, who has been murdered (by the Pope's nephew, Caravaggio incorrectly thinks, who also desired her). The painter's male lover, Ranuccio, has been jailed for the crime. Later in the film, Ranuccio, who has hitherto resisted Caravaggio's advances while loving Lena with the painter in a peculiar ménage-à-trois, confesses to Caravaggio that indeed it was he who committed the murder so the two men could love only each other. In response, the horrified artist stabs Ranuccio to death. Is Caravaggio cursing a God who permits Lena's murder? Or is the curse (also?) against the deity's very worldly representatives, such as Del Monte, the high and mighty who exploit the poor and innocent, setting off this disastrous chain of events?

Yet Del Monte is kind as well as decadent. He is sympathetically portrayed by Jarman although the young Caravaggio, whom he has lifted out of the gutter, thinks the cardinal only (whether correctly or not is ambiguous) admires his art to get to his body. Ironically, the mature Caravaggio is able to recruit partners of his own with the wealth he has earned from patrons whose love of art is closely linked to their lust for male artists and models. Is Caravaggio cursing the cardinal for introducing him to the man he (incorrectly) thinks murdered his woman — symbolically, for turning him into a lover of men to survive and advance — or for seducing him into a sterile, perverted world of high culture which hypocritically denies, rejects, represses, and ultimately murders the genuine life-impulses of ordinary folk upon whom it depends for its sustenance? By having the Pope appear at a party dressed as a satyr, Jarman perfectly symbolizes his ambivalence about the courts of the Italian Renaissance. He notes the inconsistency of a religion and society that deny legality to same-sex love (for the clergy, any sexual fulfillment) yet practice it behind closed doors. Yet such elites throughout history have also granted a measure of tolerance to homosexual desire and fostered a great artistic tradition without which there would be no gay past at all.

Alternatively, before the cut to Del Monte, Caravaggio appears to be cursing his audience. For it is the greater society's suppression of same-sex love that inhibits Ranuccio from coming out, turning his passion to violence, much as with Caravaggio himself. Straight prejudices force gays, even in the highest circles such as the Papal court, to live in darkened, claustrophobic, if at times decadent spaces and to disguise their feelings. Religious art becomes an excuse to celebrate the male body (today, pornography and athletic competition fulfill that function). This semi-secret world is perfectly symbolized by Caravaggio's canvases where only a small ray of light illuminates an interior. The world out-of-doors, the sky — Caravaggio considered the color blue to be "poisonous"[28] — rarely enters. Caravaggio's color scheme typically employs an infinite chiaroscuro of dark red and reddish-brown — the colors of earth, not the blues, golds, and whites of Heaven — much as Rembrandt uses black, relieved only by that single ray of light falling on the bodies of his subjects.

5. ❧ Caravaggio

Caravaggio's unusual use of colors suggests that in addition to denying Christian transcendence, he may also have been rejecting a comparable alchemical transformation. As the historian Jason Kelly has argued, in my view definitively, this hermetic scientific tradition was certainly the inspiration for the work of the British painter J. M. W. Turner.[29] Alchemical paintings stress the transformation of earthy browns and reds into lighter tones of white, yellow, and blue before attaining transcendence symbolized by gold. Caravaggio's patron Del Monte was an adept of alchemy judging by the writings and pictures of alchemical masters in his library.[30] Furthermore, the Knights of Malta, or the Knights of St. John ("the saint Jesus loved" according to the Bible) with whom Caravaggio stayed from 1607–1608 in the hopes of becoming a member of their order, were not only rumored to be homosexuals and atheists (their historian G. Legman makes a case for the fact they were) but also practiced alchemy.[31] Count Cagliostro, a Freemason accused of dabbling in the "black arts" in the late–eighteenth century, learned alchemy in Malta from the Grand Master.[32]

Caravaggio's arrest in and escape from Malta indicates that he was no more comfortable with alchemical transcendence than with Christian transcendence, for the earth colors red and brown dominate his paintings.[33] He rarely uses the "poison" blue, symbol of sky and Heaven, the color most associated with the Virgin Mary's robes in pre-modern art. His figures frequently seem crowded or pressing against claustrophobic settings from which there is no escape. Jarman has gold, symbolizing either alchemical transcendence or Christian saintedness in haloes, appear as parody in the film as money: the coins with which Rinuccio and Lena shower each other, and those which are placed on the dead Caravaggio's eyes. The real gold, or light and fire brighter than the sun, comes from the body of the beloved (in this case male) in his paintings, a frequent theme in Italian Renaissance love poetry. Michelangelo, for instance, wrote, "If the heart is seen in one's face, in one's eyes, I have no more evident sign of my heart's flame... looking on the pure fire which burns me."[34] Similarly, Guido Cavalcanti wrote: "Your face is more resplendent than the sun." [35] Caravaggio's bodies are much brighter than the sources of light from the outside which at first glance appear to be illuminating them. Jarman thus uses the colors of alchemy to account for Caravaggio's denial of either alchemical or spiritual transcendence and his difficulties with both Roman law and the Knights of Malta. Interestingly, Jarman was also intensely interested in alchemy, and chose the color and title *Blue* to signify "the universal love in which man bathes ... the terrestrial paradise" in the film which depicted his blindness, approaching death from AIDS, and belief that paradise is terrestrial, if it exists at all.[36]

One aspect of Caravaggio's "naturalism" particularly shocked his contemporaries. He took his subjects from the poor people and rough characters whose company he enjoyed. Guilio Mancini complained that a courtesan was his model for the Virgin Mary, suggesting Jarman's identification of her with Caravaggio's lover Lena.[37] Giovanni Bellori blamed Caravaggio for "seeking out filth and deformity."[38] Those who pleased Caravaggio the most were "men, who like himself, were also belligerent," according to the acerbic Baglione,[39] "his young friends, mainly lusty fellows, painters, and swordsmen, who had as their motto *nec spe nec metu*— without hope or fear," reported Joachim von Sandrart.[40] These are the words Jarman has inscribed on the dagger from which the "distracted, restless ... barbaric and brutal [painter,] indifferent to his own existence ... was never separated."[41]

Jarman follows as closely as possible contemporary belief that Caravaggio generated his canvasses strictly by imitating life. Scenes in the film turn into works of art. The director correctly stated that his script was "based on a reading of the paintings rather than the biographies,"[42] although the accompanying book shows Jarman knew the scholarship well. Nigel Terry, who played the painter, even "bore an uncanny resemblance to the only portrait we have of Caravaggio."[43] No sooner do we see Caravaggio mourning the dead Lena, observing the Pope on his throne, or looking at Cardinal Del Monte reflecting on the skull of "Vanitas," among many other shots, than the film brings to life Caravaggio's method of painting exactly what he saw. Before our eyes, the shots turn into what seem to be the masterpieces themselves, although they are of course facsimiles. Nearly the whole film is shot in claustrophobic spaces, evoking a world reminiscent of Caravaggio's paintings.

By using the street gang members and lower classes of his day to signify Christ and Biblical figures, Caravaggio transfigured the poor and immoral into saints. Furthermore, many of his greatest paintings are wondrously erotic portraits of young boys and men or seductively androgynous figures like the Cupid of *Amor Vincit Omnia* or the *Lute Player*.[44] Whether the subject is classical or Christian, Jarman decodes Caravaggio as arguing that what the high and mighty really want is to enjoy the bodies of beautiful young people. Art, culture, and Christianity are all pretenses. As the novelist Edmund White reported that the French thinker Michel Foucault once remarked: "I've been trying to do intellectual things that would attract beautiful boys."[45]

The debate over Caravaggio's naturalism can also be viewed as the pictorial equivalent of a centuries-long debate in Italy over what language best expressed the highest ideals. Dante was Caravaggio's first prominent

5. ∞ Caravaggio

literary predecessor in that regard: his use of the Italian vernacular in *La Commedia Divina* paralleled his support for an Italian ruler to seize secular power from the Holy See in *De Monarchia*. By the sixteenth century, the controversy had shifted from Latin vs. Italian to whether elevated, formal Italian was better than more plebeian, local, or vulgar dialects. The Frenchman Michel de Montaigne (1533–1592), whose first volume of *Essais* appeared in 1580, shortly before Caravaggio began to paint, offered in "Of the Education of Children" the sixteenth century's most eloquent defense of down-to-earth language and the people who used it: "In language, to study new phrases, and to affect words that are not of current use, proceeds from a puerile and scholastic ambition. May I be bound to speak no other language than what is spoken in the market-places of Paris.... Whilst they at the upper end of the table have been only commending ... the flavor of the wine, many things that have been very finely said at the lower end of the table have been lost and thrown away." Remembering that Montaigne's most famous essay speaks sympathetically of the customs "Of Cannbials," we may (without looking for too exact a parallel) regard Caravaggio as the French thinker's illustrator.[46]

A disproportionate number of Caravaggio's paintings are nudes. His classical subjects are Bacchus, Cupid, and Medusa, respectively the god of excess and revelry, the god of love, and a terrifying symbol of vengeance and death.[47] His religious paintings include breathtaking male nudes, some of whom appear as sword-wielding executioners at the martyrdoms of aging saints. In fact, as the long scenes in which Jarman has Caravaggio painting seductively posing, nearly naked models suggest, not only the product but the process of art is intensely erotic. "The moment the model was taken from him," Bellori notes, "his hand and his mind became empty."[48]

Yet sex, which Caravaggio is soon enough able to buy once his career has taken off, is not enough. Jarman interprets the painter's work psychologically to symbolize Caravaggio's frustrated quest for true love, which in turn generates his well-documented intense melancholy, professed indifference to art, and violent rages. At one point, the painter states: "Upon my bed at night I sought him whom my soul loves, I sought him but found him not."[49] Jarman imaginatively suggests that an old Cardinal Del Monte may have been Caravaggio's model for St. Jerome, sitting dejectedly at his table, attempting feebly to write. The skull traditionally symbolizing the "Vanitas" of human desires sits atop a stack of books and manuscripts. Del Monte laments: "Years ago, when we first met, I dreamed of paintings I could love."[50] He foolishly trusted that art and learning could substitute for the ecstasy he craved through the reciprocated love of a beautiful young man. Del Monte speaks this line to Jerusaleme, Caravaggio's mute servant, toward whom he expresses both emotional and sexual affection. If a real Jerusalem or Holy City exists, it is through such an empathetic friendship, not in the treasures of Del Monte's palace or as a work of god after the Second Coming of Christ.

Jarman effectively portrays the intense, unfiltered eroticism of lower-class life through scenes such as boxing matches of sweaty, half-naked men, and Ranuccio and Lena — a laborer and prostitute who loved each other and both of whom Caravaggio loved — having sex in a haystack as they shower themselves with the gold coins the painter paid him for modeling. Caravaggio's relationships with the lower orders convey authenticity in the film, unlike the delicious sense of perversity and power as old notables persuade the young and beautiful to do their bidding, both in going to bed and in posing for erotic art. In a transvaluation of values, it is the rich and powerful, trapped in robes, palaces, and rituals, who live vicariously through the possession and depiction of those whom they simultaneously court and exploit.

The aristocrats also fear the lower orders, and manipulate them shamelessly if secretively to preserve their power and pleasures. "The Holy Father and I will turn a blind eye to Sodom as long as you make it worthwhile by bringing the riff-raff to Church, and placing them in awe of the power of the Holy Father," Cardinal Scipione Borghese informs Caravaggio.[51] Crossing and recrossing boundaries between the poor and disreputable he used for models and with whom he spent his spare time, and the highest circles of the Papacy which supported his work and facilitated his experiences with his lovers and associates, Caravaggio served as an elite tool for co-opting potential popular discontent. Common folk who saw themselves and their representatives "honored" through transfiguration into saints and heroes by a "gracious" elite — today, they play football or pop music or appear on talk shows — are likely to continue feeding the hands that pinch them. The Pope says as much in a conversation with Caravaggio immediately following the audience with Borghese: "Revolutionary gestures in art are a great help to us. But you hadn't thought of that, you little bugger. Keeps the quo in the status. Never heard of a revolution made with paintbrushes."[52]

Not only has the violent Caravaggio been bought off, but by "elevating" the lowly through his art he is granting them symbolic representation that poorly compensates for their lack of power and miserable lot. Over the centuries, "radical" artists and intellectuals, from Voltaire to many modern academicians, feted and institutionalized by elites, have rendered themselves irrelevant in improving the lot of those for whom they pretend to speak. Echoing elite voices and performing for the upper crust, such men of art and letters nevertheless succeed in earning historical fame through the applause of successive generations of intellectuals who have been similarly paid to "keep the quo in the status."

But we cannot blame them for selling out. Hence the paradoxical, complicated view of history Jarman is always presenting. Selling out is not only possible for gay people, but desirable and frequently unavoidable, as coming out would have meant ostracism or death in most times and places. We can only understand their plight, recognize that it resonates with contemporary problems, and tell their hidden stories whenever possible to construct a better future. As Jarman writes:

> Michele is a strange mixture of vanity and humility, with a confidence born of extreme doubt; a much quieter man than his biographers have allowed, secretive and withdrawn. The sudden aimless outbursts in a bright undifferentiated world are balanced by the darkened studio, where a controlled light shines that tells the story. The story, as it grew, allowed me to recreate many details of my life and, bridging the gap of centuries and cultures, to exchange a camera with a brush.[53]

Jarman catches the paradox that even limited freedom for practitioners of same-sex love depends on a world that openly condemns people for whom it harbors secret attractions, "a conspiracy between Church and gutter" as the malicious yet truthful Baglione puts it in the film.[54] Jarman has the young Caravaggio, who is both pornographer and prostitute, tell an English hustler who buys his paintings in order to obtain access to his body: "Io son oggetto d'arte.... Ed io son molto caro," the last word a double-entendre in Italian, as is the English "dear," which means either expensive or beloved.[55] Jarman brings to life the homosexual, hedonistic circle of Cardinal Francesco Del Monte that commissioned many of Caravaggio's works, but it is a closeted, claustrophobic world from which even the Holy Father and his cardinals cannot come out. Reality is in nature, in the street: "Madonna, Queen of Heaven," Cardinal Borghese greets the prostitute Lena, model for Caravaggio's Mary.[56] Art, which seeks to be true to reality and is coveted by the rich as a symbol of their desires, is a poor imitation of life. Hence Van Mander recorded Caravaggio's "belief ... that all art is nothing but bagatelle or children's work, whatever it is, and whoever it is by, unless it is done after life.... He is one who thinks little of the works of other masters, but will not openly praise his own."[57]

From a necessity he transformed into a virtue, Jarman's creative process in making *Caravaggio* mirrored the painter's own of elevation of social refuse into high art. Taking seven years (1979–1986) and produced with a modest budget of £475,000, *Caravaggio* used largely unknown actors and props gathered from second-hand shops and garbage: "There are palaces and prisons, the catacombs and the Vatican ... in the large derelict warehouse down at Limehouse Studios in London's dockland, which is stacked with rubbish and old discarded sets."[58]

Jarman also creatively used occasional but stunning anachronisms to signify that the attractions, repulsions, class structure, and sexualities of his own era do not essentially differ from those of the Renaissance. The virile stud Ranuccio rides a motorcycle. In a hilarious imitation of Marat, the soon-to-be assassinated French revolutionary leader as painted in his bathtub by David, the critic Baglione pecks away at a typewriter. The richest banker in Rome, Vincenzo Giustiniani, computes his wealth on a gold pocket calculator.

Yet the most important distortions Jarman deliberately introduces are only obvious to those who have gone back to the sources he carefully credits at the front of the book accompanying the film's release. According to Van Mander, the Ranuccio Caravaggio murdered was not a laborer who was his model, lover, and rival for Lena, but a "well-bred young gentleman" from Terni whom the painter killed following a dispute over a wager on a game of *palla a corda*, a sort of tennis. And the real life Pasqualone was not, as Jarman has it, the older boy who initiated the young Caravaggio into the joys of same-sex love, the ideal love for whom the painter longs throughout the film. He was a Roman notary whom Caravaggio mugged one night, striking and injuring the back of his head with a weapon, perhaps a sword, following "words on account of a girl called Lena," whom Pasqualone identified in court as Caravaggio's "girl."[59]

Jarman reinforces his three main themes by violating reality so obviously for those who consult the record, but (unlike the anachronistic objects signifying his characters) so invisibly to those who do not. First, he is hinting that the underlying motive for these attacks, and hence the violent temper that led to Caravaggio's exile and death, were not the pretexts of a tennis game or a few remarks about his girlfriend. Caravaggio's fondness for ball games reflected the desire to enjoy male bodies. Turning to Caravaggio's concern for Lena's reputation, we note that his art celebrates the male, not the female, body. Lena was either a secondary interest or represented Caravaggio's attempt to hide from himself or others his true love which he could not publicly reveal. Repression of same-sex love, Jarman argues, leads to violence both by and against those who wish to practice it. Caravaggio "became the most homosexual of painters ... in a hostile environment [where] this extreme of self-analysis becomes self-destruction. It's worth noting how many 'gay' artists die young: Murnau, Pasolini, Einsenstein, Fassbinder, Marlowe, Orton, and Caravaggio."[60]

Second, Jarman's film lowers Lena's status, as she is not explicitly referred to as a prostitute in Pasqualone's complaint. Ranuccio is degraded from gentleman to worker and Pasqualone from notary (a more important position in Latin than in Northern European countries) to farm boy. Thus the film emphasizes that desires which can be acted out in popular culture are given exalted facades by the upper crust.

Third, Jarman's distortions implicitly make the epistemological point that he explicitly articulated in his description of a later film, *Edward II*. "How to make a film of a gay love affair and get it commissioned? Find a dusty old play and violate it.... Marlowe outs the past — why don't we out the present? That's really the only message this play has."[61] Jarman thus believes that "violation" of a text is necessary to reveal its true meaning, especially when dealing with a subject such as same-sex love which could only be expressed surreptitiously throughout most of human history.

Reconfiguring and mixing up the stories of Lena, Ranuccio, and Pasqualone with tales of murder surrounding Caravaggio, Jarman invites speculation as to the nature of Caravaggio's psyche. Why would he avenge Lena by killing Ranuccio? The latter is freed from jail thanks to Caravaggio's influence, exits his cell with the seductive double-entendre "I'm out," and then offers himself to Caravaggio? "Did Ranuccio Thomasoni love Michele Caravaggio?" are the last, enigmatic words of the book Jarman wrote to accompany the film.[62] Not Jarman's only message, but his principal one, is to lament how a world of subterfuge, hypocrisy, and jealousies, engendered through suppression of homosexual desire and intensified by the flaunting of money and class privilege, has infected both Renaissance society and our own. The paradoxical side of this message is that such suppression has in turn produced great art, both his own and Caravaggio's.

The film's ending again reinforces this dual message, and recalls the first scenes where in flashback, the dying Caravaggio remembers buying Jerusaleme, a poor, mute boy, for thirty pieces of silver, the price Judas received for betraying Christ.[63] Jerusaleme, the Holy City, that is the (City of God or the chosen people in a sinful world, is happy working for Caravaggio, goes to bed with him, mourns his death, and tells his story. He is saved not through Christ, but by a man who paints himself as Christ's betrayer and denies Christianity. (The boy is Caravaggio's "New Jerusalem.") The good is thus identified with Caravaggio's popularly-based art and atheism rather than their sublimation into Christianity and high culture which distort and obscure the beauty we can find in life through genuine human relationships. As Jerusaleme's grandmother tells the comprehending yet silent child: "The stars are the diamonds of the poor. Rich men hide their diamonds in vaults, embarrassed to compare them with the riches of the Lord that sparkle in the sky." If there is a God, Jarman thinks he is to be sought in nature rather than culture (which bores Caravaggio when Del Monte tries to teach him reading and philosophy).

At the end of *Caravaggio*, Jarman has the painter's servant hand signing, employing the language of the deaf and mute, to convey a final message in the background behind a procession of mourners bearing away the artist's body: "There was much more but time has not permitted. That chapter I will write tomorrow. Death is all things we see awake, all we see asleep is sleep. Rest in peace."[64] Jerusaleme's gestures are hurried, desperate, barely to be discerned. A mute servant tells Caravaggio's story in film, through signs of the painter and his world rather than through his own voice, and carries on his work, much like Jarman himself in the film. Caravaggio's art must be understood by deciphering his paintings and interpreting his silence. His message must be discerned through signs that can only with difficulty be detected.

Jarman's and Jerusaleme's carrying on of Caravaggio's work can barely be made out behind the Christian religious ceremony which is burying the painter, both literally and symbolically with respect to his true intentions. Special knowledge is needed to understand a Jerusaleme transvalued as the object of homosexual desire. Such wisdom can be acquired by those with voices who take great pains to empathize with the voiceless — with a Caravaggio who was forced or preferred to speak only through signs; with his heirs who are silenced, whose stories are either suppressed or distorted behind a cacophony of mainstream art, society, and religion; and ultimately with a Jarman whose complex meditations on morality, culture, and history can only be discerned by decoding his films and his writings in tandem with the historical evidence on which they are based.

6

The Angelic Conversation: Queer Dee and Shakespeare?

&

Jarman's film *The Angelic Conversation* can only be understood if we realize he borrowed the title from the Elizabethan sage John Dee, whose works he studied intensely and whom he portrayed as a character in *The Last of England*. In 1581, at the age of fifty-four, Dee, an immensely learned scholar, owner of England's finest library, and intimate of Queen Elizabeth and her court, ceased what we would term scientific investigation and publication. Renouncing the laborious pursuit of knowledge through empirical studies, for the remaining twenty-seven years of his life he employed the services of three skyrers, or astrologers, in an attempt to communicate directly with the angels. His sprawling account of what is usually called *The Angelic Conversation* was published in 1659, a half-century after Dee's death, by Meric Causubon as *A True & Faithful Relation of What passed for many Years Between Dr. John Dee (A Mathematician of Great Fame...) and Some Spirits....* In this work, Dee prophesied wars and plagues, good fortune for some and bad for others, as the second part of the lengthy title — *Tending (had it succeeded) to a general alteration of most States and Kingdomes in the World* — advertised. Also included were a grammar of the angels' language and descriptions of the specific celestial beings who supposedly visited Dee.[1]

Dee had a reputation as a sorcerer even before he tried to contact the heavenly hosts. Both Causubon and his contemporaries regarded Dee,

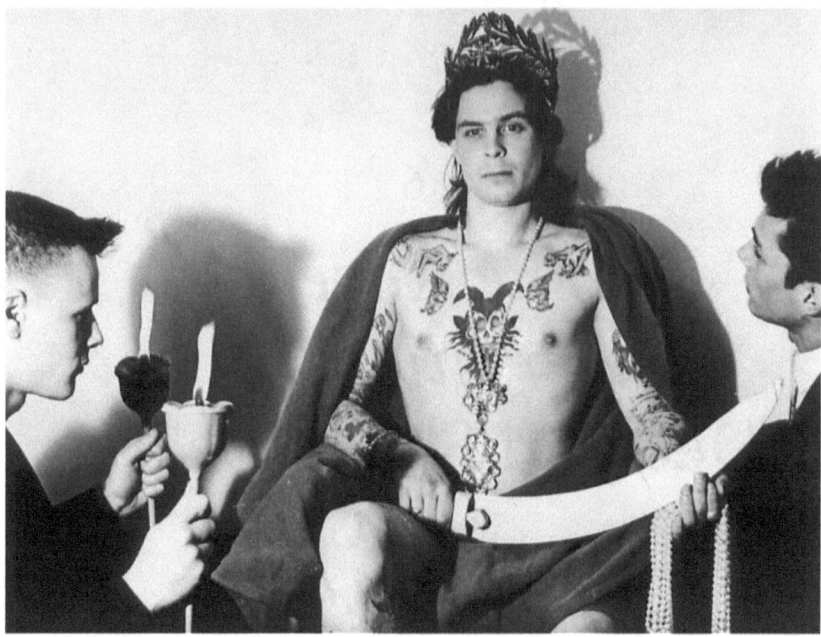

The characters who find solace in the protection of their ruler obtain a consolation denied to the two lovers, who only briefly meet and then go their separate ways. (*British Film Institute, Posters and Designs.*)

especially after the prophecies failed to come true, as being in league with the devil. The people who lived in the vicinity of his mansion at Mourtlake (on the Thames south of Kew Gardens) even mobbed his house in 1583, shortly after he and his family left for six years in Europe. Although unpublished, his "conversations" circulated widely in Elizabethan intellectual circles as well. Thus, it is quite possible Dee served as a secondary model for Christopher Marlowe's *Doctor Faustus*, probably written in the last year of playwright's life (1592–93) when the first English translation of the German Faust legend was published. Marlowe makes this explicit connection by adding "angelic conversations" to the German story. Not only does Mephistophilis tempt Faust, but good and bad angels explain to him the effects of accepting or rejecting the diabolic offer. Unlike in Goethe's more famous version, Marlowe's Faust is damned, the fate most Elizabethans would have attributed to Dee.

The parallel between Dee's wanderings on the Continent from 1583 until he returned to England in 1589 and Faust's adventures further suggests that the Elizabeth magus may have contributed to the story of one of the most famous recurring literary figures in modern history. Like Faust,

6. ~ The Angelic Conversation

Dee met rulers and nobles. In addition to his family, Dee departed with two younger men — Albert Laski and Edward Kelly. These men, who teach him the art of necromancy, correspond to Valdez and Cornelius in Marlowe's *Faust*.

Jarman entitled his film of gay love frustrated and thwarted, in which fourteen of Shakespeare's sonnets are read (by actress Judi Dench), *The Angelic Conversation*. He therefore suggests homosexual attraction may have been one of the mystical experiences for which Dee yearned, one motive for his travels with Laski and Kelly. Making a film about Dee, and connecting it explicitly to Shakespeare's and implicitly to Marlowe's presumed homosexuality, Jarman continued his project of "Queering the Renaissance," to cite the title of a scholarly collection of essays edited by Jonathan Goldberg[2] with a similar purpose.

Jarman strongly criticized academics who denied that Shakespeare was "queer"— they "might have their professorships in literature but they haven't got their O levels in life." Comparing the Sonnets to Renaissance portraits, he argued that "no [one] would deny that the boy you see in a Bronzino existed," although some scholars continue to maintain that the "he" of Shakespeare's Sonnets was a mere "convention." It did not matter whether Shakespeare actually had sex with the object of his desire or not — "it's quite possible to be a celibate queer."[3]

Before Dench reads the first sonnet, the first two lines of sonnet 151 appear on a black screen:

> Love is too young to know what conscience is,
> Yet who knows not conscience is born of love?

Of the fourteen sonnets Jarman uses, only this one is not read aloud, and this is the only instance in which the first two lines alone appear. The unread remainder of the sonnet explains why Jarman limits himself to this fragment: its final line reveals it has been written for "her," and Jarman wants to stress that while Shakespeare may have loved women too, he definitely was attracted to men. Thus, heterosexual love remains unspoken, silent, much as homosexual love would be in most cases. Jarman is reversing the traditional notion that Shakespeare must be presumed heterosexual:

CONCLUSION OF SONNET 151

> Then, gentle cheater, urge not my amiss,
> Lest guilty of my faults thy sweet self prove.
> For, thou betraying me, I do betray
> My nobler part to my gross body's treason;
> My soul doth tell my body that he may

> Triumph in love; flesh stands no farther reason,
> But, rising at thy name, doth point out thee
> As his triumphant prize. Proud of this pride,
> He is contented thy poor drudge to be,
> To stand in thy affairs, fall by thy side.
>   No want of conscience hold it that I call
>   Her "love" for whose dear love I rise and fall.

This sonnet resounds with sexual innuendo, as much as any Shakespeare ever wrote. He writes of how "flesh" (the penis), rises, stands, and falls at hearing his beloved's name. The first and second lines above (the third and fourth of the sonnet) deny that there is any sinfulness in sexual feelings or activity, a point Jarman and other queer theorists have stressed in writing, film, and their personal lives. The two lines Jarman does put on camera, thus, make the point that conscience, or morality, may be the result of our attraction for others — that the body comes first, then the mind and its rationalizations.

As the music (performed by Coil) begins, we see a young man looking longingly through the window of a Renaissance building. Its panes resemble a jail cell or wire fence, for only later in the film is he freed, or "outed," from the building, that is, his fears and inhibitions, and allowed to meet his lover. The melancholy tones, visual image, and sonnet set the tone for the entire film in which music, screen and text reflect each other throughout the film. Dench then reads the first sonnet (number 57):

1. Sonnet 57

> Being your slave, what should I do but tend
> Upon the hours and times of your desire?
> I have no precious time at all to spend,
> Nor service to do, till you require.
> Nor dare I chide the world-without-end hour
> Whilst I, my sovereign, watch the clock for you,
> Nor think the bitterness of absence sour
> When you have bid your servant once adieu;
> Nor dare I question with my jealous thought
> Where you may be, or your affairs suppose,
> But, like a sad slave, stay and think of nought
> Save, where you are how happy you make those.

Interestingly, alone among the fourteen sonnets he chooses to have read aloud, Jarman omits the final two lines of this one. Perhaps he intended the two lines he projected at the outset to complete the standard fourteen. More likely, as a firm believer people should love and enjoy their sexuality, is the possibility that he did not consider love "a fool" as the omitted conclusion suggests.

> So true a fool is love that in your will,
> Though you do anything, he thinks no ill.

Throughout this sonnet, the young man pining at the window is revealed as the absolute slave of the person that he loves. This gender-neutral poem thus completes the thought of the initial two lines from sonnet 151. Both describe the helpless slavery of those in love to the one who is beloved, but it will turn out the object of desire is male rather than female.

Upon the conclusion of sonnet 57, for the first time, Jarman displays a shining sphere several inches in diameter. (Later, a globe and a flat rectangular mirror will be added to complete the references to John Dee's fortune-telling tools for conversing with angels.) A young man (although not the loved one) dressed in Elizabethan garb holds the mirror. His movements are cryptic: is he working the magic that will bring the two lovers together, or is he shining a light on the troubled young man which prevents him from revealing his hidden sexual desires?

The second sonnet links the Elizabethan and present eras as times in which people are "enslaved," fenced-in, and subject to controls which makes same-sex love extremely difficult to obtain. Although basically intended as a "gentle film," "a love story" which evokes through its settings "the land of England that was once the home of dryads and nymphs," Jarman writes that "destruction hovers in the background of *The Angelic Conversation*." We move during the reading of the second sonnet from the "mysterious landscape" and "the very fine Elizabethan mansion" to a radar antenna in motion. Throughout the film such threatening modern symbols periodically reappear: "the radar, the surveillance, the feeling one is under psychic attack; of course we are under attack at this moment."[4] Surveillance and obstacles to homosexual passion exist in both societies: when the second sonnet (number 90) concludes, we hear industrial music and see the young man walking along a barbed-wire fence, its chain-link support resembling the crossed glass panes of the Elizabethan mansion.

2. Sonnet 90

> Then hate me when though wilt; if ever, now;
> Now, while the world is bent my deeds to cross,
> Join with the spite of fortune, make me bow,
> And do not drop in for an after-loss:
> Ah, do not, when my heart hath 'scoped this sorrow

> Come in the rearward of a conquer'd woe;
> Give not a windy night a rainy morrow,
> To linger out a purposed overthrow.
> If thou wilt leave me, do not leave me last,
> When other petty griefs have done their spite,
> But in the onset come; so shall I taste
> At first the very worst of fortune's might,
>   And other strains of woe, which now seem woe,
>   Compared with loss of thee will not seem so.

At the end of this sonnet, the young man indeed appears as the slave suggested in the first sonnet. He is carrying a heavy barrel. His labored steps contribute to the irony Jarman intends: he is trudging along the coast at Dancing Ledge, a mysterious landscape Jarman loved so much that he used it as the title of one of his books. But to someone who can neither find nor express love, a landscape that should dance is but the site for sorrow. As during the previous sonnet the setting is murky, limited to variations on two colors shrouded in mist. The young man is joined by his eventual companion, but both are bearing weights and breathing heavily. Their panting exposes them as "slaves" to a love they cannot find and a system which burdens them with both toil and homophobia. Neither their love nor the landscape which mirrors it can be fully and beautifully revealed. The men never appear in the same frame and wander as if lost. The second man carries a heavy log — Jesus seems to be carrying his cross. As they struggle to keep their footing on the rocky coast of Dancing Ledge, they also recall Sisyphus and his struggle to push his rock uphill. By equating the struggles of past and contemporary homosexuals with such primordial emblems of suffering, Jarman is reinforcing a theme he uses repeatedly that appears most spectacularly in *The Garden*, where a contemporary dual homosexual Christ is persecuted by policemen.

Indeed, what appears to be a police car and policeman appear briefly as Dench reads the third sonnet, increasing the atmosphere of surveillance and oppression. Fog permeates the screen, although it lifts briefly from time to time as the sonnet's words suggest even the shadow of the lover's presence brightens the day. Both men's shirts now open a little as well. However, such relief from the oppressive mist is brief.

3. Sonnet 43

> When most I wink, then do mine eyes best see,
> For all the day they view things unrespected;
> But when I sleep, in dreams they look on thee,
> And, darkly bright, are bright in dark directed.

6. ☙ The Angelic Conversation

> Then thou, whose shadow shadows doth make bright,
> How would thy shadow's form happy show
> To the clear day with thy much clearer light,
> When to unseeing eyes thy shade shines so!
> How would, I say, mine eyes be blessèd made,
> By looking on thee in the living day,
> When in dead night thy fair imperfect shade
> Through heavy sleep on sightless eyes doth stay!
>   All days are nights to see till I see thee,
>   And nights bright days when dreams do show thee me.

The tenth line indicates a change of mood. At that point, we see a man holding another shining mirror, a square one. The shining magic mirror is held aloft like a sword or chalice in a sacred ceremony, and we hear songs like Gregorian chants sung as the young men now carry torches. They have shed their burdens and are searching for each other. The music switches from melancholy, characterized by percussion and irregular sounds, to strings playing a melody that could be a love song. Jarman films the torches using beautiful black and white film. Sonnet 4 (number 53) is then read:

4. SONNET 53

> What is your substance, whereof are you made,
> That millions of strange shadows on you tend?
> Since everyone hath, every one, one shade,
> And you, but one, can every shadow lend.
> Describe Adonis, and the counterfeit
> Is poorly imitated after you;
> On Helen's cheek all art of beauty set,
> And you in Grecian tires are painted new.
> Speak of the spring and foison of the year;
> The one doth shadow of your beauty show,
> The other as your bounty doth appear,
> And you in every blessèd shape we know.
>   In all external grace you have some part,
>   But you like none, none you, for constant heart.

During the fourth sonnet, the two lovers begin to approach each other. Gloom is turning to light thanks to the torches they bear for each other. The first lover smells flowers, indicating the beauty of spring and foison (harvest) which reflect true love. Jarman arranges for shadows of the men to illustrate Shakespeare's point that natural beauty and human love reinforce each other. The sonnet also, by equating Adonis and Helen, for the first time in the film explicitly states that same-sex love is as legitimate as heterosexual desire. The first man sees his beloved shirtless, for the first time, and their eyes meet. However, the second man looks away, and soon the shirt is back on. Although the sonnet aesthetically and historically (or mythologically) justifies homosexuality, Jarman nevertheless illustrates the difficulty of practically coming to terms with it. He also has the first lover shadow-boxing against a huge fire with a stick. What he is boxing against is his own shadow, for the obstacle to his passion is not just social, but prejudices and hesitations contained within his own psyche.

Jarman replaces fire with water as Dench reads the fifth sonnet. The first lover kneels, as if praying that his companion will appear. For the first time we see the sea, albeit murkily. The film's atmosphere in general, however, despite some retrogression to darkness, is becoming clearer.

5. Sonnet 148

O me, what eyes hath Love put in my head,
Which have no correspondence with true sight!
Or, if they have, where is my judgment fled,
That censures falsely what they see aright?
If that be fair whereon my false eyes dote,
What means the world to say it is not so?
If it be not, then love doth well denote
Love's eye is not so true as all men's 'No.'
How can it? O, how can Love's eye be true,
That is so vex'd with watching and with tears?
No marvel then though I mistake my view;
The sun itself sees not till heaven clears,
   O cunning Love! with tears thou keep'st me blind,
   Lest eyes well-seeing thy foul faults should find.

However, sad music is still heard in the background, the (police?)man with the car appears again, and the torches flicker from occasional bits of light to intense flames. While the two men are drawing nearer, stumbling blocks to their meeting and consummating their love are still present. But these will soon vanish. Almost immediately following the fifth sonnet — unlike the several minutes between most of Dench's readings — Jarman selects a sonnet in which same-sex love is not only acknowledged and praised, but no longer shares the stage with its heterosexual counterpart. As the verses are read, one of the men swims, either naked or wearing only a bathing costume. The water is blue, the sky is clear, the fog is banished. Birds are heard, the music soars, and Dench recites a poem Shakespeare directed explicitly to a young man. But still the men do not touch, and one merely observes the other in the water:

6. Sonnet 126

O thou, my lovely boy, who in thy power
Dost hold Time's fickle glass, his sickle hour,
Who hast by waning grown, and therein show'st
The lovers withering, as thy sweet self grow'st;
If Nature, sovereign mistress over wrack,
As thou goest onwards, still will pluck thee back,
She keeps thee to this purpose, that her skill
May Time disgrace and wretched minutes kill.
Yet fear her, O thou minion of her pleasure;
She may detain, but not still keep her treasure.
   Her audit, though delayed, answered must be,
   And her quietus is to render thee.

Shakespeare here expresses the hope that in time, true love will prevail, and love will be consummated. The thought continues, and the beloved remains male. In the seventh sonnet Dench reads:

7. Sonnet 29

When, in disgrace with fortune and men's eyes,
I all alone beweep my outcast state,
And trouble deaf heaven with my bootless cries,
And look upon myself and curse my fate,
Wishing me like to one more rich in hope,
Featured like him, like him with friends possess'd,
Desiring this man's art, and that man's scope,
With what I most enjoy contented least;
Yet in these thoughts myself almost despising,
Haply I think on thee, and then my state,
Like to the lark at break of day arising
From sullen earth, sings hymns at heaven's gate;
   For thy sweet love rememb'rd such wealth brings,
   That then I scorn to change my state with kings.

Before the lovers actually embrace, however, Jarman brings on three more characters, suggestive of the state of kings. He tells us that here he integrated the Anglo-Saxon legend of "The Wanderer," which probably dates from the eighth century, into his film. In the chaotic state of a country torn by war between many small kingdoms and the need to defend Britain against the Vikings, "a wanderer on earth, remembering hardships, the violent assaults of enemies, and the extinction of loving family," mourns that the days of his youth when his "generous lord entertained him at the banquet" have disappeared. He longs for the old comradeship, to kiss his lord upon the knee, but instead there is only desolation everywhere: "There is now not one living being to whom I dare plainly express my heart."⁵

Jarman illustrates the ephemeral state of earthly security and bliss by having the three men kiss a globe, a whirling ball, which the ruler holds on high. He is covered with mysterious tattoos, and the other men pay homage to him. He holds a sceptre in the manner of a huge penis, while one of the men kisses his knees, as "The Wanderer" describes. Then the man's lips move all over the ruler's body, who is also gently anointed with water. Much as the two lovers will meet each other in the water, water symbolizes the love of the men for their ruler. Jarman is illustrating that unexpressed homosexual love, in addition to or instead of the wealth of kings, is a principal attraction of people at royal courts for each other. The affection of the three men also suggests that a realm symbolized by justice and acceptance of homosocial if not homosexual companionship, as "The Wanderer" suggests, is vanished, or nonexistent. Jarman wrote that he hoped to depict "service willingly given, not exacted. There is no compulsion in the scene."⁶ Public and personal acceptance of same-sex love are mutually necessary, for only in a society in which such love is officially sanctioned and can be practiced securely, can it "speak" and emerge from the shadows. This reticence is suggested in the eighth sonnet, which continues to focus on the ruler and his two subjects. The king throughout conforms to the unmoved person who moves others to passion described therein:

8. Sonnet 94

They that have pow'r to hurt and will do none,
That do not do the thing they most do show,
Who, moving others, are themselves as stone,
Unmovèd, cold, and to temptation slow;
They rightly do inherit heaven's graces
And husband nature's riches from expense;
They are the lords and owners of their faces,
Others but stewards of their excellence.
The summer's flow'r is to the summer sweet,
Though to itself it only live and die;
But if that flow'r with base infection meet,
The basest weed outbraves his dignity:
    For sweetest things turn sourest by their deeds;
    Lilies that fester smell far worse than weeds.

Here Jarman inserts a warning for the soon-to-be united lovers. Once their love vanishes, the pain will be excruciating, like that the Wanderer suffers in his ravaged land. Torches flicker and uncertainty reigns. Yet in the ninth sonnet, Shakespeare's number 30, Jarman describes how the happiness which will finally arrive when the men embrace and make love will cause all past sorrows to be forgotten:

9. SONNET 30

When to the sessions of sweet silent thought
I summon up remembrance of things past,
I sigh the lack of many a thing I sought,
And with old woes new wail my dear Time's waste:
Then can I drown an eye, unused to flow,
For precious friends hid in death's dateless night,
And weep afresh love's long since canceled woe,
And moan th'expense of many a vanished sight;
Then can I grieve at grievances foregone,
And heavily from woe to woe tell o'er
The sad account of fore-bemoanèd moan,
Which I new pay as if not paid before.
   But if the while I think on thee, dear friend,
   All sorrows are restored and sorrows end.

The lovers appear shirtless in the ninth sonnet. One anoints the other much as the king was anointed previously, with water from a shell. Their passion, which is exhibited as the tenth sonnet is read, is thus compared on one level with the cold ruler who does not respond to his subjects' similar caresses. The scene again becomes naturalistic.

Yet all the two men seem to be doing is wrestling rather than making love. Jarman is showing that aggression and power, although sublimated, are implicit in love-making just as sexual tension underlies the public "worship" of great men. Jarman has the men wrestle to illustrate the martial analogies of the tenth sonnet as well — that war and the ravages of time will not erase the memory of this love or the immortality of this sonnet, and, by extension, its visual depiction in film. The protracted wrestling match is one of the film's longest scenes, a symbol of the ability of love, literature, and film to outlast and overshadow monuments and memories of warriors. Wrestling is required as foreplay, just as much athletic and martial behavior is an alternative outlet for sex. But at the end of the tenth sonnet, the lovers finally stop wrestling and lay tenderly in each other's arms as Shakespeare's words proclaim that this love (between these two particular men or love of the homosexual variety in general?) will serve as the standard to which other lovers will hold themselves whenever the sonnet is remembered:

10. SONNET 55

Not marble, nor the guilded monuments
Of princes, shall outlive this pow'rful rhyme;

> But you shall shine more bright in these contents
> Than unswept stone, besmeared with sluttish time.
> When wasteful war shall statues overturn,
> And broils root out the work of masonry,
> Nor Mars his sword nor war's quick fire shall burn
> The living record of your memory.
> 'Gainst death and all-oblivious enmity
> Shall you pace forth; your praise shall still find room
> Even in the eyes of all posterity
> That wear this world out to the ending doom.
>   So, till the judgment that yourself arise,
>   You live in this, and dwell in lovers' eyes.

However, love is not an unmixed blessing. Jarman's choice of an eleventh sonnet (number 27) recalls Plato's point in *The Symposium* that to be in love is to be miserable, always longing for the beloved and fearing that love will not last. Shakespeare compares the toil of day with the sleeplessness of a troubled lover at night. Jarman has a man play a trumpet, from out of nowhere, to suggest the precariousness of peace and quiet:

11. Sonnet 27

> Weary with toil, I haste to my bed,
> The dear repose for limbs with travel tired,
> But then begins a journey in my head
> To work my mind when body's work's expired;
> For then my thoughts, from far where I abide,
> Intend a zealous pilgrimage to thee,
> And keep my drooping eyelids open wide,
> Looking on darkness which the blind do see;
> Save that my soul's imaginary sight
> Presents thy shadow to my sightless view,
> Which like a jewel hung in ghastly night,
> Makes black night beauteous and her old face new.
>   Lo! thus, by day my limbs, by night my mind,
>   For thee, and for myself no quiet find.

Still, during the eleventh sonnet, the predominantly grainy, foggy set yields to nature as the lovers kiss, an act they have not performed before. "Ghastly" night literally yields to beauty.

In the twelfth sonnet (number 61) the men kiss again to the sound of running water. The setting is natural and attractive, and beautiful blossoms eclipse the radar signal, which appears again as the words "watch" and "watchman" recall the surveillance which hindered true expression earlier. Jarman intended the end of the film to show how the "hovering, external violence" symbolized by the antenna "is cauterised by the blossom, which obliterates the radar" and "takes over."[7] But since I viewed the film before I read the commentary, I interpreted the scene differently. (Jarman himself wrote that "I came to the ideas after I made the film.[8]) The sign of surveillance can be seen lurking behind and undercutting the message of the flowers — Shakespeare, or Jarman, the true lover, fears that he must perpetually "watch" a lover who does not love him as intensely. Even in an ideal world, with societal repression of homosexuality but a memory, internal surveillance over a relationship in which one of the parties loves more strongly must take its place. As the poem ends, the beloved walks away with his back turned.

12. Sonnet 61

Is it thy will thy image should keep open
My heavy eyelids to the weary night?
Dost thou desire my slumbers should be broken
While shadows like to thee do mock my sight?
Is it thy spirit that thou send'st from thee
So far from home into my deeds to pry,
To find out shames and idle hours in me,
The scope and tenure of thy jealousy?
O no! thy love, though much, is not so great.
It is my love that keeps mine eye awake;
Mine own true love that doth my rest defeat,
To play the watchman ever for thy sake:
 For thee watch I, whilst thou dost wake elsewhere,
 From me far off, with others all too near.

In sonnet 13 (number 56), the lover prays for his beloved to return; he kneels in prayer at the side of Dancing Ledge, the stark yet spectacular cliffs and beach where they first met.

13. Sonnet 56

Sweet love, renew thy force; be it not said
Thy edge should blunter be than appetite,
Which but today by feeding is allayed,
Tomorrow sharp'ned in his former might.
So, love, be thou; although today thou fill
Thy hungry eyes even till they wink with fullness
Tomorrow see again, and do not kill

> The spirit of love with a perpetual dullness.
> Let this sad int'rim like the ocean be
> Which parts the shore where two contracted new
> Come daily to the banks, that, when they see
> Return of love, more blest may be the view;
> > Else call it winter, which being full of care
> > Makes summer's welcome thrice more wished, more rare.

At the poem's end, we see the original manor house. But now the first man is "out" — of doors — a sign that he has acknowledged his true feelings and come "out." He fans himself, he sits in a leisurely manner to contemplate the terrain. He is still hot with love and the thirteenth poem takes place in summer. Jarman lingers long on the palatial grounds, to show that wealth and a beautiful landscape are no substitute for love that blossomed on the beach back when the men were "slaves" to the world and to their love. However, walking around the estate, he cannot recover his lost love, although he recalls their brief moment of bliss as he looks into the lily pond. No longer do the lovers frolic amidst the wild ocean waves. Only an image of the beautiful man he saw swimming remains.

His hopes are in vain. The summer of love at the ocean is, as the final poem reveals, a brief encounter. The beloved's beauty fades: the moment of passion endures but an instant, never to be recovered. The lover swims a bit, alone, and then repeatedly sniffs the flowers to remember his experience. The beloved's image returns for a while, but then the frame is frozen and the picture ends as the last sonnet's final word — "dead" — ends the "angelic conversation" and the film.

14. Sonnet 104

> To me, fair friend, you never can be old,
> For as you were when first your eye I eyed,
> Such seems your beauty still. Three winters cold
> Have from the forests shook three summers' pride,
> Three beauteous springs to yellow autumn turned
> In process of the seasons have I seen,
> Three April perfumes in three hot Junes burned,
> Since first I saw you fresh, which yet are green.
> Ah! yet doth beauty, like a dial hand,
> Steal from his figure, and no pace perceived;
> So your sweet hue, which methinks still doth stand
> Hath motion, and mine eye may be deceived:
> > For fear of which, hear this, thou age unbred;
> > Ere you were born was beauty's summer dead.

6. ❧ The Angelic Conversation

Jarman leaves us with the brief memory of an intense encounter too long delayed, too soon vanished. Unlike his other films, historical references are scarce. Societal obstacles to homosexual love occur in Anglo-Saxon times, in the Renaissance, and again in the modern world. Subtly, Jarman shows us that given public mores, it has been almost impossible for men to express their true feelings. Hence the great sadness of this film, the long delay in gratification, and its quick departure.

But even these encounters occur thanks to a magical mirror of the sort John Dee used to transport himself to other ages, a mirror which ultimately deceived him as his angels were wrong about the future. For true homosexual love to flourish requires something of a miracle, for a John Dee to leave behind the "real" world for one where he dwells with the angels. Jarman is telling us, here as elsewhere, to discard the personal and societal inhibitions which prevent love from flourishing beautifully and naturally. Only rarely do the film's colors seem natural and the flowers and the ocean appear in their true splendor, and only rarely does the music express either sweetness or (when the lovers embrace) a sense of triumph, which suggests that every experience of true love is a miracle, that also enables us to see the true beauty of nature and music. Try enjoying them when you are miserable! Since such experiences are so fleeting, they need to be cultivated and cherished, rather than rendered obscene as they are by a homophobic social order which deserves that epithet for itself.

7

The Tempest: From the Renaissance to the Present

              ಐ

Jarman wrote that his film *The Last of England* was intended as a sequel to his version of *The Tempest*, the Shakespeare play his class read in college.[1] "Should there be great calm, after the stormy weather?" he asked, which could signify either the storm that cast the Milanese adrift or else their tempestuous quarrels preceding the shipwreck. "Did Miranda's marriage solve the world's problems?"[2] Jarman asks. He considered "stormy weather" a real possibility following Miranda and Ferdinand's wedding: "The world doesn't see heterosexual union as a solution any more."[3] Elsewhere, Jarman stated that "in my film *The Tempest*, the three-hundred-odd years of the play's age — it was premiered in 1611— became its period."[4] "Stormy weather" stretches from Shakespeare's age to our own, and is the title of the song Jarman substitutes for the masque of the ancient gods at the play's end.

    Jarman's main model for Prospero is John Dee, confidant of Elizabeth I, adept in alchemy, and leading figure in the Elizabethan "police state."[5] The setting for Jarman's adaptation is the early seventeenth century. Prospero reads and works his spells out of Cornelius Agrippa's 1631 book, *Of the Occult Philosophy*. Indoor scenes of his run-down mansion are set in Stoneleigh Abbey, a Renaissance country house where *The Tempest* was actually performed in 1612 for Elizabeth, the future "Winter

7. ✤ The Tempest

Elizabeth Welch had been singing on the British stage for over four decades when Jarman cast her to sing "Stormy Weather" as sailors danced the hornpipe to substitute for the usual masque at the end of *The Tempest*. The title of her song carries the subtext that all will not be well with the quarreling characters. (*British Film Institute, Posters and Designs.*)

Queen" of Bohemia and daughter of James I.[6] But Jarman planned to costume Prospero like Robespierre, the French Revolutionary leader, and indeed this ultimate "mad" scientist with rats in his hair looks like an eighteenth century rebel.[7] (He was played by Heathcote Williams, a real-life anarchist and playwright.[8]) Jarman's Prospero thus represents both esoteric learning and the effort to reshape the world to fit a particular doctrine.

The remaining characters embody three centuries of history. Miranda and Ferdinand belong to the ancient regime, as do the other aristocrats. But the young couple eventually adopt Prospero's progressive line. The comedians and Caliban are nineteenth century workers (Caliban is also an exploited colonial), Ariel and the sailors twentieth century minions of the elite. Jarman makes sure that the clothes, thoughts, and behavior of each character suits an important group of people in modern history. In ninety minutes, he is giving us a whirlwind tour of Western civilization since the Renaissance.

To make this film, Jarman "cut away the dead wood ... so that the great speeches were concentrated. Then the play was rearranged and opened up."[9] Paradoxically, Jarman was thereby being "authentic" in the best sense, for in Shakespeare's time plays were rewritten for specific actors and settings, boys played men, and the written text could be varied much like the props available in different settings.[10] Critics who complain of this inauthenticity are being inauthentic in their very complaint.

Whether Jarman was familiar with the writings of Michel Foucault (he did not write about them, at least in the published works, although they were very much in the air in the late seventies and early eighties), this version of *The Tempest* is the visual equivalent of Foucault's theory of the Enlightenment project (as he always called it).[11] Amazingly, when reflected on, Shakespeare's seventeenth century play can also be plausibly interpreted as demonstrating that "reason" and "science" were not so much ways of making knowledge generally available, but "occult" practices, as Agrippa's title suggests, esoteric languages that enabled an elite to exercise power, to discipline and punish "Others." A great deal of the history of Elizabethan and Jacobean England anticipated the next three hundred years. A centralized state was seeking to contain opposition from Parliament, Roman Catholics, Puritans, the lower classes, and the provinces. The morality of enslaving people of other nations was discussed, although the process accelerated. Political thought was borrowed from the Italian city states, pointing the way both to Machiavellian politics (*The Prince*) and republican patriotism (Machiavelli's *Discourses*). Weak or indifferent kings could bring down the state. Was the bookish James I possibly another model for Prospero? In any case, to present (consciously or not) this Foucauldian interpretation, Jarman stands on their heads the traditional conceptions of Shakespeare's characters: "Our Prospero is young and healthy, the first time he has been cast that way," and the costumes "are a chronology of the 350 years of the play's existence.... Beside him Ariel seems wan, world-weary. It's a subtle reversal of the accepted order."[12]

As Jarman's *Tempest* opens, we hear what turns out to be Prospero's heavy breathing gradually becoming louder than the storm at sea he has ordered. Prospero's breath is the word, the command, all that is needed to put science into action, and in this instance, to launch a catastrophe. All the film's outdoor scenes are a sickly blue, a color Jarman later used in his final film, *Blue*, to depict the void seen by the blind, and which he also used sparingly to depict disease and death in *Caravaggio*, citing the painter's supposed remark that the color blue was "poison."[13] At the same time, the indoor scenes effect the alchemical transformation Agrippa's work discusses: earth colors (browns and reds) are transformed through fire into gold. (Jarman claimed not to have studied Jung's works on alchemy until the mid-1970s, and that he had arrived at a comparable color scheme "quite unconsciously," thereby illustrating Jung's notion of the collective unconscious.[14]) In short, in the modern world nature becomes subordinate to artificial human creation. There are no real flowers in this film, only artificial ones in the final scene.

Neither Shakespeare nor Jarman disguise the hypocrisy and conspiracy that pervaded the age of Machiavelli. The two leading characters are Italian princes who exemplify characteristics of *The Prince*, a work well-known and studied in Shakespeare's England. In place of the old regime Prospero uses his books, which Caliban rightly calls the source of all his magic, to reduce the world to slavery. The centralized state that relies on knowledge and language is but a change of masters, a different form of power, as Foucault would put it. The modern ruler offers different carrots and sticks to different sorts of people. Caliban, naked in his natural state as ruler of the island, wears a black jacket and looks a bit like nineteenth century working man under Prospero. His speech consists mostly of curses, whereas Prospero's words to him are mostly threats, a fair description of the reality underlying the deferential performances of capitalist class relations. (When Miranda asks Prospero why he keeps Caliban, her father responds that he not only does all their work, but he is their only subject. Shakespeare knew a master needed a slave two centuries before Hegel did.) For Jarman, Caliban clothed and at labor represents the century of industry (he stokes the flames which provide the energy for the island). He speaks imperfectly and unpleasantly, for lower-class or rebellious speech is rarely tasteful. When Caliban uses his natural voice, untaught and unintellectual, Jarman presents this voice graphically as the highly emotional and moving laughter, weeping, and other sounds he utters when he is neither cursing nor plotting rebellion. Caliban has, Shakespeare tells us, learned speech imperfectly, and regrets that he has learned it at all: he has learned enough to obey, to rage and threaten destruction, but not enough to plan the revolt that might free him.

Jarman's Caliban not only signifies the working class, but also an exploited colonial population Shakespearean scholars plausibly find represented in the play.[15] Caliban's mother came from Africa. Prospero's island is in the "Bermoothes" or Bermuda of the "brave new world," a term coined in this play by Shakespeare. The Bard thus presents him as a black slave brought to America, whereas Jarman depicts him as a white "wage slave." Jarman offers an interesting variant on Prospero's comment that he has enslaved Caliban as punishment for lusting after his daughter Miranda. This is one aspect of the Christianize-civilize argument used to justify slavery and subsequent forms of racial domination, the stereotype that non-white men yearn for white women. (Shakespeare does not tell us whether Prospero is telling the truth, although a superficial reader would not realize how this prejudice is conveyed by innuendo.) Jarman's Miranda, however, enjoys Caliban's advances secretly. She kicks his buttocks and chases him out of her room while she is bathing. But then one asks: how did he get inside in the first place, and why does she seem to enjoy the experience so much once he has left? Although ugly, Caliban is lusty and funny in a way that Miranda's future husband, the stilted Ferdinand, is not. Caliban embodies popular culture, Ferdinand high society. Miranda, at least at first, seems torn between her pseudo-Afro dreadlock hairstyle (representing nature and suggesting some affinity for Caliban) and her dress, standing for civilization, which is in tatters from the beginning.

For Jarman, the shipwrecked prince Ferdinand turns the frisky Miranda into a fellow domesticated product of Prospero's Enlightenment project. Ferdinand has been cut off from the established order, and is washed up naked on the island in the manner of Robinson Crusoe. He is at once enslaved by Prospero and set to chopping wood. Caliban and Prospero talk of beating him, but instead, as Ferdinand is standing naked in a corner, and (it seems) is prepared to be whipped, Prospero hurls clothes at him. Unlike the physically coerced Caliban, the educated, higher-class worker who has mentally submitted to the establishment works in the hope of advancement in the system, which is precisely what Ferdinand achieves. His exploitation is clothed, that is hidden, whereas that of Caliban, the lower classes, and people of color is not. On the island Ferdinand is Lockean man, for whom capitalism works. He begins in the state of nature (literally) and acquires property and power through labor. He marries Miranda, and they revel in their bourgeois domesticity: they wear white, glittering clothes by the final scene. The "games" Miranda fears Ferdinand will play with her turn out to be merely chess and badminton.

For Jarman, Ariel represents Propsero's intellect. Under Sycorax, the pre-modern sorceress, he was stripped, chained, and ultimately imprisoned in a tree, much as the pre-modern intellect was subservient to arbitrary and magical powers. Now he is free — to do what his master commands. To achieve the "liberty" Prospero keeps dangling before him, Ariel enacts his master's wishes "to the syllable." Language controls Ariel, the modern man who serves his master in hopes of reward, although when he hints at rebellion the iron fist (Prospero threatens to imprison him again) behind the promises of liberty appears none too subtly. At one point Jarman has Ariel imprisoned in a pile of hay, both a mockery and suggestion of his former appearance when confined in Sycorax's oak. Since unlike the powerful oak the hay could be cast off with one shrug, Jarman is suggesting that actual physical coercion need rarely be applied to the technocrats and intellectuals who serve the modern world's powers-that-be so faithfully.

Unlike Ferdinand, Miranda, and the exiled Milanese nobles, neither Ariel nor Caliban have been brainwashed to internalize Prospero's domination and revalorize it as morally good. Jarman has Ariel fulfill Prospero's bidding sadly. Ariel wears "the most modern of our costumes, a workman with kid gloves, he could be teasing together the parts of a computer in a dust-free factory." Later he appears as a head waiter. At the play's end, when he is free, Ariel sings "Merrily, merrily shall I live now" with "melancholic wistfulness."[16] In Jarman's modern world, the intellect still has the same function it did before: for the most part it serves as the slave of those who would subvert it for their own ends.

The lower classes, represented by Stefano and Trimalcho, are buffoons. They want to rule but thanks to their drunkenness are prone to absurd fantasies and lack realistic plans to wrest power away from Prospero or the aristocrats. Even joined with Caliban, their efforts at revolt are pathetic: they are the proverbial drunken mob in miniature. Similarly, in Margaret Thatcher's England, when Jarman made the film, socialism had come to little, with a good many workers being seduced by the good life and turning Tory. Caliban — so easily intoxicated like the Native Americans he in part represents — follows these false leaders whose efforts only lead them to be exiled from the good life on the island, at least as Prospero programs it.

The upper classes, the old aristocracy, for their part include a scheming priest and a soldier (the two bulwarks of ancient regime society), the dotty old king they manipulate, and Gonzalo, the councilor who speaks of Utopia, a society of abundance without repression. Note that Prospero greets Gonzalo in the final scene as a friend. Indeed they must be, for if rulers and their publicists did not extend the Utopian dream of prosperity and freedom to their subjects, Prospero's books would be of little value in persuading others to dance to his tune.

Or rather, before the dancing starts, to remain immobile until Prospero decides to "free" his subjects to attend a carefully choreographed pageant. Prospero's magic freezes the other characters: after they are released, they are only free to act when they behave as he wants. Otherwise, as with the corrupt priest, they are tortured until they see the light. Jarman has the priest gnawed at by dwarf women who resemble Velasquez's famous painting of *Las Meninas*. As in Jarman's *Jubilee*, the dwarf represents the underside of court life, basically, the keeping of "cute" little people as pets. (Caliban too, is similarly dehumanized, whether by Prospero who calls him the devil's child or his own allies who call him "monster.") But it turns out the cleric only imagines the pain: as Foucault noted, we only need fear to keep us in line and will accept the order that represses us. Physical pain is rarely necessary. At least, as Jarman implies at the play's end, most of us are satisfied with the illusion of freedom if that order provides frolics and material abundance.

Jarman plays three pieces of music toward the end of the film which progressively approach the present and grow increasingly ironic in the contexts in which they are placed. The aristocrats are tormented, quite appropriately, to the Overture to Rossini's *The Barber of Seville* when they first enter Prospero's palace. Based on a play by the French Enlightenment thinker and revolutionary Beaumarchais, this opera is about a barber, a man of wit and intelligence, who manipulates the silly upper class figures he encounters. Next the mariners, whom Shakespeare summons from their ship, appear in Jarman's version as members of the modern Royal Navy. They dance with ever-increasing frenzy to the tune of "Hora Staccato" as performed and orchestrated by the popular musician Zamfir. Their dancing is devoid of real emotion, they move like automata (although once the dance is over, some of them become affectionate toward each other; they're on their own time). Given the sycophantic aristocrats and the attractive (but completely programmed) sailors, Jarman is satirizing Miranda's honest statement, "O brave new world that has people such as this." This precision dancing is art for people who like military parades and Vegas shows.

The pièce de résistance, however, is the singing of "Stormy Weather" by actress-singer Elisabeth Welch, a black woman who had made her stage debut singing that very song by Cole Porter in 1933.[17] But her skin has been whitened, she wears a golden headdress, and she blends perfectly into the blinding white and gold light of the final scene. The headdress is strangely reminiscent of the sorceress Sycorax's hair, although cleaned up. Sorcery, disguised perhaps as entertainment, is indeed required to keep the Brave New World in line. And sorcery is exactly what Welch performs, with her extraordinarily seductive singing. She sings of stormy weather with a smile on her face. Her manner, although not the words of the song, conforms to the general meaning of Shakespeare's original masque ("Lis replaced Iris, Ceres, and Juno," Jarman noted),[18] which is to serve as prelude to a calm voyage back to Europe and prosperity and peace all around.

Welch seems to be the African, non–European who has been co-opted as a star performer, but she and Jarman give us an opportunity to read beyond presentation of the song to think about the actual words. Put to one side the manner of Welch's delivery and consider the words of the text: "The blues came in and met me when he went away, Stormy Weather." Thinking about the words is not easy given her casual demeanor and her subtle interaction with the attractive young sailors who seem to be hinting that many of them are, literally, "closet" subversives. Immediately after Welch's number, Ariel walks sadly away, whether or not he will provide the calm voyage Prospero demands now that he is off the island. Jarman thus brings us back to the tempest at the beginning of the film and the outdoor sequences, all filmed in blue. The blue(s) literally come in, the "poison" blue foreshadowing the "Stormy Weather" ahead. And there will be plenty of storms in the centuries between *The Tempest* and Jarman's next major film about his own time—*The Last of England*. Tempests will rage between old regime and Enlightened elites, between popular culture and high culture, between classes, between the imperialists and their colonies—all of which Jarman reads imaginatively, yet sensibly, into the text by reversing the usual appearances, lighting, and line readings of Shakespeare's play.

At the end, Jarman's Prospero himself tells us the Enlightenment project is a bust, "the stuff dreams are made of." On his desk is a bust, in fact, of Mausolus, the occupant of the prototypical "mausoleum" at Halicarnassus which was one of the seven wonders of the ancient world,[19] the world's largest and most elaborate tomb.

8
Wittgenstein: The Grey Flame and the Early Twentieth Century

——————— ଏ ———————

Jarman's *Wittgenstein* offers yet another example where Jarman laid commentary on commentary. Entrusted in 1993 with filming a life of the twentieth century Austrian philosopher for Britain's education channel, he was also provided with a script by the Marxist literary critic Terry Eagleton. Jarman promptly rewrote it, retaining only small portions. Eagleton sharply criticized Jarman at the time, but was more gentle in his published introduction to both scripts. Eagleton points out that whereas Jarman constructs a biographical montage of the philosopher's whole life, he himself sets his script entirely at Cambridge, introducing Ludwig Wittgenstein's (1889–1951) fascinating life through points in conversations among philosophers and students. Jarman's Wittgenstein, on the other hand, does not arrive at Cambridge until the film's twenty-fifth scene, after which the director intersperses Eagleton's dialogue with more scenes of his own devising. As Eagleton commented: "My own script strikes me as reasonably strong on ideas but short on dramatic action; Jarman's, minus my own interpolations, seems to me just the other way round." Whereas Eagleton tried to introduce "something of the verbal tautness, wit, and pointedness of Wittgenstein's philosophical style," Jarman's "fanciful, whimsical" film compensated for its loss of "sensibility, in exchanging sharp for broad humor, [by gaining] immensely in visual and dramatic interest."[1] Both

Jarman dressed the young Wittgenstein in gold and a military helmet to indicate his family's great wealth and a primary source of it — munitions making. Later, the philosopher would be clad in grey. Jarman arranged the film's mostly primary colors against a stark black background to illustrate Wittgenstein's own theories of color. (*British Film Institute, Posters and Designs.*)

versions, Eagleton concluded, were needed to understand this complex and unusual philosopher.

Eagleton wrote a script for intellectuals; set in the academy, his story places the world of ideas at the center of Wittgenstein's life. Drama arises through debate and argument: indeed, this script would work well as a play. Eagleton may be correct in showing that what really matters about

Wittgenstein are his ideas, without which he would be only one case, and at that a mild case, of the madness that ran rampant through one of the wealthiest families in the Austro-Hungarian empire (two certainly, and perhaps three, of his brothers committed suicide). Would we care much about Socrates if he were only a critic of Athenian democracy, about Jesus if he were another Jewish revolutionary, or Michel Foucault if he were merely an eccentric French professor who went wild in San Francisco?

Yet Eagleton too realizes that the "dramatically interesting events of Wittgenstein's life ... left their indelible mark on what philosophy he produced." Here Jarman comes into his own, asking what sort of a person would insist that "philosophy was just a by-product of misunderstanding language," of no real use, and that "I've spent most of my life groping down a blind alley."[2] Jarman begins not with Wittgenstein's thought, but with his life and his homosexuality. In this, Jarman's approach is truer to Wittgenstein than Eagleton's: "'I want to get rid of the age-old picture of the soul brooding in isolation,' said Ludwig. He wanted a public discourse."[3] (Both Jarman and Eagleton, it must be noted, rely heavily in their respective scripts on Wittgenstein's own words and on observations by those who knew him.)

Wittgenstein's unusual discourse, Jarman intimates, was shaped by the various contexts in which his largely unfulfilled homosexuality was played out. He is first presented, literally, as the golden boy, his body dripping with jewels and crowned with a golden helmet. The members of his family are attired like Roman aristocrats, wearing togas and golden helmets and armor. They appear as the epitome of power and wealth. Their initial identification as Romans, conquerors, and oppressors as well as agents of civilization, symbolizes their effort, in company with many successful nineteenth century Jews, to hide their ethnicity. They listen to Paul, Ludwig's brother, a world-renowned concert pianist who lost an arm in the First World War (Ravel then composed the "Concerto for the Left Hand" for him), play an intermezzo by a family friend, Johannes Brahms. The piece is quiet, introspective. Their mood suggests the detached contemplation of beauty, rooted in a timeless tradition. Their religion, the insanity that will destroy many of them, Paul's lost arm, and Ludwig's abandonment of this world are all absent. What seems to count is the gold and the isolation from suffering it is supposed to bring.

Jarman's unusual and bold color scheme — bright primary colors transposed against black — comes straight out of Wittgenstein's *Remarks on Colour*. Reading Wittgenstein, in fact, inspired Jarman to scavenge bookstores all over London to find works on color throughout history. His own book *Chroma*, about the various significances of different hues, appeared shortly after the film and shortly before his own death.[4] For instance, that Jarman drapes the Wittgensteins in gold is not only an obvious symbol of their wealth, but an allusion to Ludwig's observations about gold in his treatise. When Wittgenstein writes, "It is easy to see that not all colour concepts are logically of the same sort, e.g. the difference between the concepts 'colour of gold' or 'colour of silver' and 'yellow' or 'grey,'"[5] we can decode this statement as a reflection on his family's privileged position. "The rich are not like you and me," as F. Scott Fitzgerald once said. At the same time, the wealthy's claim to distinction is materialistic and superficial, a *surface* effect — a word Wittgenstein uses twice in his discussion of gold: "We speak of the 'colour of gold' and do not mean yellow. 'Gold-coloured' is the property of a surface that shines or glitters." And "*Golden* is a surface colour."[6] Gold cannot convey artistic feeling, emotional depths, or accurately describe reality, even when this reality is the very color itself: "There is gold paint, but Rembrandt didn't use it to paint a golden helmet."[7] We might add that in medieval art, gold is the halo crowning saints: it resolves, or cancels out reality, embodies transcendence, serenity, the otherworldly, the non-human.

In turn, Jarman's first remark on gold and silver in *Chroma* derives from Wittgenstein: "What is it that separates silver and gold from the colours? ... Is it because of their lustre or their value?" Although most of Jarman's examples refer to Midas and Croesus, how "gold steals souls in Siberia" and "rushes in the Yukon," he also notes: "Gold have I none, but I have golden oldies, memories, and silence. Gold is not a colour, but it nestles up to the colours and shows them off."[8] As with Thomas More's gold-rich Utopians who made children's toys and slaves' chains from the metal, "gold" is a community construction. This construction not only blinded the Wittgensteins to reality, it led to their greatest crime: Ludwig's sister Helene traded the family assets in America to the Nazis to guarantee their safety. Hitler and his supporters could relish the irony that Jewish gold helped to fuel the holocaust. Jarman, paraphrasing Wittgenstein's dictum, "Of that which one cannot speak one must remain silent," states: "Of Helene we will remain silent,"[9] which is all the mention she gets in the film. The truth can be learned in Ray Monk's fine biography, which appeared in 1990 and which Jarman read before making the film.[10]

Ludwig, after his brief golden appearance, wears nondescript open-collared white shirts and grey jackets for the rest of the film. As a schoolboy, he utters a silent scream — as does Tilda Swinton in her protest against the slaughter of World War I in *War Requiem*—that silences his jabbering tutors: "I was to spend a lifetime disentangling myself from my education. Quite the best to be had in Vienna ... I shared a history teacher with Adolf Hitler — what a school!" His education, in short, is unspeakable, and while the poor boy Hitler could not possibly have shared the Wittgensteins' tutors, Jarman is saying that — born in the same year of 1889 in the same Austria — to a large extent they were shaped by similar circumstances. Young Ludwig then fills a blackboard with Stars of David and pretends to shoot the tutors with an imaginary gun. The Stars reveal the Wittgensteins' hitherto-concealed Jewish origins as well as Ludwig's affinity with the Biblical King David, who loved Jonathan. The stars are "yellow," Jarman stresses, not gold, foreshadowing both the insignia of concentration camps and a genuine color, indicating Wittgenstein's rejection of his family's wealth and search for truth, perfection, and a moral life.[11]

In contrast to the gold of the Wittgensteins and the bright colors of the Cambridge academics is the incessant black background Jarman uses for the film. Jarman commented that "for this, the lack of budget came in handy," because there simply was no money for sets. However, the director also thought poorly fabricated imitations of early twentieth century interiors would compromise his purpose: "My task was to make a philosophical film.... To redefine film, like language, needs a leap — in this case the black drapes, which defy the narrative without junking it."[12] It makes sense to view this black as the oppressive social background of the philosopher's life, for that is how Wittgenstein himself described black as socially constructed in *Remarks on Colour*: "Black dirties." That means "it takes the brightness out of the colour.... Black is a surface colour." Wittgenstein has the same negative feelings about the "surface" color gold — that is, his family, wealth, and bourgeois society — as he does about black, and all that blackness traditionally implies in "white" Western civilization. "In paintings darkness can also be depicted as black.... The difference between black and say, a dark violet is similar to the difference between the sound of a bass drum and the sound of a kettle-drum. We say of the former that it is a noise not a tone. It is matt and absolutely black." Combining the surface superficiality of gold with the unpleasantness of noise, black is worse than neutral: it drains life from color. Wittgenstein's thoughts on black perfectly encapsulate Jarman's opinion of the homophobic bourgeois society that made life miserable for the philosopher.[13]

Among Wittgenstein's philosophical works, Jarman is most interested in the *Remarks on Colour*. More accessible than most of Wittgenstein's writings, it provided Jarman with the opportunity to construct a cinematic context that aids in understanding the philosopher's difficult thought. It is noteworthy that in the year of Jarman's death, 1994, several months after he made *Wittgenstein*, his own remarks on color appeared.

8. ⁊ Wittgenstein

Chroma poetically and historically illustrates Wittgenstein's conclusion that we learn the meaning of colors "through language-games in which, for example, things are put in a certain order ... through agreement with other people."[14] Jarman dazzles us with hundreds of examples of how colors mean different things in different contexts to different communities. There is no "essence" of a color — or of anything outside a communally constructed "language-game." In Wittgenstein's words: "I think that it is worthless and of no use whatsoever for the understanding of painting to speak of the characteristics of the individual colours." Similarly, in music, "It is completely wrong to speak of the character of the minor mode in general. In Schubert the major often sounds more sorrowful than the minor."[15]

Jarman employs dark colors — black, brown, grey, deep blue — to depict Wittgenstein as he serves in the First World War, teaches at a rural school, spends time alone in Norway, applies to work as a laborer in the Soviet Union, or lectures to gaudily clad Cambridge students and faculty. Wittgenstein likes these colors, as he notes in his remarks, reversing the way people usually think about color in an effort to show ideas of color are not innate or absolute: "Why can't we imagine a grey-hot? ... Why can't we think of it as a lesser degree of white hot?" "Imagine we were told that a substance burns with a grey flame. You don't know the colours.... it would mean nothing."[16] In light of these remarks, Jarman seems to have accomplished the impossible. He has done what Wittgenstein asked us to imagine: to give "grey" a powerful meaning, providing coloristic significance for Wittgenstein's own life that negates the philosopher's despair, that dramatically illustrates his point that "Everything grey *looks* as though it is being illuminated."[17] Jarman's Wittgenstein burns with a grey, intense flame: his sincerity is superbly portrayed in actor Karl Johnson's desperate efforts to reach philosophical truth. Grey is the color Jarman gives to Wittgenstein most often. To stand out against it, economist John Maynard Keynes, whose "mixed economy" combined the principles of capitalism and socialism, appears in pastels drained of life. These colors also reflect his dry, affected personality and the way he masked his homosexuality behind marriage to a Russian ballet dancer.

Grey Wittgenstein also far outshines the bright red academic robes of Bertrand Russell, a high-living radical activist, and the (usually) flaming red and pink dresses and absurd hats of his lover Lady Ottoline Morrell. "Terry [Eagleton] is Bertie and I'm Ludwig," Jarman once remarked half in jest. One of the reasons he made the film was "I love the idea that Wittgenstein hated the Bloomsbury set and their threadbare veneer of culture."[18] One of the two passages from *Remarks on Colour* Jarman quotes in *Chroma* concerns the "nature" of Red: "For if someone has mastered the use of what looks red — or indeed what looks red to me — he must also be capable of answering the question, 'And what is Red like?' and 'What does something look like when it turns Red?'"[19] The phoniness of Russell, a radical activist and theoretical socialist who lived a life of aristocratic leisure and delighted in wit and irony, comes through brilliantly (in both senses of the word). His sign is a color that usually signifies earth, anger, blood, or life, but through Jarman's wizardry and effort to bring Wittgenstein's theory of color to life, red becomes the most artificial shade imaginable. The contrast becomes even more marked when Wittgenstein appears before a large red flag as he applies, without success, to work as a laborer in the Communist Soviet Union.

Jarman writes of Wittgensteinian grey in *Chroma*, but doesn't confine it to one chapter ("Grey Matter") as he does with the other colors. He includes a long poem comprising most of the section on "Iridescence" that could fairly be described as a tribute to Wittgenstein as Jarman filmed him. Jarman writes of "the sad eyed chameleon/ volcano grey ... grey is his coat/ and grey is his heart/ grey-eyed chameleon in deep grey thought." He begged for a rainbow to "wash away/ the grey in my life/ the grey of the day," and was blown away to where he discovered "a lustrous shell/ rainbow bright/ Mother of Pearl."[20] Jarman not only writes of Wittgenstein, he explicitly identifies with him as a creative gay outcast searching for truth and a better world while others lived for money and easy sociability. "I have much of Ludwig in me. Not in my work, but in my life.... The cinema was Ludwig's escape. Mine, a garden."[21] That the "grey chameleon" finds the Mother of Pearl while the people who dwell in light and luxury do not even search for it completes the filmmaker's empathy with his subject.

From the start Jarman uses Wittgenstein to exemplify their mutual theory that "we learn to use words because we belong to a culture.... In the end we speak as we do, because of what we do.... I want to start from our culture, our shared practical life together, and look at what we think and feel and say it in these very public terms."[22] The paradox of Wittgenstein's life was that he was never comfortable with any real public. He found his academic colleagues superficial and insincere. He termed Cambridge a "brothel," bereft of oxygen, and filled with "drunken chit-chat."[23] Yet Wittgenstein's mentality and demeanor also alienated him from the "real" people into whose midst he would, without success, seek solace. The film accurately sums up his feelings about teaching young children: "I kidded myself that my background and class weren't important but I stood out like a sore thumb in these provincial schools. The parents hated me and called me strange. I felt guilty for years. Somehow I had failed — morally." When he complains about his sins and how he cannot tolerate dishonesty, Keynes warns him: "You are suffering from a terminal case of moral integrity. If you'd just allow yourself to be a little more sinful, you'd stand a chance of salvation."[24]

To demonstrate his morality, Wittgenstein gave away a vast fortune, periodically tried to join the working class, and urged others to do likewise. He asks rhetorically in the film: "How can I be a logician before I am a human being? The most important thing is to settle accounts with myself?" Wittgenstein explained his volunteering to fight in World War I as an "escape" to war — "Standing eye to eye with death will give me the chance to be a decent human being." Manual labor was another escape.[25] Wittgenstein's homosexuality added to the estrangement of an Austrian in Britain. His "escapes" can be interpreted not only as efforts to find genuine camaraderie but to place himself in situations — the army and the factories — where men's bodies in good shape were on display.

Wittgenstein persuades his best student, Johnny, to return to his working-class roots and become a mechanic, who unlike a philosopher does something "useful." Jarman contextualizes this much-criticized advice by having Wittgenstein articulate his homosexual proclivities, and guilt expressing them, more explicitly than the philosopher would have done to others, or perhaps even to himself:

> Philosophy is a sickness of the mind. I mustn't infect too many young men. How unique and irreplaceable Johnny is. And yet how little I realize this when I am with him. That's always been a problem. But living in a world where such a love is illegal and trying to live openly and honestly is a complete contradiction. I have known Johnny three times. And each time I began with a feeling that there was nothing wrong. But after, I felt shame.[26]

Unable to rid himself of socially constructed guilt for his feelings, Wittgenstein ruined his own life and Johnny's by sending him away. Meanwhile, he gained satisfaction from suffering — in a "moral" cause, to be sure — while vicariously enjoying the experience of Johnny's engagement with physical labor. By articulating what Wittgenstein dared not, Jarman displays the tragic consequences when homosexuals are confused and made to feel guilty by internalizing the norms of a homophobic society. In this context, Wittgenstein's dexterity in decoding language games appears as a desperate attempt to avoid coming to terms with his desire for same-sex love, to avoid dealing with the constraints placed on him by society, and to escape serious thought about whether a homosexual (or, alternatively, the society that represses him) can be moral. Silence equals misery, if not death.

To "out" Wittgenstein, Jarman has the philosopher's college students clad in sports clothes, for the most part jogging suits that vie with Russell's red robes for sheer brightness. The presence of their athletic if concealed bodies provides the real attraction for a gay man teaching youths, Jarman indicates. Just as Wittgensteins' anachronistic togas point to the past, the late-twentieth century jogging suits herald the future where casual and increasingly revealing dress has become the norm. To be sure, we rarely see a male body shirtless in this film, and then only when Wittgenstein is making love. The jogging outfits, like the togas, mask reality, in this case sexual. They also symbolize how difficult it is for a man of intellectual bent, such as Wittgenstein, to find students with whom he can communicate, as many students are more interested in athletic and sexual sports than language games, and not terribly interested in complex and not particularly attractive professors.

In addition to looking at Wittgenstein's own life, Jarman placed his subject's personal and intellectual problems in a tradition of queer thinkers. Repression may have produced personal misery for the thinkers, but paradoxically it has been responsible for some of the glories of civilization. Jarman remarked in the introduction to his script that the "explanation of Colour is Queer," noting the interesting fact that the world's major theorists of color have been predominantly homosexual. These included "Leonardo in his notebooks, [and] Newton's *Optics*" along with Wittgenstein. "Leonardo experimented with colours and boys. He looked the world in the face," whereas "Ludwig and Newton shared a repression. Isaac worked without stop. Ludwig found a black hole in his words. For this there was no language."[27] In his writings, Wittgenstein never mentioned homosexuality, and rarely touched on the ethical questions which vexed his life apart from the "language games" of philosophy. These were the issues "of which he felt compelled to be silent."

In *Chroma*, Jarman extends the pantheon of queer investigators of color to include Aristotle and Renaissance thinker Marsilio Ficino, and, by implication, himself. In *Remarks on Colour*, Wittgenstein refers to communities of the colorblind, blind, mental defectives, and even a Martian to suggest that only those who are outside the mainstream are prone to question its assumptions: "We might want to say: If there were no such humans, then we wouldn't have the concept of *seeing*.— But couldn't Martians say something like this? Somehow, by chance, the first humans they met were all blind."[28]

Wittgenstein considered himself as odd as such a hypothetical Martian. In his despair, he wrote, "That which I am writing about so tediously, may be obvious to someone whose mind is less decrepit."[29] This is why Jarman introduces a Martian into his film as the only being who can carry on a discussion with Wittgenstein rather than simply admire or be puzzled by him. On his deathbed, Wittgenstein wanted to "compose a philosophical work which consisted entirely of jokes," but unfortunately had no sense of humor.[30] Jarman, through the Martian, absent from Eagleton's more literal script, supplies that humor: "Wittgenstein believed in the green valleys of silliness rather than the heights of intellect.... The period in which Ludwig lived was obsessed with Martians.... Mr. Green—holds a glass to the film. He reflects light back into the lens"—at the end of the film, quite literally.[31] The Martian appears first to the young Wittgenstein, asking him how many toes do philosophers have. They then play a language game. When Wittgenstein replies ten, the Martian responds: "That's how many humans have." When Wittgenstein replies philosophers are human, the Martian retorts: "Oh dear, does that mean Martians can't be philosophers?" The humorless young man replies "Oh god," a groan of anguish which could also be a double-entendre, that he is not only upset, but has in fact met and failed to recognize a divine being.[32]

The Martian returns at the film's end and has the last word: "Hail Chromodynamics, Lord of Quantum. This is Quark, Charm and Strangeness reporting. Concerning the philosopher Ludwig Wittgenstein. Deceased. The solution to the riddle of life in space and time lies outside space and time. But as you know and I know, there are no riddles. If a question can be put at all, it can also be answered."[33] With this ending, Jarman, in a paradoxical, Wittgensteinian way, presents color as holding the secret that bridges the world of physics and the realm of beauty. The new, what we now call postmodern world, which Wittgenstein's philosophy implied although he did not probe the science behind it, accepts uncertainty and variety as the price of freedom, meanwhile rejecting the notion that the correspondence of the real world to metaphysical absolutes is a fit subject of inquiry.

In both the film and in *Chroma*, Jarman is denying the self-proclaimed "decrepit" Wittgenstein's lament that all we can do is decipher the rules of the games we play. Rather, the disabled, the queer, are peculiarly sighted and gifted: they appreciate the beauty of the world, symbolized by color, all the more because they are excluded from the consensus society flatters itself that it has easily achieved. As Wittgenstein wrote: "We speak of 'colour-blindness' and call it a defect. But there could easily be several differing abilities, none of which is clearly inferior to the others."[34] It was Wittgenstein's tragedy, and glory, that he simply did not rage against the stupidity which repressed him. Although he showed what passed for truth to be a "language-game," reaching after much agony what semioticians and deconstructionists pretend to take for granted these days, he realized with Nietzsche that a terrifying void opens if we believe that God is dead and nothing is certain. The fictional Keynes caught Wittgenstein's dilemma in a speech Jarman borrowed from Eagleton:

> There once was a young man who dreamed of reducing the world to pure logic.... Countless acres of gleaming ice stretching to the horizon. So the clever young man looked around the world he had created, and decided to explore. He took one step forward and fell flat on his back. You see, he had forgotten about friction.... So the clever young man sat down and wept bitter tears. But as he grew into a wise old man, he came to understand that roughness and ambiguity aren't imperfections. They're what make the world turn. He wanted to run and dance ... But something in him was still homesick for the ice, where everything was radiant and absolute and relentless. Though he had come to like the idea of the rough ground, he couldn't bring himself to live there. So now he was marooned between earth and ice, at home in neither. And this was the cause of all his grief.[35]

Wittgenstein demanded of himself that he not only criticize others, but himself as well. To speak authentically, he had to share the sufferings and persecutions of others. To be a repressed homosexual was not enough. It is Jarman's glory that he was able to decode Wittgenstein, one of the most theoretical of philosophers, and relate the philosopher's writings to his personal life and the great historical and ethical problems of the early twentieth century. As Wittgenstein noted: "When you want to know the meaning of the word, don't look inside yourself, look at the uses of the word in our way of life. Look at how we behave."[36]

And how did Wittgenstein behave? When he didn't seek suffering, he sought escape, much as Jarman did with his gardens, paintings, and films. The worlds to which Wittgenstein had easy access, the Viennese aristocracy and the British university, he considered false and unsatisfying. As a youth, he sought escape by trying to design a better sort of airplane. Had he succeeded, he would have merged his desire for utility with his philosophical investigations. At the end of the film, as the philosopher lies dying, we see his youthful self return. For the first time in the film, the oppressive black back-drop gives way to a real sky as the young man flies away with the aid of a contraption he planned but never realized, composed of wings and balloons.

Wittgenstein could never fly away. He kept returning to Cambridge, to philosophy. Even though both were unsatisfying, they gave him the only "home" — even though he denies it in the film with the words "God help me!" — he ever had.[37] He never attained the synthesis of dream and reality, thought and technique, happiness and authenticity promised by his flying machine. As a homosexual philosopher living in a society that criminalized his behavior, this was impossible. Jarman, and our Martian observer, suggest that "the riddle" can be answered, that these dichotomies can be reconciled. But whether they will, and when, remains an open question. Humanity led of necessity by courageous queers and their straight allies will answer it one way or another through its collective endeavors.

9

War Requiem: The Long Shadow of the Great War

༄

The opportunity to film Benjamin Britten's *War Requiem* presented Derek Jarman with the prospect of reflecting on war, human nature, and history in a complex setting of many layers. First, Britten (1913–1974), a gay British composer, interspersed the text of the traditional Latin Mass for the Dead with the poems of Wilfred Owen (1891–1918), a (probably) homosexual army officer killed during the last week of World War I. Britten's *War Requiem* was first performed at Coventry Cathedral in 1962 to mark its reopening for use following the German bombing in World War II. The Cathedral's ancient ruins were preserved, but complementing them now was a modern structure reflecting on the meaning of the bombing and the war for Christianity and humanity. Soloists in the performance were soprano Galina Vishnevskaya, a Russian survivor of the Second World War, baritone Dietrich Fischer-Dieskau, a young German soldier during the war, and tenor Peter Pears, Britten's lifetime companion, who stands for a British soldier, although neither Pears nor Britten did military service. In 1989, Jarman set his film to the recording made at the time of the first performance.

Britten's music mirrors the Owen poems on which it comments by showing how war does not repudiate, but evolves out of civilization's most venerable institutions. Owen writes of an unprecedented catastrophe

9. ✥ War Requiem

Jarman castigates a British establishment that could still preach nationalism uncritically and enjoy life as it sent young men off to the horrors of the Western front. (*British Film Institute, Posters and Designs.*)

unleashed by old men, a church, and capitalists insensitive to the death and slaughter of the young. He contrasts their suffering with previous history and prewar domesticity to bring home the horrors of our century. Britten similarly highlights Owen's poems by intertwining them with the text that Christians have traditionally used to pray for salvation. But the composer sets his music *against* the Requiem's Latin words, causing us to question the promise of eternal peace. The Kyrie (Lord have mercy, Christ have mercy) and Agnus Dei (Lamb of God, who takes away the sin of the world, grant us peace) are probably the briefest and quietest settings ever made of what are usually major sections of the mass. They can barely be heard and make little impression amid the tumult. On the other hand, the Sanctus (Holy Lord, Heaven and earth are filled with your glory, Hosanna in the highest) consists of the soprano raging against desperate martial music: here is the Lord's glory, or thus have we corrupted his earth. By treating the Requiem's promises of mercy, peace, and paradise with searing irony, Britten implies that such prayers, or at least the traditional religious context in which they occur, are futile.

Jarman develops in turn a commentary on Britten's commentary on Owen's commentary on World War I. As he put it: "Owen took on the war; Britten, Owen and the mass: I'm taking on all three."[1] The director compares the slaughter of the war with the persecution of homosexuals and the AIDS epidemic of his own time. Britten dedicated the *Requiem* to four friends who died in the Second World War, Jarman the film "to all those cast out, like myself, from Christendom. To my friends who are dying in a moral climate created by a church with no compassion."[2] Jarman adds to Owen's and Britten's meditation on the two world wars footage to show the relevance of their poetry and music to the "wars" of our time, not only against AIDS but in Vietnam, Cambodia, Afghanistan, and the possibility of nuclear annihilation. Jarman then goes backward from Owen's verses, taking his critique of the slaughter of the young and innocent back to the murder of Christ, who ultimately appears as identical to the Unknown Soldier whom Britain, like other nations, buried to remember those it could not identify.

Jarman's commentary on Britten begins even before the music starts. The film opens with a simple but spectacularly moving reading of much of the Owen poem "Strange Meeting," with which Britten concludes the *Requiem*. The speaker is the great actor Laurence Olivier, in his final film role and himself near death, whose characterizations, staging of plays, and film work have been among the glories of modern British civilization. Here he plays an aged veteran who has remained, crippled and confined to a wheelchair, for the seventy years from the end of World War I until the making of Jarman's film in 1989. He nostalgically fingers his medals, which a nurse, Tilda Swinton — who appears as nurse, companion, and mourner throughout the film — helps him pin on his sweater before they go for a walk. Olivier shows her an old miniature of a nurse he remembers from the war, noting the resemblance. Swinton's multiple roles signal the continuity of the experience of war throughout the century. She offers the perspective of a woman who can only comfort, mask her eyes, stop her ears, or scream (silently, that is, ineffectually), all of which she will do in the film, against the senseless murders of men. The veteran recites that "it seemed that out of battle I escaped." Olivier emphasizes the word "seemed," for the veteran's obsession with his medals and his immobile legs insure that the war of seven decades ago remains the central incident of his life.

Yet despite the horrors Jarman shows on the screen and Britten conjures up with his music, the memory and nature of war is left mixed, or open, in this first scene, for those who have not heard the *Requiem* or seen the film before. Later in the film Olivier stares in horror as a latter-day Abraham ignores the angel and slaughters Isaac to symbolize the nature of war in which an older generation massacres a younger one in the name of God. (One of Britten's most moving works is the canticle "Abraham and Isaac" based on the biblical incident.) At the beginning, however, the old man is proud of his decorations. Jarman writes, "It's difficult to understand the gung-ho mentality with which the young men of 1914 went to war, pleased to sacrifice themselves on the altar of King and Country." Jarman recognizes martial impulses latent in everyone: "There is a fatal attraction which this violence conjures in all of us," he noticed when a friend asked him: "What really is the difference between watching a snuff movie and watching this film?" With war as the peak experience in the lives of those who survived, peace can only be anti-climactic, "the profound dull tunnel," to which the veteran "seemed" to escape. Hence, the British and American Legions and veterans organizations throughout the Western world — which in Germany, Italy, and elsewhere merged with fascist political movements — spoke of "keeping the spirit of the Great War alive."[3] After 1918, for the first time in modern history, national leaders sported plain military uniforms rather than gentlemen's high fashion or the formal military dress of the higher ranks.

Jarman lets the veteran speak before Britten's music begins because he wishes to include four lines from the Owen poem with which the *Requiem* ends, but which Britten omits. After seeming to escape the war, the old man finds himself in a tunnel filled with the victims of wars present and past. One figure bestirs himself in this trench of the dead, so similar to those of the First World War. Then Olivier speaks the words Britten omits, which become for Jarman the key to understanding Owen, Britten, and war:

> And by his smile, I knew that sullen hall,
> By his dead smile I knew we stood in Hell,
> With a thousand pains that vision's face was grained;
> Yet no blood reached there from the upper ground.

Britten, however, leaves out these critical verses because he does not choose to leave us in Hell, but in peace. He draws back from his anger and irony at the end of the *Requiem*, unable to set Owen's final terrifying vision, in which young men who have lived in the Hell of the trenches and then died nevertheless remained smiling, the memory of their sacrifice failing to penetrate human consciousness in a meaningful way — that is, persuading the world to achieve peace. Britten concludes instead with Owen's reconciliation of the two soldiers, British and German, in which the words, "Let us sleep now," the last line of his poem "Strange Meeting," mingle with the comparable, final words of the Latin Requiem, "Requiescant in pace" (rest in peace). The ending contradicts the tone of anger and irony which dominate most of the work. Jarman, on the other hand, refuses us this consolation, although he loved Britten's music and used it in several of his films because its nostalgic, melodic, and formal aspects "made the perfect foil to my intuitive film-making."[4] Jarman believes Britten compromised Owen's vision, just as his willingness to compose music for the powers that ruled Britain, who outlawed his sexual orientation for much of his life, compromised his principles. Jarman concurs with poet W. H. Auden's criticism of Britten "as a 'queen's man' hell-bent on papering over his insecurities in the bosom of the Establishment and its church.... How would Owen have coped with the powerful [people of the world, at the Coventry ceremony] celebrating his poems in this way, when he was [in his poetry] burning all memorials, flags, and even the forefathers themselves? Would he be lulled by the Kyrie as they were?"[5]

Jarman is true to Britten even in his refusal to introduce homosexual elements into the film. Nudity is infrequent, and when it occurs, it is logical, symbolic, and only faintly erotic. Some men are shirtless as they try fruitlessly to remove the mud of the trenches; the Unknown Soldier appears as a Medieval or Renaissance Christ. The scenes in which men interact are more homosocial than homosexual. Jarman downplays the sexual attraction, if any, between Owen and the Unknown Soldier: a hint of eroticism comes across when Owen removes a thorn from his foot and takes a little too long, and when the Unknown Soldier as Christ bears Owen's body. But so much more could have been done with young men alone, in the most dreadful circumstances. In this film, same-sex love, for those who know about Owen, Britten, and Jarman, is dramatically conspicuous by its absence. Jarman accurately represents the repression which society placed on Owen and Britten, forbidding them to express their feelings publicly. He reflected on this problem in the book accompanying the film:

> What is the relationship of the artist to his creation? They were at it again last night on TV, denying that Britten's sexuality had anything to do with [his opera] *Billy Budd*.... Someone went on to say that if Britten had chosen universal themes (i. e. heterosexual relationships), he would

have been a greater composer.... It is vital to underline yet again that art is the spark between private lives and the public.... A Tory MP stated that my sexuality was 'chemically unbalanced, not part of the Almighty's plan' and that it was his 'duty to protect the nation from deviants' like myself, and, by implication, Britten and Owen. There are far too many who promulgate the gospel of love with hate filled hearts.[6]

Jarman, and by extension Olivier playing the old veteran, voice the message from which Britten shies away: that we have been living in hell since the World War, an interpretation which is finally revealed as the veteran's own innermost feeling when he stares in horror at the scene in which Isaac is in fact sacrificed rather than spared by a modern Abraham. This hell can take many forms — repressed and oppressed homosexuality, war, destruction of landscape — all present in the film. The tunnel resembles the trenches, but it is a dead end, the hell of war, and the hell where, once war has ceased, the memory of war is all that remains. As for those who have survived or lived in the world the war gave us, we have been condemned to "hopelessness," to "undone years." Never again would the world know how Owen "went hunting wild after the wildest beauty in the world." "Of my weeping something had been left," Owen states through the veteran's voice. This something was "the truth untold ... the pity of war distilled," but this too "must die now."

Jarman includes the poem's last words as Britten did not to drive home the truth that the world did not effectively remember the First World War and its horrible consequences. It built monuments, forgot, and went at it again and again. The veteran suffered, ignored, for three score years and ten, the traditional human lifetime, beyond his moment of triumph and tragedy. He lives in a nursing home, with only his nurse to comfort him. Jarman thus sees himself as "an interpreter ... a bridge to other audiences and other times," such as the late-twentieth century, when "a surprisingly high percentage of British schoolchildren do not know where Britain is on the map ... and fewer still will know about the two world wars, let alone those nearer in time."[7] The veteran ends his monologue with the untold truth about the war which Owen expresses and Britten fears to articulate. Jarman's film finished Owen's poem, the soldier's real verdict on his insane enterprise, whereas Britten did not. After we see the ever-increasing destructiveness of future wars on the screen, we learn that those who forget their history are doomed to repeat it. In future generations, never knowing the innocence of the pre-World War era, "none will break ranks," Jarman predicts, and given overwhelming public enthusiasm for the Malvinas and Gulf Wars in Great Britain and America, respectively, in recent times, he has a point.

Jarman brings these subsequent wars to life. He is especially adept at showing how, whether Soviet, Vietnamese, British, or American, the soldiers march in step and look the same. He intersperses shots of parades with scenes of men helping their fallen comrades. As in World War I, the humanity of ordinary soldiers contrasts vividly with the mass destruction willed by their leaders. But the world has learned nothing. Jarman writes that all viewers could see on television during the Malvinas War of 1982 was the victory parade: "You would think you were back in the 1890s, as the guards trotted by in their nineteenth century uniforms."[8] While Jarman remarks ironically that America "showed too much" to the public in the Vietnam War, he lived to see that "error" rectified as the triumph in the Gulf War of 1991 appeared as antiseptic and easy as the British reconquest of the Malvinas.

Nothing so symbolized the age of innocence, and arrogance, that preceded World War I — and now has come back as the young are not taught meaningful history — than the publicity surrounding the launching in 1912 of *Titanic*, the largest ship the world had yet seen. In Owen's "Strange Meeting," the word "titanic" appears to describe modern wars; in another poem of Britten's, "The End," the Earth speaks of how there is no resurrection: "Mine ancient scars shall not be glorified,/ Nor my titanic tears, the sea, be dried."[9] Owen's use of the word "titanic" and his allusion to the sea, rather than any number of plausible synonyms, recalls the sinking of *Titanic*. The ship symbolized the hubris of a civilization confident in its greatness and ability to conquer nature: its captain plowed full speed ahead into a field of icebergs and most of the passengers were lost because lifeboats were deemed unnecessary on an "unsinkable" ship. The charge through the ice field anticipates the endless frontal assaults of the Western Front. *Titanic* embodies the proud and prosperous world that went to war in 1914, its destruction a harbinger of the collapse of the society that built her.

Jarman reveals the world before the war explicitly in addition to making sure we are aware of the "titanic" catastrophe itself. He also offers a fictional narrative for Owen's brief life that corresponds to the words of the poems Britten integrated with those of the Latin Requiem. These scenes are lit brightly — too brightly — and the red, white, and blue colors of the British flag predominate. Patriotism, it seems, blinds people to reality. Young Owen washes clothes with his mother and nurse. The sheets hung out to dry will retrospectively resemble the sheets in the hospital ward where nurses care for the wounded, and then the shrouds worn by the dead. In the book accompanying the film's release, Jarman describes their concentration on "domestic duties" as "sacramental" — the symbolic reenactment of a cosmic truth.[10] The cleanliness of the nurses' ward and of the Victorian home contrasts with the ineradicable filth of the trenches. Jarman nearly always shows the soldiers caked with mud. Their efforts to wash in what little water is available appear pathetic, touching attempts to reclaim the order and purity of a lost world.

Quoting Bertrand Russell, Jarman noted in the course of the filming that "if our century had ... unmasked the humbug, it had also squandered the beauty of the world." For all his radicalism, Jarman had a deep affection for the people and landscape of traditional England, which modernity and progress were destroying while substituting huge, sterile structures to put in its place. "As I wandered through the Romney Marshes in the autumn, taking the landscape footage for the film, I found only one house that still had a real cottage garden, with vegetables, flowers, and butterflies. Surely, the task of the next century must be to protect what remains."[11] Or, as Owen put it in "Strange Meeting," "Men will go content with what we spoiled."

Jarman filmed *War Requiem* on the grounds of Darenth Park Hospital in Kent, which was undergoing demolition even as the filming occurred. The very process of filming symbolized a desperate attempt to save what little was left, which is the best one can do with the England Jarman both loved and idealized, although not uncritically. The rubble which surrounds several scenes eerily connects the devastation of war with that of the "progress" that will substitute a much-needed hospital with an office building or parking lot. The setting could be a symbol for the message of the entire film—that the Western world's ruling governments' principal contribution to civilization has been death and destruction in various forms. (They have no right to take credit for the achievements of writers, scientists, and artists who are most often their adversaries.) Jarman states:

> My chief critics ... would be laughed out of court by any living culture. Except Britain — creaking with 'success' into the twenty-first century; shored up by ... obsessive secrecy, and a government pledged to no freedom except in the marketplace; a land in bondage to the estate agent, PR, and runtish Tory MPs whose faces are deep in the trough, selling off the Welfare State our fathers and grandfathers died to create, to line their pockets. What patriots these? Doesn't it strike you as odd that after eight years of economic growth [in the 1980s], a booming economy, and a population (we're told) richer than ever, that no money can be found to help the weak and disenfranchised? Or for any of the very real and pressing needs of hospitals and other public institutions."[12]

Jarman foretells the tremendous fires that rage through the film by showing us three children who weep over the death of a teddy bear they burn as they "play" war. The two boys are dressed as British soldiers, one in World War I garb, the other in Napoleonic or Crimean-era style, and a girl resembles a nurse. Later, in the extended footage of post–World War I warfare, Jarman inserts a few frames of boys playing soldiers with toy guns. The attraction of war for children as a diversion from the monotony of everyday life mirrors the seductiveness it holds for adults.

Jarman also constructs a parallel life for a German soldier. We see him as a child, too, playing with his mother and trimming a Christmas tree. This unthinking childish reverence for Christ becomes especially poignant when it turns out that the Unknown Soldier he accidentally kills is, at least symbolically, Christ. The circumstances of both the British and German soldiers' deaths are as absurd as can possibly be imagined. The German soldier is playing an old piano in the snow, perhaps a Christmas song at Christmas time. The Unknown Soldier comes upon him, but instead of stabbing or shooting him in the back playfully tosses a snowball. This scenario is plausible, as during World War I the armies took Christmas day off, played football, and threw snowballs.[13] The German responds in kind, but in the frolic the Unknown Soldier unfortunately backs into some barbed wire and bleeds to death. Coming upon the scene, Owen stabs the German.

The scene of the Unknown Soldier's death, which Jarman entitles "Crucifixion" in the accompanying text, is set to Britten's moving "Lacrimosa," or "Day of Weeping." It is followed by a companion scene, perhaps the most powerful in the film. The next section of the Requiem is humanity's plea for liberation from death, "as was promised to Abraham and his seed." Here Britten inserts Owen's poem "The Parable of the Old Man and the Young," which retells the story of Abraham and the sacrifice of Isaac. Jarman has an up-to-date Abraham, dressed as a Church of England bishop, build an altar and bind Owen himself as the sacrifice. He uses "belts and straps" from an army uniform, and surrounds the altar with "parapets and trenches" before asking God where is the lamb for the burnt offering. An angel, the child who also plays young Wilfred, wearing painted cardboard wings and a halo, points to a "ram" caught in a thicket — of barbed wire, a frequent symbol in Jarman's film to depict the constrained existence of modern humanity. Owen calls this beast the "the Ram of Pride"— meaning if only the politicians and generals would kill their pride they could avert the murder of millions. But the ram reminds the viewers of the Unknown Soldier himself and the conclusion, although chilling, is foreordained: the old man "slew his son, and half the seed of Europe, one by one." Instead of bringing the salvation of Isaac and future generations promised to Abraham, the official representatives of Christ in the twentieth century have rejected the choice of the ram and prefer to kill their own children. Owen recalls this sacrifice again in the poem which accompanies the Agnus Dei, "At a Calvary Near the Ancre": " But His disciples hide apart;/ And now the Soldiers bear with Him./ Near Golgotha strolls many a priest,/ And in their faces there is pride,/ That they were flesh-marked by the Beast/ By whom the gentle Christ denied."

Watching the sacrifice are four caricatures of fat capitalists, smiling, smoking cigars, and applauding. The quartet has appeared once before in the film, also as observers, at the point where Jarman presents Owen's poem "The Next War." They work behind the scenes and never do anything on screen, much as in the real world where few people can name the head of the Bank of England or General Motors as opposed to their visible, political front men. After Owen describes how soldiers become friendly with Death, he writes, "We laughed at him.... No soldier's paid to kick against his powers," at which point several hideously costumed and made-up music hall girls begin to dance the can-can in front of a plump satire of a seated Britannia as the capitalists laugh and cheer. (Jarman had used a similar parody of Britannia in *Jubilee*.) This burlesque is the only "kicking against the powers" going on. It also shows how the masses are amused with cheap entertainment that diverts their attention from what they need to know to save their lives. In his screenplay, Jarman quotes Owen's poem "A Terre" (To Earth) and urges us to "spit" [what our leaders want us to do back to enemies] in their faces": "Little I'd ever teach a son, but hitting,/ Shooting, war, hunting, all the arts of hurting./ Well, that's what I learnt — and making money." Owen would not teach his son to make money, but to turn the aggression the master class encourages against itself. [14]

"The Next War's" final words predict the future conflicts Owen, Britten, and Jarman illustrate through their art: "We laughed, knowing that better men would come,/ And greater wars; when each proud fighter brags he wars on Death — for Life; not men — for flags." Owen here is simultaneously praying that men will actually war against Death — that is, not go to war — but ironically implying that their pretended motivations for murder will become loftier as the means of destruction increase. The likely outcome, as the poet concludes "At a Calvary Near the Ancre," is that "the scribes on all the people shove/And bawl allegiance to the state." Jarman's footage and commentary on the wars since 1918 chillingly reveal the truth of Owen's bitter prophesies.[15]

In addition to capitalists, religious leaders, and popular culture, high art also conspires with nationalism and war. Jarman puts Britten's chorus on screen twice. Thirty men and women from a Bach Choir, immobile and in the foreground, sing the *Dies irae, dies illa* (Day of wrath, day of weeping) as men charge across no-man's land and fire roars across the landscape. Elite art carries on oblivious to the horror of war, sublimating it for audiences which believe that music can in fact convey terror, or that feeling weepy during a requiem for fallen youth is all the penance their murderers need. As Abraham sacrifices Owen, the boys' choir stands still and does not mime the words they should be singing on the soundtrack. Rather, as Jarman writes, "They stand like a chorus in a Greek tragedy and observe the burial with accusing faces."[16] Yet the music goes on, and they continue to stand still. Silence Equals Death. Art which does not protest whatever catastrophe an age is undergoing—war, AIDS, environmental destruction—consoles and contributes to complacency.

In contrast with the soothing irrelevance of much official art, the grotesque capitalists, and the symbols of nationalism—Jarman cuts to the stiff-upper-lip faces of George V and British military leaders as he intersperses the bloody results of their policies—are the moving human and religious images interspersed throughout the film. The Unknown Soldier washes the feet of a fellow soldier much as Christ did those of his disciples; his own feet bear the stigmata from his barbed-wire "crucifixion." Jarman modeled several scenes on paintings or works of art to provoke reflection on how traditional religious themes are reflected in the lives of people in our own times. Based on an unknown twentieth-century artist's conception, the Unknown Soldier appears as Christ wearing a crown of thorns, carrying Owen's body as the Madonna traditionally bears Christ in the Pietà. The soldier is laid out for his tomb in imitation of Charles Sargent Jagger's Hyde Park Tomb of the Unknown Soldier. And he appears for a brief moment in glory, holding the banner of St. George—England's patron saint who slew the dragon—at the film's end in imitation of Piero della Francesca's *Resurrection*.

But is there a resurrection? Jarman plays the final scenes in the "profound dull tunnel" about which Owen writes in "Strange Meeting." These are the lines with which Olivier ends his opening monologue, and which Britten leaves unsaid. The Unknown and German soldiers are reconciled, and the German soldier participates in the resurrection by blowing the last trumpet. But he does so as a child who finds a discarded bugle in a pool of water, suggesting the notion of rebirth is childish. The German soldier offers red poppies to the Unknown Soldier, who is now laid out on his tomb like the dead Christ in numerous medieval and Renaissance tomb scenes rather than as the triumphant figure of the Resurrection. The nurse and his mother offer white poppies. The Unknown Soldier has vanished, and in his place stands a lighted candle. The nurse then closes the door on the sepulcher.

9. ✤ War Requiem

Jarman's film began with a lighted candle, but it was snuffed out before the old veteran began his monologue. We are left, at the end, with a vanished Christ and a candle in an airless tomb. How long can it last? Jarman ends with images of Christ's Resurrection and Death, the Biblical order reversed. These occur in gloomy settings that contradict the salvationist triumphalism of the traditional church. Only the precarious, precious candle, which we ourselves light in the midst of darkness, snuffed out at the beginning of the film, rather than the risen Christ, remains to light our way after the World War. The "rest in peace" with which the Requiem ends for Jarman is the peace of the grave, not of the New Jerusalem.

10
Jubilee without John Dee? Modern Times

―――――――――― ❧ ――――――――――

Had I betrayed Punk...: 'Derek the Dull Little Middle-Class Wanker'? Or had Punk betrayed itself? How could you fight success? ... Some aristo on a fallen estate, that's how I consoled myself in the face of so-called Social Realism, that was never real.[1]

In 1977, the year in which Britain celebrated Queen Elizabeth II's twenty-fifth year on the throne, Jarman made the bitter film *Jubilee* to show the devastation being inflicted on Britain in the name of progress. The destruction was especially apparent in his own neighborhood, the south bank of the Thames in London, where he successively moved from studio to studio in a neighborhood of old warehouses that were being demolished and, in some cases, suspiciously burned to make room for modern monstrosities. In an unpublished note, he dedicated *Jubilee* to "all those who secretly work against the tyranny of Marxists fascists trade unionists maoists capitalists socialists etc ... who have conspired together to destroy the diversity and holiness of each life in the name of materialism."[2]

Jubilee shows the absurdity of much contemporary culture by reversing expected roles. "All the positives are negated, turned on their heads," Jarman explains. The main characters are "amazons [who] make men

10. ⚭ Jubilee

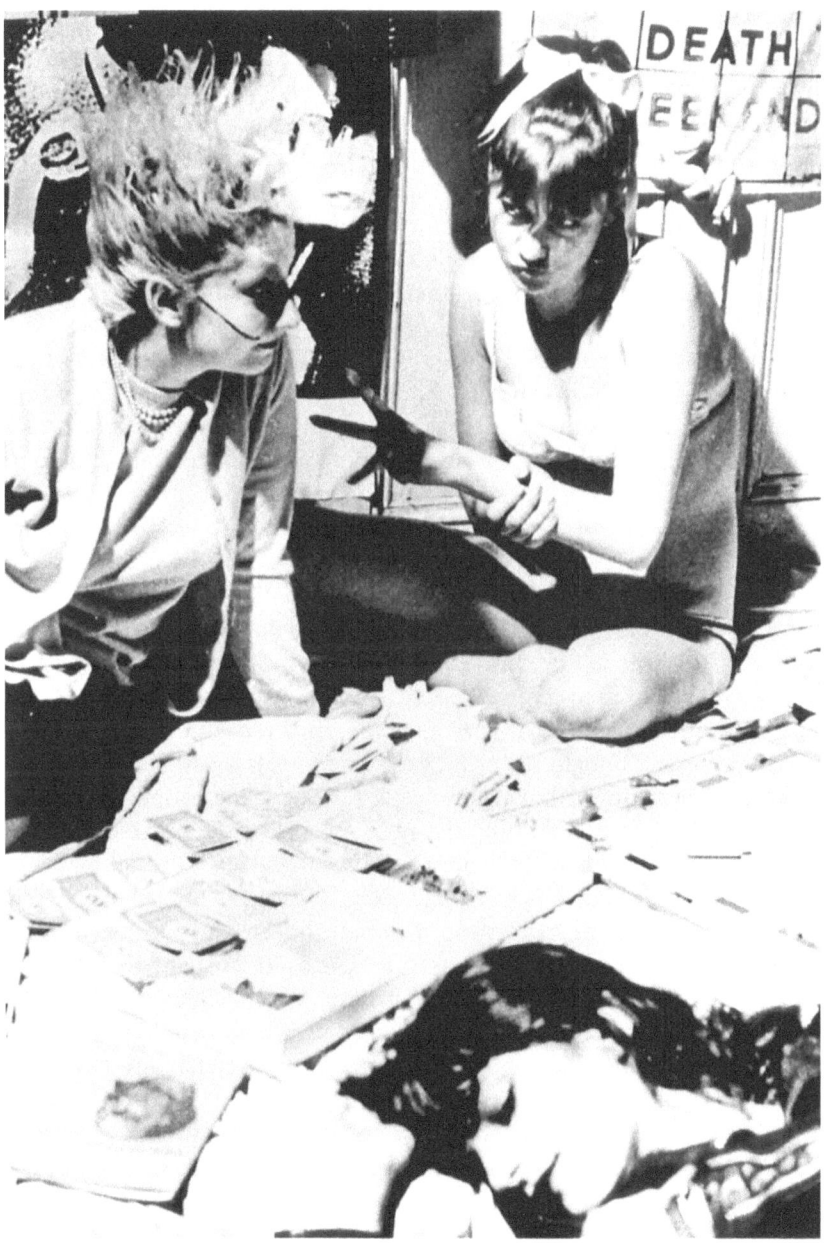

Jarman juxtaposed the vibrant yet ultimately futile punk scene, which flourished in 1977 as Queen Elizabeth II celebrated her twenty-fifth year on the throne, with its establishment critics. (*British Film Institute, Posters and Designs.*)

uncomfortable, ridicule their mad pursuits."³ A group of urban misfits—punks, musicians, and terrorists—fight the police state only to be co-opted by it. Persecuted homosexuals alone resist the wasteland that is offered as the promised land by the then-dominant Tory party. Jarman rejects the present for the past, and juxtaposes the reign of Gloriana, the first Queen Elizabeth, to the "decline and fall" he observes in his own lifetime. In the film he incorporates "the streets and warehouses in which I had lived," and "a mass of Xeroxes and quick notes on scraps of papers, torn photos, and messages from my collaborators." "The progressive merging of film and my reality was complete."⁴

To be sure, Jarman is no reactionary or imperialist. A mute, dwarf serving woman shadows the first Elizabeth. Her presence calls attention to the class structure that underlies the golden age. "Huge spectral hunting dogs which tower over" Elizabeth remind us that force contributed to her achievement. Nevertheless, her England bettered rather than hurt most of the population. Furthermore, she tolerated religious differences among Protestants and prevented what may have been a Catholic majority from rebelling, no mean achievement when these factions were tearing each other and nations apart all over Europe. As Jarman has Ariel, the spirit who leads her into the present, express it: "Consider the world's diversity and worship it, by denying its multiplicity you deny your own true nature."

Without knowledge of what England once was and might be again we are powerless to fight the evils of our own age. Jarman is acutely aware of how attitudes toward or ignorance of history shape people's behavior. In *Jubilee* the "historian" Amyl (Nitrate), played by the punk singer Jordan of the Sex Pistols with an appropriate hair-style and facial makeup, shares a flat with Mad, a pyromaniac, Bod (Bodicea—"Queen of the New Age"—named after the courageous Britannic queen who resisted, in vain, the tyranny of the ancient Romans), and Chaos, their silent French maid who stands for the world outside of Britain. That Jarman associates the voice of "history" with the drug amyl nitrate, which people use to keep themselves stimulated at concerts and discos, suggests that late-twentieth century radicalism, like the "Mad" violence and cult of "strong" women who improve their "bods" and imitate men (Bod sometimes wears masculine attire) may be revolutionary in theory but can easily be co-opted in practice.

Amyl dances round a "bonfire of vanity" set "between iron sheds in a scarred industrial landscape invaded by scrub." In imitation of Savanarola's brief Renaissance republic, in which the burning of books was called the "bonfire of the vanities," books are burned along with a Union Jack. The fire is stoked by a young boy who throws his golden locks into the fire, his new coiffure signaling a "new Puritanism" which accompanied shorter male hair in seventies' England. Amyl thus celebrates the end of traditional history. "Masked figures representing art, Michelangelo's David [homosexual expression], and death watch impassively" to signify that historical amnesia wipes out beauty, freedom, and knowledge along with injustice and devastation.

Amyl's work-in-progress, "Teach Yourself History by Amyl Nitrate," deconstructs the master narrative of British glory much as the bonfire does. The Normans "screwed the Anglo Saxons into the ground," creating a two-class society which then joined together to fight the rest of the world and rule much of it for the benefit of the British elite. Then "Chaos" came, turning the British on each other in class warfare, and "England sunk into the sea." By depicting "Chaos" as a French maid, Jarman may be calling attention to how the French Revolution and France's working class helped the British realize its plight. From this perspective, England should be proudest not of its history but of the deconstructionist historian who tells the truth: Mad introduces Amyl as "England's glory who's going to tell us the exciting story of her misspent life."

Yet Amyl does not live up to expectations. Her narrative is short, simplistic, and ultimately trivial: she writes history "to compress it," as a hobby. She does not find history useful because it does not really exist—"It's so intangible. You can weave the facts any way you like. Good guys can swap places with bad guys. You might think Richard III of England was bad, but you'd be wrong. What separates Hitler from Napoleon or even Alexander? The size of the destruction? Or was he closer to us in time? Was Churchill a hero? Did he alter history for the better?" Amyl's narrative is not unreasonable: the young people who rebel against a conformist state at least do not join or salute the forces which repress them. As Amyl notes: "We're carrying on regardless, coping with misgovernment and idiocy on every side."

Amyl's ideas reflect the POSTMODERN line, a word which appears in capital letters as graffiti while alienated youths indiscriminately rob and murder both "an affluent hippy" and a wealthy woman in a Rolls-Royce. Jarman in this scene links the superficial radical chic of the prosperous sixties with modern conservatism as having nothing to offer young people in a decaying society with poor job prospects. They face what Jarman presents as a "globe blotched with a black cancer" bearing the words: "NEGATIVE WORLD STATUS; NO REASON FOR EXISTENCE; OBSOLETE." Amyl relates how as a child during the optimistic sixties she and her peers were encouraged to "make your dreams reality," but when that proved impossible people acted on their "desires"—the "me" generation. "Films, books, pictures

[and] art" became "obsolete" as people were encouraged simply to express shriveled selves bereft of the very cultural artifacts that would provide them with an alternative to the present. Amyl herself wishes to "defy gravity," which means she refuses to take life or ideas seriously and consciously lives the ironic, postmodern existence that will make it easy for her to go over to the powers she detests.

Yet Amyl is aware of a lost world. She does not rejoice when she accidentally smashes her Winston Churchill mug. She says "shit," realizing the loss of heroes — which Mad describes as "SO SAD" [capitalization Jarman's]. When she dabs herself with perfume, Amyl comments: "Carnation from Floris, not all the good things have disappeared." She will use this perfume to blind the policeman who has killed the Kid and thus take revenge. She repeats the same line as she joins the camp of the new dictator, Borgia Ginz. What we take from flowers, even the scent that remains when they are dead, is a symbol for Jarman of a world we have lost that can still inspire us to create beauty and fight evil. Jarman's own garden at Dungeness, where he carefully cultivated flowers amidst the rubble, symbolized that fact in his life. In *Jubilee*, Queen Elizabeth I—"the Virgin Queen, Astraea, paradigm of royalty," Jarman calls her — and her court alchemist and astrologer John Dee "signed" themselves with the "codes and countercodes, the secret language of flowers" to symbolize the golden age they inaugurated: "True gold of the new spring of learning." But as Dee and Elizabeth observe England's terrible modern fate, the spirit Ariel, himself depicted as a youth in a leather jacket who guides their time-travel, brings "the winter of thy flowers and the frost that secretly destroys the temple."

We can see some of these false flowers as cultivated by Max, the "malevolent" ex-mercenary who now "wars" on imaginary threats to his garden. He only grows plastic flowers—he is furious when a live bug appears in one of them and he eats the insect for the "protein." "Mad" Max cares for these simulacra as though they were real. He also consoles elderly women by calling bingo games where they relieve their loneliness, talking nonchalantly of the awful news outside and justifying the extermination of suspected subversives. What they really want is indicated by the prizes they win—a large black dildo and a male inflatable doll. What we have deluded ourselves into believing are beauty, conversation, love, and community in the modern wasteland are really artificial, pale, or perverse imitations of things past. Evil is reduced to banal chit-chat: it doesn't register. As Amyl notes: "when ... law and order were finally abolished, all those statistics that were a substitute for reality disappeared. The crime rate dropped to zero." Jarman here exaggerates the everyday practice of fabricating statistics to show things are better than they seem to be.

10. ⊗ Jubilee

Jarman contrasts the beautiful, glorious Elizabeth and Dee, who speak poetically in strains reminiscent of Shakespeare, with the second Elizabeth. (The director entitled his film about Shakespeare's sonnets *The Angelic Conversation*, a tribute to one of Dee's major works.) Dressed in a scarf and frumpy coat, she makes a brief, almost imperceptible appearance before she is gunned down by Bod as she flees. She gives way to a ferocious woman who resembles a man—Margaret Thatcher was waiting in the wings of the Conservative Party in 1977. Elizabeth II, unlike her predecessor, is of no personal consequence. Known to be sympathetic to social justice in private, the members of the royal family, in effect, no longer exist as a real force.

Jarman symbolizes the real new rulers of England in the form of Borgia Ginz, the name a composite of the Renaissance family of usurpers and murderers and the Ginza, the main street of contemporary Tokyo. (Jarman originally invented the character as a play on the name of a former roommate, Michael Ginsborg.)[5] Since both the Borgias and various Tokyo-based banks were among the leading financial brokers of their eras, international business is revealed as the power behind the scenes of the world's states in the eras of both Elizabeths. To show this is not a matter of race but of class, Jarman has a black man—the smoothest, most ironic, and slimiest character imaginable—play Ginz. His story is different than Amyl's but equally plausible: "This is the generation who grew up and forgot to lead their lives. They were so busy watching my endless movie [that] the media became their only reality and I owned their world of flickering shadows." The "sinister impresario of mediocrity ... King of Kapital and the Kathode" dwells in an empty opera house (culture is dead—Jarman designed operas) from which he directs the BBC, CIA, ABC, the KGB, and the C of E (Church of England). Media, political, and religious institutions may appear to a gullible public as either autonomous or opposed to each other, but they collectively form a world-system which compels subservience. As Ginz boasts: "As long as the music's loud enough we won't hear the world falling apart." Ginz is also identified with Judas, the betrayer of Christ, for he is the man who "picked up the thirty pieces of silver and made the movie you saw on TV."

These last words are spoken by Angel, the lover of his own brother Sphinx. They first appear "pallid and famished reading atrocities from the yellow press" while telling Mad to "Fuck off." Unlike the others, they come from a genuine working-class slum. Sphinx explains that he

> Never lived below the fourteenth floor till I was old enough to run away.
> Never saw the ground before I was four, just locked alone with the telly

all day. The first time I saw flowers I freaked. I was frightened of dandelions.... Everything was regulated in that tower block, planned by the social planners to the lowest common denominator. Sight: concrete, sound: the telly, taste: plastic, touch: plastic, the seasons regulated by the thermostat. Once a year my mum and dad dusted down the plastic Christmas tree and exchanged pathetic presents. Didn't know I was dead till I was fifteen. Never experienced love or hate. My generation's the blank generation.

Yet Angel and Sphinx do not settle for their lot, mock it ironically, or turn to mindless violence. Combined, like the dual Christ in Jarman's *The Garden*, their names stand respectively for the religious achievement of love, morality, and self-transcendence and civilizational achievement of intelligent questioning, which have always called upon society to live up to its professed values. Angel leads a protest against "Cardinal" Borgia Ginz's religious values. "Save your souls. Welcome to the palace of heavenly delight," Angel preaches from a soapbox outside of Westminster Cathedral. At this point, Jesus and the twelve apostles perform a disco dance to the tune of "Jerusalem," Hubert Parry's setting of the William Blake poem which has served as the unofficial anthem of the British working class, pledging to rebuild a pastoral Jerusalem to replace the "dark satanic mills." (Jarman also dedicated the film to Blake, in addition to his contemporary heirs.) [6] The gay "angel" articulates Jarman's vision of Jesus' message: that he and his apostles had formed an alternative gay community that preached enjoyment as well as charity and tolerance towards others.

Borgia Ginz, however, arrives on the scene and co-opts even this protest, claiming it is a spectacle he has staged. As a subtext, the police who will soon murder Sphinx, Angel, and Kid — another young rebel played by Adam of the rock group Adam and the Ants — join in the orgy. The police pervert it from a celebration of love to a violent brawl, much as they infiltrated peaceful demonstrations in the 1960s to provoke violence and resentment against the countercultural protestors. As their brutal beating of Kid suggests, a suppressed homosexuality which takes a sadistic turn lies at the heart of the persecution of gays. The cop who kills Kid sneeringly refers to him as "Princess." Kid's crime is not homosexuality, although he is guilty by association with the gay brothers who believed they had a right to protest and lead their lives. Rather, he had refused to perform on Ginz's television network under the name of SCUM, about which Ginz says: "it's [the name that] all they deserve." Sphinx disentangles Kid from the cords attached to his electrical equipment and lures him away with these words: "The music industry's dead. You're better off on the streets.... He'll steal your voice and sell it. He doesn't care if the mindless public hears your words or not. He just wants to package you.... Why don't you come along and sing to me." Angel adds: "The devil said, 'I'll give you all this if you go down on your knees."

Amyl, unlike Kid, has no trouble selling out to Ginz. (Is Jarman comparing the "authenticity" of Adam and the Ants to the superficial shock value of the Sex Pistols, Amyl's real-life band?) She deconstructs rights as part of her history in her chapter on "Civilisation":

> Human beings have no rights, but some dumb fuck told them they had them. First, political rights. Freedom of speech and things like that. And if that wasn't enough they were told they had material rights too. They forgot about the political rights soon enough, but they got hooked on the material ones. One desolate suburban acre and a car. And then a TV, fridge and another car. That was by right, and the habit demanded more and more. The day came when the expectations couldn't be fulfilled any longer, and everyone felt cheated. So here we are in the present, with civilization destroyed by resentment, but since civilization was always fucking awful for everyone, who gives a shit? We're better off without it.

While an excellent commentary on mainstream society, Amyl's narrative omits the fact that history has been shaped and life meaningfully improved precisely when people, like Sphinx, Angel, and Kid, reclaim "freedom of speech and things like that" and reject self-indulgent postmodernist commentary for radical politics. Amyl has no trouble going on Ginz's show, where she performs "Rule Britannia," a song linking British "freedom" to imperial expansion and war rather than the working-class, ecologically friendly "Jerusalem." "A shell-shocked Britannia in a sea of dry ice," she spits out the song, "goose-stepping across the stage, a vision of disaster," as "Hitler's hysterical speech jabbers through the football crowds, chanting 'England! England! England!' dive bombers, explosions." As with the "radical" music of the sixties, the establishment commercialized the "revolution" against itself, turning rock stars into millionaires and reducing dissent to "art" detached from life. Jarman is here having Amyl comment on the character who is playing her: Jordan belonged to the Sex Pistols, whose irreverent version of "God Save the Queen" topped the charts in the Jubilee Year thanks to skillful promoting by the music industry.[7]

Hence it is no wonder that Adolf Hitler himself joins Amyl in Ginz's living room as they watch the official royal "Jubilee" on television. Hitler comments: "The [queen's] golden coach is so fantastic, an artist's dream. Though of course I was the greatest artist of this century, greater than Leonardo da Vinci." Joined by Mad and Bod, Amyl toasts him. His true art, of course, is the very violence in which Mad and Bod delight. Jarman suggests that their vengeance on behalf of the boys is motivated more by a thirst for blood than a sense of justice: fascisms of the left and right seek vengeance rather than a better world. For when Amyl and Bod have no other targets, they box with each other, and Mad is a pyromaniac.

At the film's end, Elizabeth I remarks to John Dee that "my heart rejoiceth in the roar of the surf on the shingles. Marvelous sweet music it is to my ears." The sea reminds her of their love of flowers, happy days at Oxford, and dreams of a better world. But now the sign of this better world is not in England, but the sea which defines where England ends. Ariel remarks that the sun is sinking, and while the west reveals "a vision of silver dew falling into a chalice flowing on a sea of pure gold," the east and north — England's most impoverished and blighted regions in the 1970s and '80s — only offer "black hoarfrost," "the sun eclipsed," "howling chaos," and "a black rain [which] falls without ceasing." The image is of the sun setting on a British Empire upon which the sun formerly never set: "Now is the time of departure. The last streamer that ties us to what is known parts. We drift into a sea of storms." The "media" have debased nature, music, art, love, religion and history to reinforce a world of capital that uses force when seduction does not suffice. Hoping against hope, Jarman fought to the end to provide the anchor in the storm that would reconnect us to other lives, other possibilities, and an alternative history.

In a lighthearted sequel to Jubilee he never filmed — *B Movie: Little England/A Time of Hope*, Jarman offered an alternative history of his own. After "Lord Protector" Ginz dies, his followers hope to apply the science of cryonics and resurrect him. However, despite elaborate publicity, the required machinery fails as the Archbishop of Canterbury tries to cover up the botched job. Meanwhile, Ginz's successors are selling off England to C. T. Slicker, Texans, the Japanese, and other rich foreigners in a parody of the privatization of state industries undertaken by the Thatcher government. No one wants the Isle of Dogs (in fact an artists' neighborhood in London where Jarman lived) so Adam (intended to be played by the singer from Adam and the Ants again) buys it for fifty pence — literally, the price of a song he was tipped for singing. He makes his aging parents King Rocker and Mary Lou, who are only interested in fifties rock and roll, its king and queen. Adam is lured to negotiate with Slicker by the latter's daughter Veronica, who betrays Adam and thus teaches him indirectly about class solidarity. Learning that his enemies will neither play by their own rules nor stop until they have acquired everything including his own worthless kingdom, Adam learns the "Internationale" from Red Flag, an old trade unionist, signifying that genuine democratic socialism is reborn.

10. ∞ Jubilee 141

A war then ensues pitting Adam and the Isle of Dogs (that is Jarman and his artistic allies) against Slicker (King Charles the Last) and the rest of England. Adam is victorious when his women warriors strip off their clothes and cause Slicker's forces to desert and make love, not war. Everyone except Slicker and his capitalist cronies live happily ever after. Did Jarman hope a reborn Labor Party and rejection of a costly, neo-colonial policy of seeking overseas prestige (hence the equation of "little England" with "hope") could rebuild Jerusalem on England's green fields? He never stopped trying. Much of Jarman's film oeuvre presents alternative histories which could or should have happened, which proves that he never bought into the ultimate cop-out: historical inevitability, the absurdity proclaimed in works such as Francis Fukuyama's *The End of History and the Last Man* (1992), which argue that bourgeois "liberalism"—which has depleted the earth's resources, created ugliness wherever it spreads itself, and enabled a minority to live parasitically at the expense of most of the world's population—is the apex of human history.

11
The Last of England: Modern Times Revisited

&

Ten years after *Jubilee*, Jarman filmed *The Last of England* (1987). Stylistically, it is very different. There is no obvious no story line. The picture is best read as a montage contrasting the blight of Margaret Thatcher's prime ministry with scenes of England earlier in the century. *The Last of England* presents the completed catastrophe that at the time of *Jubilee* was still in the making. (Part of Jarman's personal catastrophe is that in 1986, he learned that he was HIV positive.) Nevertheless, similar themes run through the two films.

As with *Jubilee*, Jarman is intensely concerned with the knowledge and meaning of history. Here, however, instead of presenting, and implicitly arguing against, a punker's view that history is meaningless, he himself narrates the story. He is seated at a desk covered with writing and art materials so he can practice his two main vocations besides cinema. A skull representing "Vanitas"—the futility of human endeavor—stares at him as it did at the learned patron of the arts Cardinal Del Monte in Jarman's *Caravaggio*. "Once, I dreamed of paintings I could love," said the cardinal.[1] As Jarman recites the first of four long poems about the contemporary state of England which shape the first part of the film, we see a handsome half-naked young drug addict—played by the ironically named "Spring"—alternatively stomping and masturbating on top of a

11. ⁑ The Last of England 143

By the mid–1980s, Jarman had written off Margaret Thatcher's England as hopelessly repressive, homophobic, and deliberately exploiting the many for the benefit of a few. (*British Film Institute, Posters and Designs.*)

thrown-away copy of Caravaggio's painting "Profane Love," — the seductive, naked Cupid on the verge of adolescence. The homosexually-inspired Renaissance could create the beautiful; the present age can only destroy. The ravaged addict replaces and defiles what should be a beautiful painting to be loved. He opens this tragic film as the representative of a lost generation to be mourned.

How much can, and should, we remember of England's past in the face of the contemporary catastrophe? "Imprisoned memories prowl through the dark," Jarman begins before complaining, "Aw, fuck it." Nevertheless, he continues with the poem and the film in spite of this apparent confession of futility — or does the expletive express a "what the hell" attitude to proceed in spite of everything? For the first part of the film, nearly all of the scenes shot in the present are in fact dark — black and white, shades of grey, brown, and a smoldering fiery red — in contrast to the vivid, pleasant memories of an earlier age. These are represented by Jarman's parents' colorful home movies of his childhood. Then, flowers bloomed. Now, Jarman pastes dead blossoms into a book. "Poppies and corn cockle have long been forgotten here.... The oaks [symbol of England's glory] died this year." In *Dancing Ledge* he added: "The TV replaced the hearth in the fifties. Where the fire had nourished dreams, allowed the mind to wander like the flickering flames that danced in the coals, the TV numbed the mind."[2] The present, *The Last of England,* is filled with rats, goblins, ashes, and rattles of death. The weather is changing: "they say the ice age is coming"; black hail falls. "Spring lapped the fields in arsenic green," a double-entendre referring to the young addict who is raving, shooting up, and masturbating. Here is a new meaning of green, for "on every green hill mourners stand and weep for the last of England" as Shakespeare, "the Swan of Avon, dies a syncopated death."

In place of England's green fields, oaks, flowers, and literary heritage stand the ruins of modernity. Thatcher's economic policies in the eighties led not only to the destruction of traditional England, but even modern factories and housing projects degenerated into slums and then ruins. These are the settings for Jarman's film. Jarman and a boy hold aloft a torch, searching like Diogenes for something amid the rubble — truth, beauty, decency, perhaps. Jarman appears wearing a large miter, a dunce cap or the hat victims of the Inquisition wore in their death processions. The torch remains aloft at the film's end, as a rowboat with several people dressed in white moves quietly in Stygian waters. Jarman adapted that image and title of his film from a painting by Ford Madox Brown, "The Last of England."[3] Here, nineteenth century emigrants leave behind the poverty and oppression of a land that offers them nothing. But the image also resembles Gustav Doré's nineteenth century engraving for *The Divine Comedy* of Dante's descent into hell. Only now the innocent are damned. Britain is, literally, going to Hell.

Jarman's second poem, and his tone in reading it, switches from sorrow to anger. "My teacher said there are more walls in England than in Berlin," he begins, indicating that post-industrial England's real problem is not Communism abroad, but repression and ugliness at home. Refusing to be "your clean-limbed cannon fodder for the drudgery nine to five," Jarman and his fellow critics, artists, and punkers linked service to the establishment in war and Cold War with the wasting of life in everyday business activity. We see people walking home at London rush hour, in front of St. Paul's Cathedral, which sits in the background as high-rise monstrosities threaten the church from all sides. The fruit of "malevolent bureaucrats mutated large as dinosaurs,/ A thin yellow pus dripped through exhausted institutions.... What were we to do in the crumbling acres — Die of boredom?" Jarman asks, before giving his generation a difficult and perhaps impossible mission: "Recreate ourselves emerging from the chrysalis all scarlet and turquoise." But it was to no avail: "even our protests were hopeless/Neat little marches down blind alleys."

This is "The Wasteland" of T. S. Eliot's poem, which ends "not with a bang but with a whimper," as Jarman quotes Eliot's "prophetic voice." He also cites Allan Ginsberg's "Howl" to stress the human wreckage accompanying the landscape: "I saw the best minds of my generation destroyed by madness, starving, hysterical, naked." Later, Jarman will show us a naked, homeless man, ravenously devouring a cabbage from a garbage can. "Gather everything you throw out of your dream houses/Treasured your trashbins, Picking through the tatters of your life." (Jarman said: I myself saw a naked, homeless man under a railroad bridge in Washington, D.C., less than a mile from the United States Capitol as I wrote this chapter.)

The cabbage matters. In the third poem, Jarman writes: "Where's hope? The little white lies have carried her off beyond the cabbage patch." Hope lies, if anywhere, in remembering the past, in scavenging among the trash — that is, in a critical awareness of history — since the previous generation was "busy squandering our threadbare patrimony (on the atom?)." The homeless man and his rage become symbols of Jarman's generation: the young man who is shot at the end of the film also sorts through rubble, searching for something. So did Jarman himself, who made his films at wrecked industrial sites, used recycled home movies, and found his props and costumes at flea markets and thrift shops. To put a Marxist twist on it, the material conditions of Jarman's film-making mirrored the message he sought to convey: that all the late-twentieth century had were ruins, relics, and remembrances to reconstruct itself.

Jarman pins the blame for this situation squarely on the agents of a perverted progress: government bureaucrats who would fib about threats at home and abroad and extol the value of replacing old England with standard international high-rises and housing developments. "Lies," "evasion," and "bribery" became "normal." World War II was one lie. Japan, represented in the film by Emperor Hirohito and the person whom one British lady calls "his Empress, Nagasake" "stole the patterns" from the British Empire by going imperialistic. Jarman misnames the empress for two reasons: to illustrate people's ignorance of the world in which they live and its history, and to call attention to the site where the second atomic bomb was dropped. Jarman blames expenditure on the atom, symbol of Cold War "defense," for much of Britain's impoverishment: she tried to remain a great, that is to say, imperialist, power despite the economic debacle of World War II and the dissolution of the empire. Hence Jarman writes: "The bomb [was] dropped with regular monotony," signifying both its threatened use and the devastation England inflicted on itself. Living in the shadow of a nuclear reactor, he could see the triple threat of the world's annihilation, the waste of valuable resources on unusable weapons, and the destruction of the landscape through "progress" symbolized by nuclear power.

In league with the government were the capitalists themselves and the religious fanatics who confused the economic and foreign policies of the English-speaking nations with the will of God. As the homeless man tears into the cabbage symbolizing his and England's hopeless situation, we hear voices praising Jesus and asserting that he will rise again. At the same time, beautiful bracelets and necklaces with preposterously huge numbers of jewels are advertised at "bargain" prices on what sounds like shoppers' television.

Jarman says in the film that everywhere "citizens stand mute watching children devoured in their prams." We see an old man wheeling a pram through the darkness, carrying a torch that no longer illuminates, in contrast with children playing in happier times. Children figure prominently in the film. They are numbered among the homeless; they play in filthy streets with old shopping carts; they frolic amidst barbed wire as Jarman flashes back in a home movie to where barbed wire supposedly protected children at a military base. If the present generation has no patrimony, the next will not even have the memory of one. "Tomorrow has been canceled due to lack of interest," Jarman cites an anonymous graffiti that parallels Eliot's and Ginsberg's wisdom.

What is replacing community, concern for the quality of life, education, and tradition is mindless patriotism: "and in the despair all you did was celebrate the Windsors once again." Jarman links the fanfare surrounding the royal wedding of Charles and Diana with the celebration of the easy victory over the Argentines in the Malvinas, or Falklands. As in *Jubilee*, we also hear chants of "England" presented as voice-overs to speeches of Hitler. These cries are coming from one of the soccer games — we hear the ball put in play — which became increasingly violent as the economy worsened while chauvinism increased in the early eighties. In *Jubilee*, Hitler remained a passive observer, appearing only at the end to praise the "art" of the 1977 celebration. Here, he is an actor, his speeches substituted for Thatcher's racist, anti-gay, and anti-welfare state policies to call attention to the fact that repression has become respectable — it need not wear a military uniform and rarely raises its voice. The footballers provide the Nuremberg rally, their "Englands" merging into "Heils." Hitler has conquered us.

Military uniforms are indeed present in the postmodern dystopia. Guns are brought in where official gobbledygook fails to mystify. The film's masked soldiers appear to be terrorists; it seemed so until near the end of the film, when three bourgeois women dressed in black mourning ask their leader: "Did you enjoy the Falklands? Preparing for the next one?" The real terrorists are those military and police forces which sustain a terroristic civilization. The women bring a wreath of poppies to an underground tomb, reminiscent of the three Marys who came to mourn Jesus. (The British memorial to the soldiers who died in this war is in the crypt under the altar at St. Paul's.) But these satanic black Marias do not weep; they encourage the soldiers to keep up the good work. We remember Jarman's first poem: that poppies are "long forgotten," but "the boys who died in Flanders,/ their names are raised by a late frost that clipped the old village cross." The late frost is the "icy" weather of Jarman's own time, where empathy has vanished. The deadly spirit of patriotism which motivated the First World War still exists, only the cross is now "clipped." The poppies do not live: they float on the Styx as the boat rows off to Hell in the final scene.

The spirit of old England, which in *Jubilee* Jarman brought back to life through Queen Elizabeth I, appears in *The Last of England* with numerous shots of the statues of Queen Victoria, first Empress of India, and the elephant that decorates the monument in front of the Royal Albert Hall. A living Elizabeth has been replaced by cold marble. Soldiers from India march on parade, their kilts and identification with the empire appearing ludicrous amid the devastation with which Jarman intersperses it. Elgar's "Pomp and Circumstance" March, "Land of Hope and Glory," praying that "God who made her [England] mighty [would] make her mightier yet," a march whose words are obnoxious for their strident imperialism, becomes absurd when played in the context of a post-colonial, postmodern little England. A fat, laughing man, looking almost like a baby, laughs as he twirls the "cancerous" globe Jarman depicted in *Jubilee*. He could be a cruel god, a caricature of Winston Churchill — who tried to preserve the empire after winning the war — or an emperor with no clothes. Even when England was great, she built her empire by exploiting much of the world: without an empire, left to her own resources, she became weak and pitiable. Thatcherism appears an absurd effort to regain the worst of England's past.

And absurdities abound in *The Last of England*. A "Disco Death" dance features both men and women, masked, naked, their bodies glowing red, writhing as one man — ludicrously dressed as a female ballet dancer — performs some classical steps. The Smiths, a band with which Jarman worked, perform the song "Vicar in a Tutu," calling attention to the repressed homoeroticism and homophobia within the Church of

England. Alternatively, the tune may hint that the true vicar (or representative) of Christ is African Bishop Tutu. The scene also shows Jarman's recognition of the anachronism of celebratory art in a hideous world. Two soldiers dance together, a bitter reflection that whereas a young homosexual is executed, "male bonding" is tolerated in other contexts.

These bitter comic dance scenes foreshadow a far more powerful one near the film's end. A young bride, mourning her husband's death at the hands of the soldiers, performs a powerful "dance of death" and shreds her wedding dress. The music is from Diamanda Galas' "The Mask of the Red Death," a "Mass[k] for a Time of Plague." In this work, Galas, a performance artist who insists her compositions be played "at maximum volume," is a beautiful woman who appears topless and covered with spots to simulate a person with AIDS. She dedicated this work to awakening the world to the murder of people with AIDS through inferior care, social indifference, and homophobia among the world's leading nations. Jarman recognized a kindred spirit in her refusal to renounce rage or succumb to despair. By employing an excerpt from her "Mask," he linked the Thatcher-Reagan policies of war on other nations and war on the poor to their scapegoating of people with AIDS and homosexuals. In addition to Galas, we see a graffiti "UB-40," yet another group of radical musicians Jarman honors as fellow rebels against the present who have not sold out to the art-music-media establishment.

The confusion of gender manifested by the male ballerina also appears in Jarman's parody of two weddings: Charles and Diana's and the marriage of the young man later killed by the soldiers. The bride in both is played Tilda Swinton. The "bridesmaids" are fat, hairy men who wear enormous wigs. Their costumes are no more absurd than the wigs and archaic regalia which persevere in the courts and ceremonies of an England that is, literally, going to Hell. The wedding takes place in the shell of an old building as the "Dies irae" [Day of wrath] plays in the background, at once an appropriate commentary on the situation and a critique of the inability of traditional church music to provide solace in an era of economic hardship and violence. The behavior of feminized males is the converse of England's support for the masculinized female Margaret Thatcher. At the same time, the bride's mourning for her husband could also reflect Princess Diana's sympathy for people with AIDS and others.

The real subversive, aside from Jarman himself, is the young man who is killed. The masked soldiers leave the drug addict alone. He is no threat to anyone except himself, for drugs are cheaper than prisons in neutralizing the young and angry. The youth who digs in the ruins hoping to find something of value, who makes love to an apparently dead soldier sprawled on a Union Jack — the soldier revives and enjoys the experience — and who marries rather than goes off to war is shot by a firing squad. Anyone who tries to resurrect a lost England, has homosexual tendencies, and opposes the latest patriotic adventure has no place in the new world order. (Jarman intersperses cries of "Order, Order, Order" with the fascist chant of "England" and the sounds of cash registers clinging.) The executioners consist of British soldiers who follow the commands of a man with Hispanic features wearing a beret. Following the Falklands/Malvinas motif, he may be considered an Argentine, and the scene Jarman's scathing comment on the whole war. England thought it had called the tune and had won. In fact, it really had followed the cues given by a terrible dictatorship — which started the war in the hopes of bolstering its fading control. Both governments murdered their own in equally obscene causes — regenerating the popularity of reactionary governments. England succeeded whereas Argentina, by losing the war, set in motion a movement toward democracy.

The Thatcher regime, like Reagan's in the United States, enacted economic policies which created a large class of homeless people and subsistence workers. Both rulers also spouted a philosophy of blaming these people for their plight, symbolized by increasing police repression and incarceration, which Jarman shows us. Public hatred of the poor appears in a graffiti: "SQUATTERS WILL DIE." Jarman parades before us a group of mostly women and children, blacks as well as whites, but also including young, middle-aged and old men, who are being herded by soldiers out of their substandard housing to make way for more monstrous edifices. He calls them "Refugees," even though they are exiles within their own country, to emphasize both their plight and the irony that Thatcher and Reagan were far more hospitable to the "political refugees" fleeing "Communist" governments than to internal refugees from their own economic policies. For the rest of the movie, these people mostly sit around, guarded by soldiers, despair in their eyes, a fair approximation of the fate of the unemployed who are blamed for their situation and made to feel worthless. Gunfire is heard from time to time, a sign of contemporary urban violence. The guards kill a young man with a Mohawk haircut — the fate of those who refuse to be "devoured in their prams" or who go beyond the "neat little marches" the government permits to prove that dissent can exist (as long as it's inconsequential).

Jarman focuses long shots on these casualties of capitalism as Marianne Faithfull sings the "Skye-Boat Song." A beautiful Scottish tune, both infinitely sad and yet somehow consoling and lilting, it was written in the wake of the Jacobite Rebellion of 1745. The lyrics of the first stanza ask that a small boat convey Bonnie Prince Charlie to safety on the Isle of Skye, that the "lad born to be king" may return and deliver Britain from her [German and aristocratic] rulers. But Charlie's task was as hopeless as the fate of these refugees, and the second verse more appropriately describes the present and future: "Loud the winds howl,/ Loud the waves roar,/ Thunderclaps bend the air;/ Baffled the foe,/ Stand on the shore,/ Follow they will not dare." The only boat in the film, however, is the one somberly rowing off to Hell as the film ends.

Jarman ends with storms and catastrophes depicted in fast-forwarded images. As he writes in the film's third poem: "The world's curling up like an autumn leaf/The storms come to blow it into the final winter." He revives this image in the final poem — "The frosty heart of England blighted each spring leaf"— which also refers to the ruined life of "Spring," the name of the youth who plays the addict. The only live flowers in the film are those from the old home movies. Elsewhere, dead poppies, symbols of death, are laid on the tomb of the Falkland veterans. Jarman carefully preserves a single leaf in an album, a relic of times past. "Cold, cold, cold," a refrain appearing several times in one of Jarman's poems in *The Garden*, which he filmed several years later, is the atmosphere of *The Last of England*, an ironic comment given global warming and the presence of fires in both the film and the world. The refugees shiver in heavy coats: small fires warm the poor as they do in Third World countries. The world ends without a future, with nowhere for the refugees to go.

12
Neutron and *Sod 'Em:* Possible Futures

&

The Last of England was not Jarman's final word about contemporary society. Hope could be wrested from despair. Clearly, he continued to make films, struggle for gay rights, and work at his garden until he died. Discovering he was HIV positive in 1986, he set himself "a target: I would disclose my secret and survive Margaret Thatcher." Once he did, he remarked: "I have my sights on the millennium and a world where we are all equal before the law."[1]

Neutron, a script Jarman did not film, refers of course to the neutron bomb, the latest in destructive atomic technology as of 1983, when he wrote the script. The neutron bomb kills people but leaves property intact, the perfect symbol for the capitalist world-system that invented it. The material of the film, however, is a dramatization of the psychologist Carl Jung's book *Aion*, first published in 1951. Aion, in Greek, means "age," a period of history possessing a coherent identity. Based on studies in alchemy and astrology, with which Jarman was familiar, Jung saw world history evolving in two thousand year cycles: the Age of Pisces, which began with the birth of Christ, and marked the development of both Christ and Anti-Christ as symbols, would yield in or about 2000 CE to the Age of Aquarius, a notion subsequently adopted by the "New Age" movement. Jung noted that Christ and Anti-Christ, while regarded oppositionally by an institutionalized Christian church and the Western philosophy accompanying it (which divorced a heavenly spirit from earthly matter) were really essential to each other (as in true Christianity and alchemy) and their harmony would be revealed in the new "Aion." Matter and what the Age of Pisces has branded as "evil"—sexuality, violence, enjoyment of earthly pleasures—form an integral part of the human soul and need to be incorporated into a non-destructive view of the universe, and not obliterated or degraded as the "absence" of the good. But in the first two millennia CE, an "anti-Christian era" paradoxically claiming to be true to the spirit of Christianity has "degenerated into rationalism, intellectualism, and doctrinarism (that most unspiritual of all the spirit's manifestations), all of which leads straight to the tragedy of modern times now hanging over our heads like a sword of Damocles.... The present age must come to terms drastically with the facts as they are, with the absolute opposition that is not only tearing the world asunder politically but has planted a schism in the human heart. We need to find our way back to the original, living spirit which, because of its ambivalence, is also a mediator and uniter of opposites."[2]

Jung symbolized this opposition to "establishment" Christian idealism as the lapis, a brilliant stone, and also as the serpent—representing both fecundity and evil, initially a bright shining being in the Garden of Eden. In *Neutron*, Jarman agrees with Jung that we need to synthesize mind and spirit to achieve psychological unity and a better world. But he is unsure of the outcome. *Neutron* can be read as foretelling either catastrophe or salvation.

In *Neutron* Jarman embodies Jung's earthly and active principle as a radical revolutionary with a bad reputation. He is called Topaz rather than the obscure "lapis." We meet Topaz when he shoots bullets into the limousine in which Aeon—an artist—is sitting while waiting for fuel at a gas station. Topaz—a character Jarman first invented in a play he drafted as a student[3]—rages as the embodiment of the depths of society and the need for violence to disrupt a world which reserves its resources for the wealthy. Aeon on the other hand conforms to the artist described by Viv in *Jubilee*: "Artists become blood donors—their life blood drips away.... And the people who control the world make it [art] as inaccessible as possible by driving artists into corners."[4] Aeon's synthesis with the activist Topaz is required to "release energy" and "recreate ourselves as artists," the synthesis Jarman achieved in his own life. In fact, Jarman based the Topaz-Aeon dialogues on conversations he, an artist of middle-class background, had with a working-class friend, Lee Drysdale, a member of the Workers' Revolutionary Party.[5]

Jarman described *Neutron* as illustrative of "a conflict between the active and contemplative life," whose representatives meet "in a desolate shadowy world, a purgatory where neither of them has an audience."

During the course of the film, Topaz and Aeon "criss-cross each other's lives in perpetual conflict," although "at the end we discover they are the same person."[6] At intervals, a radio spouts prophecies from the Book of Revelation "which is worked as science fiction." In each instance, Topaz emerges as the defender of justice who tries to do something about suffering, while Aeon strives to win beauty from the wreckage — Jarman intended to make most of the film at a "junked-out" power station and "in the wasteland around the Berlin Wall."[7]

The contrasts between the two form much of the film. Topaz accuses Aeon of longing for "the good old days, when all was fair in love and war, when the poor were shot, and the rich went sailing.... Some of us picked up guns and turned on them. We knew who the enemy was. While you sang about the end of the world we fought to save it."[8] Aeon denies that this is true, weeps, and turns the horror into art. Next Aeon and Topaz encounter one of the many starving, miserable children who represent the world we have left them. It is Aeon who notes that the boy is cold, while Topaz offers him his jacket. The child, however, bites the hand that clothes him. As the end approaches, Topaz warms himself by a fire and masturbates, glorying in heat and sexuality, while Aeon shivers, warms a pail of water instead, and bites his fingernails. He uses the water to shave. The artist fears sensual experience, or an unruly appearance with his face hairs out of place, yet anxiety over his mission compels him to spoil his fingers. It is difficult to find much sympathy for Aeon in the screenplay, for Topaz's criticism rings true and he is willing to act. Aeon metaphorically fiddles as Rome burns. Perhaps Aeon as played by David Bowie, as Jarman intended, could have made us change our minds, although significantly, Bowie himself would have preferred to play Topaz.[9]

At the script's end, both Aeon and Topaz address a crowd shouting Hosannahs. They meet in a pink marble bunker, which has various resonances. Since much of the film is set in Berlin, the architecture reflects the monumental emptiness of Albrecht Speer's Nazi visions. Jarman has us listen to "The Muzak of the Spheres," a play on both Speer's name as pronounced in German (Shpeer) and his architecture, the concrete equivalent of muzak. But the bunker is pink: the color of homosexuality, and the site on which Christ, his two halves reunited (Aeon and Topaz) appears — either to redeem or destroy the world. Both Topaz and Aeon denounce the contemporary world, whereupon Aeon shoots Topaz before undergoing a transformation in which Aeon, in dying, assumes the stigmata of Christ on his palms. Christ and Anti-Christ, spirit and matter, art and action, the homosexual and the homophobe, the holocaust of Nazism and the Christian apocalypse emerge in a synthesis.

After the apocalypse, the world "drowns in blood."[10] But then we hear the sound of a lark, and see a medieval pilgrim walking in the sunlight surrounded by white doves. One interpretation of this ambiguous ending is to note that a reborn world glories both in the asceticism of pilgrimage and the luxury of the sun. Humanity embarks on a new journey, perhaps the journey implicit in Christianity at the beginning but derailed by theologians who split mind and matter, soul and body, allowing the world to go to hell in its own way as it concentrated on saving souls at the expense of rebuking injustice. But perhaps Jarman is instead, or also, recalling the innocuous public image of the religion whose anti-materialist biases were responsible for all the trouble in the first place. Religion has a good reputation, more identified with the quiet monk than the ferocious inquisitor or corrupt cleric. Had *Neutron* been filmed, Jarman's intention might have been clearer.

Sod 'Em (that is, Sod-omize 'Em, a British equivalent of Fuck 'Em, or even more strongly, Fuck 'Em Up the Ass), written in the late eighties, moves beyond the bleak ending of *Jubilee* and the ambiguous conclusion of *Neutron* to a tentative affirmation of human struggle to better the world. This epithet undergoes transformation in the script. Beginning as a curse, a metaphor for the attitude of Thatcher's Tory party's policy toward the lower classes, it emerges, if followed literally, as a means of joy and salvation. First, Jarman presents Thatcherite Britain as spiritually kin to Nazi Germany. People carry identity cards, the royal family (for its mildly socialist tendencies) is reduced to a soap opera, and "derelicts, drug abusers, homosexuals, and card carrying members of the Labour Party have been quietly removed." A young homosexual, Edward, shivers in a cell, singing "Gay, gay, gay/Think on dreadful doomsday," as the film opens.

Jarman next imagines a possible holocaust for homosexuals, moving along parallel lines with the fate of the European Jews. We see the holocaust through Edward's eyes: he frequently uses the words of Christopher Marlowe's *Edward II* to compare the fate of that English ruler and his supporters with the "Genocide" (personified as a character in the script) overtaking homosexuals. First comes "Section 28," a British law which forbade teaching positive aspects of homosexuality in schools. Jarman juxtaposes it to Kristallnacht of 1938, when Germans encouraged by the Nazis terrorized Jews as a prelude to murdering them. Next "gangsters" assault the welfare state and, given an impoverished majority, established rule based on "fear"—of "the loss of a job," of "appearing different," of an "imagined enemy." "Born-again christians" burn books such as Marlowe's *Edward II* and the works of Oscar Wilde and Shakespeare: these "inheritors of a genocidal religion, that ruthlessly exterminated whole populations in its lust for expansion." Money becomes the measure of all things, as Margaret (the grim) Reaper (Thatcher) explains in a Christmas speech:

> At Christmas it behooves us to think, be it ever so briefly, of the unfortunate. Those who have fallen by the wayside. Before we pass by, as pass by we must, on the other side of the highway, to get back to God's true purpose on Monday, cultivating the garden of England with our baskets of currency, planting our stocks and shares, ensuring the good life.... We thank HIM for THE COUNTRY that coined, such a marvelous word COINED ... COINED FREEDOM."

The horrors continue as Margaret declares herself dictator, inaugurates a millennium of good housekeeping, has Edward killed in the manner of Edward II, and prepares to burn Betsy Battenberg (Queen Elizabeth) at the stake for proclaiming "LONG LIVE THE REVOLUTION" that breaks out. (Jarman rejected an ending for *The Last of England* in which the queen leads an aristocracy into "Laguna"—perhaps somewhere in the Third World where criminals and other undesirables may find asylum—where their imperial assets are still safe.[11] But at the last moment, God, a lady with a long beard, advised by an angelic host of famous homosexuals— Shakespeare, Newton, Wilde, Byron, Luchino Visconti, and Plato—whisk Elizabeth from the flames and send Reaper, Genocide, and the Archbishop of Canterbury to Hell. Then begins a drag ball in Heaven as Shakespeare proclaims, "All's Well That Ends Well." The script ends with Edward and his lover in bed, having tea. It was all a dream.

The Last of England is indeed a dream, but all dreams require interpretation. Is the happy ending a dream of two people living in an England that commits genocide against homosexuals and their supporters? Or is it possibly a real outcome, symbolically expressed—that by evoking the ghosts of homosexuals past and putting gender stereotypes behind us we can reach something approaching a true millennium? God tells Edward and Johnny to "wake up" just before they awake and the vision dissolves. It is at least plausible, that Jarman concludes with the hope that homosexuals will wake up, envision a possible genocide, and be able to ensure that it remains a dream rather than another holocaust. In *Neutron*, he hypothesized that a world ripe for revolution would fall victim to its own false consciousness and outmoded traditional values. In *Sod 'Em*, he turns the tables: a world in the grips of conservatism can still be saved. But it takes a miracle. Perhaps Jarman thinks women, as his transgendered god suggests, will be the key to sympathizing with rather than persecuting homosexuals.

Jarman veered between these two views. He did not "sell out" to the film industry but made his films on shoestring budgets as suited himself: "I could have been much more effective in the short term if I had joined them," he told an interviewer. "On the other hand I would have made no serious intervention if I had." He was sure his films would be remembered in the long run — at least at one point, he agreed with critic Howard Brooker's remark that *The Last of England* was "the greatest film to be made since the move into sound."[12] But Jarman also feared "time [was] running out, desperation for a generation.... You are talking to someone who is desperate, who is near to tears."[13]

Yet as the intervention of the "good angels" who advise God suggest, Edward's nightmare can perhaps be avoided by resurrecting the hidden queer past Jarman's collective work shows us was so instrumental even in the triumph of the very civilization which condemns it. To an interviewer who remarked that Jarman's films had "very little hope in them," the director responded, "the activity is the hope.... If I were negative, I would have stopped, committed suicide! ... At ten I'd seen the very extremities of wealth and poverty in Pakistan ... there are no such problems in Great Britain, just inequitable distribution."[14] Jarman hoped that his legacy would inspire others: "But as I leave you Queer lads let me leave you singing. I had to write of a sad time as a witness.... May you of a better future, love without a care and remember we loved too. As the shadows closed in, the stars came out."[15] Remarking on a gay pride march in London in June, 1989, Jarman commented joyfully that Jesus "would join this march ... for we know that the castle of heterosex has its walls of tears and dungeons of sadness. We can laugh at the house of cards called the Family. We demand one right — 'equality before the law' — and the end of our banishment from the daylight."[16] This right had yet to be established, either in Britain or America, as the first draft of this book was finished on New Year's Day 2001, the first day of what ought to have been celebrated as a new millennium.

13
Blue: "Our Time Is the Passing of a Shadow"

The color blue was of special significance to Jarman: it represented the infinite as both possibility and "poison," as he quoted the artist Caravaggio's supposed opinion of blue.[1] In this film of 1993 Jarman and three friends and former collaborators — John Quentin, Nigel Terry, and Tilda Swinton — recite the text over a continuous blue screen. At the film's beginning, blue represents the promise of life: "You say to the boy open your eyes," but "When he opens his eyes and sees the light/You make him cry out." Sight is accompanied by pain from birth, but we only focus on the positive, ignoring the cry: "O Blue" is invoked, much as a deity, to "come forth," "arise," "ascend," and "come in."

Jarman, however, does not film a progression from birth to death: rather, the film recounts the poisoning of blue and the tragedy of life from the perspective of Jarman himself as a dying AIDS patient who is in the process of losing his sight. As the color "seen" by the blind, blue appears over and over again as a metaphor for the perils and unhappiness of human life. Only on occasion does happiness, again connected to the color blue, visit our troubled existence.

In recording his descent into blindness and death, Jarman juxtaposes his private fate with the events of the public world. As his diaries indicate, the news of atrocities in former Yugoslavia and terrorist attacks in

Britain itself punctuated the days he spent in the hospital and caused him to reflect on the relationship of his personal history, and of those people with AIDS, to the more public events of the world.[2] History, which had meant so much in his other films, is now subordinated to his-story. Immediately after the boy's birth, Jarman takes us to a cafe where young refugees from the early 1990s war in Bosnia serve him coffee: one of them notices that he has put his clothes on backward and, since no one else is there, he removes them and "put[s] them right." But what is Jarman "putting right" in *Blue*? The clothes-changing episode suggests to him that our perception of history, and the public world, are shaped by and subordinated to our own personal concerns. The Bosnian refugees only remind him that his imminent death causes others' problems to fade in the face of his own: "What need of so much news from abroad while all that concerns either life or death is all transacting and at work within me." No sooner does Jarman express this thought than he is nearly run over by a bicyclist, which plunges him into a "blue funk."

Blue achieves its power precisely through the equation and juxtaposition of private and public suffering. The AIDS epidemic should move us to intervene — take in victims, protect the helpless, fight the murdering virus — like the slaughter in Bosnia ultimately compelled similar reactions on the part of the NATO powers. Jarman equalizes both of these horrors by narrating them with roughly equal emphasis on a screen of unchanging blue, in which accounts of global problems alternate with the director's sometimes excruciating description of his struggle with AIDS. Later, Jarman compares his seven-year bout with the syndrome as of 1993 to World War II, where soldiers only faced death for six years: "A bullet in the back of the head/ Might be easier/ You know, you can take longer than/ The second world war to get to the grave." *Blue* hopes to elevate the personal sagas of people with AIDS to the consciousness of those who write the grand historical narratives. Jarman thereby questions the modernist confidence that seems to have revived in the late-twentieth century — that apparently well-off people in First World countries can sit securely in their happiness and either pity or condescendingly interfere with the fate of the less fortunate. But we are not all, or even most of us, well off: the victimized are all around us, and in the end we are all dead.

From his "blue funk," Jarman takes us to the hospitals where he is treated first as an outpatient, and then, as the disease worsens, where he is permanently confined. Efforts to cure him fail: he explains how the doctor shines "a terrible blinding light" into his eyes, temporarily producing his soon-to-be-permanent sightlessness and "blue" vision. In what is by now apparent as a stream-of-consciousness narrative, Jarman takes his mind off the pain by remembering blue skies, butterflies, dreams, and music ("the blues"), all symbolized by the blue flower, delphinium. Blue appears to those in the prime of youth and health as "universal love," "the terrestrial paradise." He links love and beauty through the image of bathing in the sea.

But Jarman's blue skies yield immediately to a "howling gale": too soon, as he noted in *The Garden*, does old age come upon his generation. There is little time to savor life's joys for people with AIDS, and Jarman's cottage at the beach where he constantly heard the "roaring waters" only reminds him of "the voices of dead friends." Ever more softly, he speaks their names over again three times, as if trying to preserve their memory. Later, when he is briefly cheered by his sun-flooded hospital room, memories of laughter and the hope that "each word [can be] a sunbeam/Glancing in the light," yields to the realization that when "blue stretches, yawns, and is awake," the words he hears are again the voices of his friends "buried" and "dead" which offer no consolation to someone who will share their fate.

For Jarman insists that our death marks the end of the world for each of us. After remembering his friends, he imagines the "world's last night." The sun fails to rise "thrice denied by cock crow/In the dawn's first light." Having compared his personal fate to the dying country of Bosnia, Jarman recalls Peter's denial of Jesus just before the latter's death. To deny Christ is to deny resurrection, eternal life, and meaning for human history. To those familiar with his other films, Jarman reinforces his atheism and contempt for traditional Christianity, thereby re-emphasizing the point he just made — that "paradise" is "terrestrial" and is the fruit of human love.

Again the doctor examines Jarman's eyes: different images come to mind. The shining light is now "atomic bright" and his diseased eyes resemble "Mars"— a "distant planet" he remembers from a comic book. But the doctor brings him back to reality — the infected retina reminds him of a pizza, causing Jarman to conclude cryptically: "Blue transcends the solemn geography of human limits"— what for some is trivial is of cosmic significance for others. To make sure we realize the true scope of the AIDS pandemic, Jarman compares it to a nuclear holocaust: "Impatient youths of the sun/Burning with many colours.... Fucking with fusion and fashion.... Cum splattered nuclear breeders." The phrase "nuclear breeders" is a double-entendre: gay men are sometimes blamed for the AIDS epidemic by straight people whom queers sometimes term "breeders." Compactly compressing multiple meanings, Jarman is on one level noting that young men who innocently and beautifully loved each other spread a disease which metaphorically raced around the world with the fury of atomic power. On the other hand, "breeder" is queerspeak for "straight person." Jarman thereby indicts the straight world both for its spread of nuclear weapons — which unlike most cases of AIDS can be morally blamed on specific people — and points out that the "cum" which infects is not limited to gays — in fact, most people with AIDS are African women and children.

After having imagined the AIDS epidemic as the equivalent of an atomic catastrophe within himself and spreading throughout the world, Jarman links these realms. In extreme pain, he senses "Ages and Aeons.... Exploding" out of his hospital room which has become ground zero. "Final judgements" have become superfluous, as "we knew that time would end/After tomorrow at sunrise," he writes, bringing us full circle to the world's last night he has already posited. In all seriousness, Jarman is telling us that we have so focused on the destructive capacities of nuclear weapons — both in building them and worrying about their use — that a relatively ignored medical syndrome may prove equally catastrophic.

Jarman spares no effort to convince us, to make us feel, that AIDS is indeed a disaster equal to the greatest in history. He delves into various aspects of the past he has treated in his other films. But now other eras and people are all imperfect approximations or intimations of his own plight. "I have no friends now who are not dead or dying," Jarman suddenly tells us, "like a blue frost it caught them." But blood as well as frost can be blue: "the blood of sensibility is blue," Jarman notes, and "I consecrate myself/To find its most perfect expression." The blue blood of nobility and the sacred vows of the religious, twin pillars of a hierarchical traditional society, are replaced by Jarman's own blood. He is on a quest, the equivalent of the sacred missions of the medieval knights, to bring home the horror of AIDS to those who cannot imagine it.

Yet Jarman realizes this horror is ultimately unspeakable, that his task is impossible. His vision is soon replaced again by the pain of medical treatment: ironically he notes that the intravenous drip in his arm "trills like a canary"— personal suffering even reduces the beautiful to a sign recalling pain. Then, having dismissed Jesus and the heroic sacrifices of Christian churches and states, Jarman turns his attention to the ancients. He will not win the battle against AIDS, he states, because "the virus was appropriated by the well — so we have to live with AIDS while they spread the quilt for the moths of Ithaca across the wine dark sea." Jarman here compactly refers to both the *Iliad* and *Odyssey* of the Greek poet Homer — himself blind and therefore granted unique insights. Homer was famous for his invocation of the "wine dark sea." Homer's sea is dark, repudiating the pleasant "infinite" dreams evoked by blue waters, and Jarman has already dismissed by implication the poet's equally famous "rosy-fingered dawn" as never to appear following "the world's last night." But the Ithacans are not the great heroes we imagine them to be, but "moths," fools who fly into flames rather than pursue heroic dreams. This would explain their participation in a Trojan War fueled by lust for wealth and women. But why does Jarman focus on the Ithacans rather than the Greeks in general? He does so to incorporate both great epics, to remind us that the traditional interpretation of the *Odyssey* celebrates the hero's return home rather than the destruction of every other member of his crew. Spreading an AIDS quilt on troubled waters is not quite as bad as spreading oil, but it hides rather than confronts the problem: "awareness is heightened ... but something else is lost. A sense of reality drowned in theatre." Jarman sees the AIDS quilt as a gesture, an effort by the healthy to confuse recognition of a problem with a serious attempt to confront a catastrophe.

Jarman flashes a welter of grand human illusions in his brief thirty-page script. Buddhist acceptance of the epidemic won't work: "The Gautama Buddha instructs me to walk away from illness. But he wasn't attached to a drip." Neither will fighting theological intolerance and hypocrisy with direct action. Jarman's vision of gay "activists invading Sunday Mass" brings to mind "An epic Czar Ivan denouncing the Patriarch of Moscow" and culminates in the question: "Will the pearly gates slam shut in the faces of the devout?" How will the future remember the queer activists of our time — as one faction in a struggle whose moral significance is long forgotten, much like the quarrels of ages past? Jarman is insisting that the heroism of the struggle for queer liberation and against AIDS must be remembered for its positive accomplishments rather than its ineffective protests.

But this particular struggle, like all others, in the long run, is futile. About halfway through the film Jarman for the first time links the colors blue and black. The ringing bell which opened the film, announcing the boy's birth, is heard again. But now "Blue protects white from innocence/ Blue drags black with it/ Blue is darkness made visible." These lines are repeated twice in succession in the script — the only such case. We can thus interpret this mid-point as the conclusion of the film's first part and the beginning of a second. Reinforcing this new direction is Jarman's posing of a question — "How are we perceived, if we are to be perceived at all? For the most part we are invisible." He follows the question with the statement (perhaps an answer?) — "If the doors of Perception were cleansed then everything would be seen as it is." But before these lines can be interpreted, we need to examine the complex historical and personal journey Jarman undertakes for approximately two pages before he redefines blue as an intensification, or even misrepresentation, of darkness and death.

The "Doors of Perception" refers to Aldous Huxley's 1954 novel of that title which maintains that we can only find true reality on the other side of reason, through mystical experiences, usually induced by hallucinogenic drugs. Jarman briefly considers that option, only to term it a hallucination in the purely negative sense. Before this dismissal, Jarman provisionally identifies the East with mysticism and the Occident with reason — provisionally because he does not accept this canard born of imperialism and ignorance, but is rather planning to refute it. What the "Doors of Perception" reveal — to Jarman as he drifts in and out of consciousness — is that "Marco Polo stumbles across the Blue Mountain," where he is inundated with beautiful blue people and brilliant blue flags. The descendants of Alexander the Great — westerners who also moved to India some fifteen hundred years before in search of profit and glory — attend to his needs.

Is their quest successful? Marco Polo sits on a lapis throne. The lapis is Carl Jung's symbol in his treatise *Aion* for the philosopher's stone, the shining (blue) jewel that alchemists sought to transform base matter into spirit. Jarman had earlier treated this symbol and its practical use — the philosophical, rather than the literal, transcendence of earthly existence through esoteric knowledge — in an unpublished script of the same title. But although Marco Polo's enthronement symbolizes a possible way out of the (literally) dead end to which blue has come in Jarman's West, the explorer's heavenly city only produces illusion rather than the true wisdom the alchemists sought. For the road to the "ultramarine" — or ultrablue or even more radiantly transcendent — people who dwell in the city of "Aqua Vitae" (The Water of Life) is "protected by a labyrinth built from crystals and mirrors which in the sunlight cause terrible blindness." The mirrors reflect "each of your betrayals, magnify them and drive you into madness."

What can this mean? There is only a guess at an answer. Marco Polo and Alexander attempted to subdue the East, not to understand it, to bring its riches home. But the wealth and wisdom of the Orient do not satisfy the imperialist; they drive him mad as no conquest can satisfy an Alexander, no quantity of wealth a Marco Polo. As literary theorist Edward Said has argued in *Orientalism*[3] — Jarman was probably aware of the concept, if not the book itself — Western man projects his own greed, sloth, sexual desire, and lust for despotic power onto the peoples of Asia. Carried away with their own delusions and occupations, the Western seekers, or raiders, can only transform the spoils of the East into reflections of their own vices. "Poets," rather than explorers and exploiters, Jarman argues, alone can "excavate" these Oriental treasures. They can take "blue ... as a word or phrase" and transform it into "scintillating sparks, a poetry of fire, which casts everything into darkness with the brightness of its reflections." In his autobiographical writings, Jarman stressed that poets and artists gave him the principal inspiration as a young man to come out and create queer paintings, books, and films, since no figures in the modern public realm dared to proclaim themselves homosexuals.[4]

The point to which the "poet" Jarman's thoughts next move, however, is a most unlikely one. In place of Alexander and Marco Polo stands "dear Miss Punch" from his own past. A seventy-year-old lesbian who rode a motorcycle and wore a beret, she was the gardener at the Royal National Institute for the Blind, where the young Jarman worked as a volunteer. (Jarman, of course, became a famous gardener.) Miss Punch, the "hope" of a young man "closeted and frightened by [his] sexuality," reminded him of Edith Piaf, the diminutive French singer whose songs—most famously "Je ne regrette rien" (I regret nothing)—expressed defiance in the face of human tragedy, especially the loss of love and lovers that made her a favorite of the similarly stricken gay community in the 1980s.

Thus, we may finally answer the questions Jarman poses before the Marco Polo/Alexander episode. An Edith Piaf surrogate, an obscure woman confident in her identity, lives a meaningful life, truly of service to humanity, without artifice and delusion, a feat unmatched by these great historical figures. For Jarman, she indeed "cleanses" the "doors of perception."

From this turning point, Jarman proceeds to juxtapose ever-intensifying delusion, or madness, against an ever-growing awareness that the "scintillating sparks" or "poetry of fire" given off by such great souls will "be forgotten.... Our time is the passing of a shadow/And our lives will run like/Sparks through the stubble." No sooner does Jarman equate black with blue than he discusses another escape from reality: prayers. He singles out appeals to St. Rita, the patroness of the Lost Cause, whose abode, like Marco Polo's destination, lies over the mountains. He harshly dismisses her as a "Graven Image," sarcastically adding that "you know the task is to fill the empty page"—the "tabula rasa" which in his *Essay Concerning Human Understanding* the British philosopher John Locke stipulated we all are when we are born, a page upon which the story of our lives will be written. Then he tells us we really should pray "to be released from image"—which, rather than reality itself, is all we can discern from the pages of our story.

Jarman clarified what he meant by "image" in *Imagining October*, where he rejected "imaging"—putting a false positive spin on a terrible situation—in favor of "imagining" possibilities for human fulfillment that realistically exist. But in *Blue* the only destiny is that when all is said and done, "Our life will pass like the traces of a cloud/And be scattered like/Mist that is chased by the/Rays of the sun." All that we cling to as real, he insists—heredity, education, vices and aspirations, qualities, our entire psychological word—are images that imprison the soul. Jarman urges instead that we become "astronauts of the void" and leave behind the "comfortable" images that "imprison" us.

The void which appears is terrifying. Jarman asks, "how did my friends cross the cobalt river [Styx]," setting out for an "indigo [blue crossed with black] shore under this jet-black sky?" Panic, inconsolable weeping, madness, petrifaction, contemplating and committing suicide are the emotions accompanying his friends' deaths, "faded like flowers cut by the scythe of the Blue Bearded Reaper, parched as the waters of life receded." The grim reaper here is conflated with the vicious Blue Beard, a figure of folklore who married and then murdered young women. The devil himself appears in the form of AIDS itself virus under the pseudonym of "Yellowbelly." He once crawled "over Eve's rotting apple wasp-like," as the serpent in the Garden of Eden, whereas in the First World War "his hellish legions buzz[ed] and chuckle[d] in the mustard gas." Now AIDS is his incarnation. Jarman fights off the madness such imaginings bring by trying to give as exact an account of his sufferings as possible: at one point, he lists no fewer than forty-one side effects of the drug he is taking, including eight involving mental delusion. It is no easy task: his bleak hospital ward reminds him of Romania, a communist nation known for its extremes of poverty, tyranny, and architectural sterility. He itches constantly: "my skin sits on me like the shirt of Nessus." A young man "frail as [the concentration camp] Belsen" walks slowly with his pajamas "hanging off him." "Once in a while"—and only then—he dreams "a dream as magnificent as the Taj Mahal." The association of historical and mythical horrors with the AIDS epidemic—and the Orientalist relief Jarman has branded as delusional when he thinks clearly—assault him and become more and more pronounced as the end draws near.

Only in one extended episode does Jarman focus on the political issues he subordinates in this film to the personal: that under current systems of caring for people with AIDS, "charity has allowed the uncaring to appear to care and is terrible for those dependent on it." Relief is doled out so sparingly that "we"—that is homosexuals who "have always been mistreated ... overreact with our thanks [whenever] anyone gives us the slightest sympathy." That AIDS patients, unlike, for instance, cancer patients, are socially regarded as pariahs rather than undeserved victims entitled to the best medical care possible is an all-too-frequent by-product of the disease. Indeed, with the exception of the ministrations of his lover H.B. and his Orientalist hallucination, the sole relief Jarman mentions in the last third of the film is a smile he exchanges with a fellow patient, whom he calls "Jean Cocteau" because of his physical resemblance to the great playwright and film-maker. The homosexual Cocteau, who made the Orpheus myth relevant for the twentieth century, anticipated Jarman's own achievement in making myth and history live again as vital elements of the present. That Jarman finds resemblances to his great predecessor in an otherwise nondescript fellow patient cuts two ways. On the one hand, it is painful that Jarman's existence in the sterile hospital setting has so deteriorated that someone with a superficial similarity to a critical figure from the past consumes so much of his attention. On the other hand, that Jarman finds in this man a common humanity and an opportunity to commiserate with a fellow patient is perhaps the film's most moving moment. Much like one of Cocteau's own projects — to relocate classic myths such as Antigone and Orpheus in the modern world, reducing (or raising) the heroic characters to a human level — Jarman has relocated Cocteau himself, and found renewed vigor, through meeting someone he can use to put Cocteau's lesson to use. Jarman here personally demonstrates and brings to life, through the narration and musical background, the empathy he is demanding from the healthy.

Blue concludes with a poetic synthesis of the two juxtapositions that have dominated the film: first, the (distantly perceived) public and historical versus the (intensely experienced) private and personal worlds; and, second, the fantasies we employ versus the reality of death and impending annihilation. Jarman begins his coda with a vision — pearl fishers in azure seas. Blue has euphemistically, seductively returned as "azure," with intimations of diving in the waters or perhaps of Bizet's romantic opera *The Pearl Fishers*. But soon these same waters are "washing the isle of the dead"— we've moved from the Indian Ocean of Nadir and Leila to the land depicted by Rachmaninoff in *The Isle of the Dead*, complete with his increasingly terrifying quotation of the "Dies Irae." "Billowing ... mournful" winds soon replace the pleasant sea breezes we enjoy, as Jarman imagines the "Lost Boys," shipwrecked, who "Sleep forever/ In a dear embrace/ Salt lips touching." He imagines a past lover of his own, "Dead good looking": the words do not even have to change to convey the shift from life and love to death. After insisting that even "Our name will be forgotten," Jarman's script ends: "I place a delphinium, Blue, upon your grave."

Whose grave is it? Is the flower being placed on the grave of *Blue* the film, or of the intimation of the infinite the color conveys? Or does it decorate the grave of one or more of the several loves Jarman invokes by name in the film? After the script ends, we hear the sound of waves fading away — perhaps the last sound that will be heard by an imaginary ear when all life on earth dies. (Jarman noted earlier that "the earth is dying and we do not notice" — a recollection of his radical ecology.) The bell rings in the film for a third time, as it had at the boy's (Jarman's) birth, and at the point where he realized that blue was really black. After the final dedication, "For H.B. and All True Lovers," blue in fact turns to black.

Yet mingled with the despair of Jarman's descent into death are the memories of his lovers, his beloved Miss Punch, and his crusade to inform the world that with AIDS it faces a catastrophe and challenge equal to any in history, one that it has been covering up and whose victims it has treated shamefully. With *Blue,* nearly the final act in his crusade for justice for homosexuals and people with AIDS, Jarman offered us his own death, described with excruciating detail, told in his own voice by someone who, the ending suggests, will be dead by the time most people view the film. The grave on which Jarman places the flower may be his own. But the delphinium stands for remembrance, not the forgetting Jarman predicts must inevitably come. *Blue* is a challenge to its viewers to continue to construct history, not as a delusional escape into imagined past glories, but as the struggle for justice and celebration of love that Jarman continues to recall even as the details of his suffering and treatment threaten to overwhelm his consciousness.

Jarman considered *Blue* "magnificent — it's the first time I've been able to look one of my films in the eye. Cinema catches up to the twentieth century, this is the first feature to embrace the intellectual imperative of abstraction, it's moody, funny and distressing; it takes film to the boundary of the known world."[5] *Blue's* effectiveness is indissolubly linked with Jarman's entire life. Its meaning rests in his audience's determination to postpone as long as possible, perhaps until the sun grills us to the roasting point or a comet collides with the earth, Jarman's ultimate judgment of the human adventure and his own: "In time/No one will remember our work…. Our name will be forgotten."

Afterword:
Imagining October

I am aware that in the course of this book, I may have been reading things into Jarman's films that he did not intend. I offer two excuses. It is impossible to discern the mental process of "intention" from either people's retrospective remembrances or from surviving evidence. Further, I am trying to study Jarman the same way he approached the figures and historical eras he filmed, that is, by constructing speculative, but I believe plausible, interpretations based on the available sources. My analyses of Jarman's historical films represent a historian's best guess at how they might yield the most significance for understanding the role of gay people in history in the hope of queering the planet — that is, for furthering Jarman's own project.

I therefore wish to conclude with a brief analysis of Jarman's twenty-seven minute 1984 film, *Imagining October*, which explicitly shows his keen awareness of the problems of historical interpretation that his films usually merely imply. Made after a trip to the Soviet Union, it honors Sergei Eisenstein, the director of the film *October* about the Bolshevik Revolution, which occurred during that month in 1917. But Jarman devotes as much of the film to a critique of modern British and American capitalism as he does to Soviet communism, just as Eisenstein, while praising the spirit that made the October Revolution, implicitly criticizes the government which it produced. Jarman thinks capitalism and communism have converged: "the very sameness of both societies," characterized by architecture of "monumental gigantism that dwarfs the human, cuts out the sunlight, monumental blunders."[1] There is implicit irony in the fact that he is *Imagining October* from the perspective of 1984, the year of the film and the title of George Orwell's imagined global dystopia.

Enforced historical amnesia is the reason people in both societies can tolerate such architectural monstrosities and the governments they so appropriately represent. Jarman accuses contemporary Britain and the United States of "crimes against genius and humanity,/ History ransacked,/ Promoting poverty of intellect and emotion." "Step forward into the past that is not," Jarman invites us in a statement that shows he is quite aware of how people construct mythical, rose-colored pasts to shape the future. He is telling us that "false imaging"—the "official story" of the past as presented by "manipulators" who would "Sooner annihilate/ Millions with Billions/ than sacrifice the profit motive"—has led most people to "image" a history that "never was" rather than exercise their imaginations in trying to figure out what remains hidden. The usual lie is to interpret the present as the worthy heir of a mythical golden age—"the merrie old land of was." Jarman uses the archaic spelling of "merrie" to emphasize the nostalgia for a "merry" old England whose poor laws, enclosures, imperialist ventures, and Industrial Revolution are conveniently forgotten. In this retrospectively invented fantasyland, "Fun, Freedom, Democracy, and the Rule of Law" supposedly mattered and still matter to more than a handful of the rich and powerful.

In the brief script, Jarman on several occasions recalls William Blake and his poetry to let us know that he knows that even two hundred years ago, England was neither merrie nor beautiful. Four lines of Jarman's text reads like "Auguries of Innocence." Compare Blake's verses "A Robin Red breast in a Cage/ Puts all Heaven in a Rage," or "The Winner's Shout, the Loser's Curse,/ Dance before dead England's hearse,"[2] with Jarman's "The harlot's cry in each high street/ Weaves old England's winding sheet" and "English Bobbies in an English street/ Defend the Rights of him they beat." Blake himself is mentioned in the script in Jarman's biting critique of the movie *Chariots of Fire*, a phrase from Blake's poem "Jerusalem," later turned into a song by Sir Hubert Parry that inspired generations of the English working class to strive for a better existence. Jarman writes: "The new British Cinema,/ Roll on, Chariots of Fire, Blake's Albion?/ Sublime introspective genius suborned/ Into the Race to Win the Race."[3] Blake was virulently anti-imperialist, but Jarman notes that his words and the film which bore them as a title were used to stimulate support for the Malvinas/ Falklands war of 1982 and thereby strengthen the anti–working class Thatcher government.

Jarman also places Blake's entire poem "O Rose, thou art sick," from "The Songs of Experience" on the screen like a silent-movie subtitle.[4] In the poem, an invisible worm is murdering the rose that has symbolized England in the past: replacing the red rose of Lancaster and the white rose of York in Jarman's time was the blue rose favored by Prime Minister Margaret Thatcher. Blue, we remember from *Caravaggio*, is the unnatural, poison color. Thatcher is both a deadly rose and the worm burrowing away at what is left of England. Jarman ironically notes that botanical gardens and horticulture flourished under her rule as the real English landscape was bulldozed in the interest of progress.[5]

Jarman almost entitled his film *Imaging October*, but there is a reason he did not. October is imagined, rather than "imaged," a word he links with "false" several times in the brief script. Imagining, on the other hand, means seeing through the imaging to the reality beneath. It requires imagination — thought, rebellion, the conscious formulation of an alternative to one's surroundings and the official imaging it contains. What is October? The promise of a better world, and the desire to act to bring it about. We see the real promise of the Russian Revolution in the heroic actions of the October days as Eisenstein presents them, not in the Stalinist consolidation.

Despite everything, that promise still remains. To be sure, you must physically, as well as psychologically, get "beyond Moscow," or the obsession with the state's formal institutions. Observing the Azerbaijanis in Baku, a beautiful, prosperous city, Jarman filmed their smiles, play, and daily lives to contrast with the sterility of other cities and the rigid movements of conscripted soldiers. People who retain some flexibility to exercise pre–Soviet customs — that is, who have preserved a genuine historical consciousness — can distance themselves from the center of power, thereby creating a space for creativity, moral, human behavior, and a decent world.

Jarman's most moving experience in the Soviet Union occurred when he observed a fabulous, elaborate sculpture an elderly man spent twenty-five years building to the memory of his daughter. Jarman used this edifice — so unlike the sterile and pretentious monuments he also filmed to illustrate "official" history — to suggest that the West and the Soviet Union offered different sorts of freedom and unfreedom, thereby countering the self-praise of both societies. He told the old gardener that in Britain, "it would be impossible to build like this ... you'd never get planning permission, it would be pulled down by the local council as a dangerous structure."

If Western capitalism distorts the past through a flood of false history that submerges inconvenient facts, the Soviet Union was no better. Like the New Leftists who were as shocked by the Soviet suppression of

Czechoslovakia in 1968 as they were by the Vietnam War, Jarman held no brief for either system. Jarman visited the library of the Soviet Union's greatest, and gay, film-maker. Eisenstein's extensive English-language collection contained a copy of John Reed's *Ten Days that Shook the World* (the October Revolution) in which a censor had obliterated Trotsky's name wherever it appeared. Jarman places an image of this censored book on the screen with the names TROTSKY and EISENSTEIN in large letters. By paying homage to Eisenstein and the unknown and unfulfilled Russian Revolution symbolized by Trotsky, Jarman found kindred spirits whose project reflected his own efforts to reclaim a hidden past to shape a better future.

He also found in them fellow adherents of a word I have not used much in this book, but which implicitly pervades every chapter: revolution. Taken together, Jarman's films put homosexuals at the center of most of the major revolutions in Western history: monotheism, Christianity, the Renaissance, the Scientific Revolution, the responses in politics, music, art, and philosophy to the First World War, and the struggle against the AIDS epidemic and for human rights in modern times. (He did not need to stress the ancient Greeks, where the connection of democracy, tragedy, and philosophy to same-sex love is generally accepted.) Like Trotsky's, Jarman's perpetual revolution continues to trouble a world which reserves the good, the true, and the beautiful for a relative few. His films and the writings and paintings which accompanied them need to be better known to inspire those who would change that.

Appendix:
Pier Paolo Pasolini, Jarman's Predecessor

Jarman termed his most important predecessor, the Italian Pier Paolo Pasolini (1922–1975), a "kindred spirit." His was the first name to come to mind when Jarman thought of "the great queer artists."[1] Pasolini's panoramic cinema, which traces human history from the ancient world to the present, clearly inspired Jarman to do likewise. However, the two directors focused on different periods — Pasolini filmed two Greek tragedies, Jarman bypassed the Greeks; three of Pasolini's works deal with the Middle Ages, whereas Jarman only approached that era obliquely — from late antiquity via *Sebastiane* and from the Renaissance via Marlowe's play *Edward II*. Furthermore, while nearly all of Jarman's films centered on the problem of same-sex love, Pasolini dealt with this theme sometimes explicitly, sometimes implicitly, and sometimes not at all. For despite the homophobia of Jarman's Britain, the sexual repression of Pasolini's Italy far exceeded it.[2]

Nevertheless, the two directors' visions coincided on several critical matters. Both sought to re-eroticize a past whose chief features in standard histories have been explained in terms of politics, religion, thought, and economics. They also showed the inadequacy of the modern world and its faith [a word used to suggest irony] in reason and technology to come to grips with the driving passions that give meaning to human existence. Each director found beauty in former civilizations and landscapes which were yet unspoiled, or only minimally so, by modernity: for Jarman, Renaissance England and the untouched seashore and gardens of England; for Pasolini, the Middle Ages, the hill country of southern Italy and the deserts and ancient cities of the Middle East and Northern Africa. Jarman and Pasolini each played characters in his own films and used elements of autobiography, as well as creative anachronism, to show how the past shaped the present. They both employed non-actors, including personal friends, in part to give their films a more realistic feeling than other works, in part because they were sometimes strapped for cash. And neither man had any use for organized religion or modern "liberal" democracy, which they saw as a disguised form of fascism. Both were radicals: Pasolini an avowed Marxist, although not an orthodox one; Jarman a perpetual protestor who detested the new wealth of Thatcherite England. Both were disgusted with the moderate reformism of late-twentieth century Italian Communist and British Labor parties.

This appendix is a brief survey of Pasolini's cinematic output to reveal the differences, as well as similarities, between his achievement and Jarman's. I do so to show that cinema, as any art form, is influenced by its own history. But an examination of Pasolini's work following my more extensive treatment of Jarman's will also demonstrate how innovative Jarman was: he went far beyond the Italian director in his use of anachronism, fragmentation of scenes and departure from a straightforward narrative, and emphatic portrayal and defense of homosexuality in nearly all his films.

The Greeks

Pasolini's *Oedipus Rex* (1967) and *Medea* (1969) adapt the tragedies by Sophocles and Euripides, much as Jarman did Marlowe's *Edward II* and Shakespeare's *The Tempest* for his films. Surprisingly, Pasolini made almost nothing of the homosexual element of Greek culture, unless the glance exchanged between Medea's brother and the attractive, nearly naked boy about to be sacrificed and a few takes that linger a bit too long on the Messenger and Oedipus are considered.

Instead, Pasolini concentrates on the class and psychological dimensions of both dramas. *Oedipus* opens with an Italian army officer, of the generation that embraced Fascism and Mussolini, abandoning his child. To some extent, Pasolini is identifying with his own childhood and personal heritage: he was born in the year Mussolini came to power. The director is also drawing attention to the sacrifices Fascism required of its children, and its fear that without murdering possible claimants to succeed the regime it cannot survive. The bulk of the film follows the plot of the tragedy fairly closely, although it omits much dialogue, and is set in the ancient world. But at the end blind Oedipus, playing his flute, is now led by a youth (the Messenger in the body of the film, who has become "Angelo"— an Angel) and appears in the modern world. First the blind ruler plays in a plaza in front of a cathedral "where the bourgeoisie can celebrate its rites and admire its own grandeur." The tourists, shoppers, police, and students who fill the square ignore the beggar (or prophet, Pasolini also terms him) playing "a song of the bourgeois renaissance (or revolution?), of the struggles for liberty."[3]

Like Jarman, Pasolini despised the modern bourgeoisie, ignorant of its own past and unconcerned about the disappearance of the attractive remnants of a historical landscape. Pasolini writes: "The most odious and intolerable thing, even in the most innocent of bourgeois, is that of not knowing how to recognize life experiences other than his own.... It is a real offense that he gives to other men in different social and historical conditions."[4] But with Oedipus' music, "all the surroundings take on a precise and emotion-laden meaning; they become memory itself, and rediscover, with their daily commonplaces, the epic qualities within them." Oedipus, in short, becomes Pasolini himself, trying to restore the mystery and magic of his story, of great works of architecture, of the grandeur of the barren African, Middle Eastern, and Italian landscapes where he set most of his films.[5]

The one line written for the Priest in the script, a small part Pasolini himself played in the film, hints at both the attractiveness and the illusory quality of the belief that truths from the past can bring meaning to the present. "He is crowned with laurel ... he seems happy," the Priest/ Pasolini exclaims when Creon returns with the news that King Polybus, who is believed to be Oedipus' father, has died, and thus Oedipus supposedly cannot be Laius' murderer. Yet the vision of happiness is short-lived as it is soon discovered that Laius is Oedipus' real father.[6]

After being ignored at the cathedral, Oedipus leaves the elegant square for the underside of modern capitalism, a landscape "cluttered with the huge, squat, and fragile outlines of factories." Now he plays "a song of popular revolt, from the partisan struggles." Yet while that tune too "seems to give its own meaning to all the surrounding elements," Oedipus is ignored by the workers and youths who play soccer: even his guide joins in the game. The soccer game provides an element of solace, "an hour of the day that still belongs to the people,"[7] but sport has become the new opium of the masses, replacing religion featured in the previous scene, for the Marxist Pasolini.

Oedipus ends where it began, with the blind musician returning to the attractive, comfortable early twentieth century villa from which he was ejected by a jealous father. Underneath the peaceful exterior of bourgeois gentility lurks the passions, along with the fascist inclinations, it tries to suppress. By choosing the voluptuous Silvana Mangnano to play Oedipus' mother and wife, Jocasta, Pasolini restores eroticism to the drama. Oedipus does not only marry the queen to rule Thebes, he is passionately attracted to an extraordinarily sensuous woman.

A similar eroticism underlines Pasolini's *Medea*, played by retired opera singer Maria Callas. Jason may seek the Golden Fleece to win a throne, but Callas (an older woman but much like Magnano's Jocasta) is a mesmerizing, if alien presence. Pasolini seizes repeatedly on those lines from Euripides' tragedy in which Medea appears as the incarnation of the "old gods." She is "wild with love." Whereas Jason and the Greeks argue and reason, Medea is "sobbing and wailing,/ Shouting shrill." Colchis appears as the antithesis of Greece: there is no dialogue there, only chanting, the wearing of animal skins, and human sacrifice. In fact, there is no city: Medea lives inside a cave. When the Greeks sail away with her, Medea becomes frantic because they simply set up camp wherever they are. "There is no center" she repeatedly cries, reflecting the fixity of the mythological world-view. In contrast, Jason has been instructed by the satyr Chiron who speaks at length about the importance of reason.[8]

Pasolini's point, like Euripedes', is that no more than ancient Athens (which has offered Medea sanctuary) does the modern Western world embody reason and justice: it can only pretend to. Jason's rationalizations pale before the justice of Medea's case, and the fact that lust for another woman underlines all his sophistries. Pasolini boldly has Glaucis die two deaths: the traditional immolation in Medea's cloak, and a modern interpretation of the flame as suicide brought on by mental anguish, which she commits by jumping off the city walls. Pasolini here underlines that the ancient story contains within it a psychological truth an earlier culture expressed more graphically. The film ends with Medea and Jason arguing with each other across an impassible flame, signifying both the chasm separating two modes of consciousness and the fate reserved for a rationalist world which ignores the "other" emotional side of life which, in fact, is the basis of the "rational" Greeks' behavior as well. Jarman, too, in many of his films, used fire to depict the ultimate fate of the modern West, and through his graphic studies of sexual perversity showed the ultimate motives that underwrote a power structure and its guardians that invent bogus theories to justify their lusts.

The Life of Christ

Unlike Jarman's *The Garden*, Pasolini's *The Gospel According to St. Matthew* (1964) does not suggest that Jesus might be gay. Dedicated to the reforming Pope John XXIII, it rather stressed Jesus as a champion of the poor and enemy of the rich and powerful. It is amazing some critics found homosexual elements in a Jesus who speaks far more harshly, or with a masculine vehemence (in both the Italian original and dubbed English translation) than the gentle saviors who soothe the bourgeois conscience in several standard epics of Christ's life. The ultimate critical idiocy was to suggest that Jesus' shawl feminized him: Jewish men *must* cover their heads and wear shawls when they pray.[9]

In fact, two of the most notable aspects of Pasolini's *Gospel* were frequently used by Jarman in *The Garden* as well: the startling yet appropriate use of different sorts of music to underline the plot, and the employment of "real" people rather than actors to play leading roles. Pasolini's diverse musical palette — Bach's *St. Matthew Passion*, the African-American spiritual "Sometimes I Feel Like a Motherless Child," twentieth century classical music by Shostakovitch, and folk tunes with a Middle Eastern tinge — convey the universality of Christ's message. They depict the more inclusive church which John XXIII sought to build. Similarly, many of the characters are played by Italian peasants: their bad teeth and rugged faces suggest the poor who were Jesus' principal audience, and underline their persistence as a majority in southern Italy well into the twentieth century, and in the world in general, probably until the end of time.

For another film about the crucifixion, *Ricotta* (the well-known Italian cheese), Pasolini was sentenced to four months in jail. Although the sentence was overturned on appeal, he was convicted "under a fascist law ... still in force" as of 1962 because "the magistrates have never been purged," for "defamation of religion."[10] In a film the director himself considered deeply religious, he makes even more explicit the class basis of a Christianity most film-going audiences in First World countries would prefer to ignore. Orson Welles plays a bored director, making a film of the crucifixion of Christ. Most of his extras are poor Italians, who are barely paid enough to survive on: their food is meagerly rationed out to them by the film company. In contradiction to the charity and love which are generally considered the message of Christianity, they are ordered about by a tyrannical assistant director. Welles — upper management — can thus distance himself from the fruits of his policies.

Pasolini uses Welles as a stand-in for himself so he can comment on the paradoxical — some would say contradictory — position of bourgeois yet radical intellectuals. They hope to liberate the proletariat, yet like other non-working class people depend on it and exploit it in their everyday life. An interview between Welles and a reporter presents Pasolini's ideology. The director states that he is offering Italians, who contain "the most illiterate lower class" and "most ignorant middle class" in Europe, an expression of "my most profound archaic Catholicism." Welles reads from the script of Pasolini's film *Mamma Roma*, explaining that "I'm a force of the past," a "poet" hoping to convey its meaning to modern people who only understand the "monstrous modern buildings" Italians and Europeans set up everywhere in the wake of the destruction of World War II. He compares himself to a "wanderer ... in search of brothers who are no more," a historian who "in the first act of post-history [would] bring to life forgotten altarpieces"— something Pasolini literally does when he plays the part of Giotto in Boccaccio's *Decameron*. He terms his public, "the average man," a "monster ... a communist, conformist, colonialist, racist [which the English subtitle mistranslates as "nationalist"] slave dealer, and socialist," before ironically remarking to his interviewer: "you only exist through my production, because the owner of your paper is the producer of my film." Pasolini here notes how modern capitalist society is so confident of its triumph that it even allows criticism of itself — where it thinks it will be confined to intellectual ruminations.

Ricotta's protagonist, who plays one of the thieves crucified alongside Christ, actually dies on the cross: he has failed to eat for a long time, and then stuffed himself on ricotta cheese, to the mockery of his fellow actors. He would have been able to eat had he not shown pity on the star's dog — whom he subsequently sells for the money he uses to buy the cheese — or had he not been forced to forego meals to participate in his scenes.

It takes little imagination to interpret *Ricotta* or to understand why it infuriated respectable Italian society: people who pretend to be Christians crucify the poor and mock Jesus every day by their way of life. Pasolini films the actors on the set, relieving themselves between scenes with sex and drink. One of the extras does a strip-tease, which might remind film aficionados of a similar event in Fellini's *La Dolce Vita*, in which people perform and observe such acts simply to relieve boredom. (At one point, Welles smiles when the reporter asks him about Fellini and responds: "He dances.") Alessandro Scarlatti's religious music alternates with frenzied band arrangements of "Sempre Libera" from Giuseppe Verdi's *La Traviata*: the latter is especially ironic because both its title, "Always Free," and the ironic manner in which Verdi himself uses it in the opera (a wealthy courtesan who yearns for domesticity pretends otherwise) contradicts the scenes in which extras scamper about at the assistant director's commands.

The extras are dehumanized, too. Pasolini speeds up the film as sheep, along with people who are ordered about like sheep, scamper to the strains of "Sempre Libera." In the film's most hilarious moment, after several assistant directors have repeated the same command, Pasolini cuts to a German shepherd barking. The shot is doubly ironic, since Germans shepherded Italians to disaster in the last world war.

Pasolini also shows the film's investors, wealthy folk dressed to the nines, who arrive on the set to celebrate the end of the shooting only to be present as the actor dies on the cross. The table at which the disciples ate their Last Supper is arrayed with refreshments reserved for them, and denied the actors playing the roles of the apostles. The post-production party is set in front of the crosses on which the three men are mock-crucified, although one of the men really is dying. The director's final line was that the poor victim had to die to receive attention, to show the world that he had lived.

The Middle Ages

Pasolini made the Middle Ages the capstone of his film career; "The Trilogy of Life"— Boccacio's *Decameron* (1971), Chaucer's *Canterbury Tales* (1972), and the anonymous *Arabian Nights* (1974) assembled by Sir Richard Burton. All three reflected Pasolini's deep interest in the Middle Ages and medieval people. He filmed them to show that eroticism, clerical and official corruption, and human nature have remained pretty much the same throughout the centuries, although the earlier age was less self-conscious and restrained in exhibiting human sexuality. The first two films are implicit responses to the furor over *Ricotta*. Pasolini is telling his contemporaries they need to remember the content of the masterworks of Western civilization; Boccaccio and Chaucer were both far more explicitly critical of the clergy of their age than anything Pasolini ever said or filmed except when he borrowed from them.

Pasolini stresses the corruption of the church by placing his emphasis in each film on particular tales which are told in fragments that begin, end, and appear in the middle of the action interspersed with the other stories. He divides his *Decameron* in two parts: the first half's dominant story describes how an evil man can fool the church into believing he is a saint, the second shows that an artist such as Giotto, played by Pasolini himself, has more faith than all the clerics in the film put together. The key Canterbury tale for Pasolini is the Friar's, which is about how the Summoner (whose own tale is not filmed) meets up with the Devil and they go around blackmailing innocent people whom they otherwise threaten to denounce for heresy. In *Arabian Nights*, the tale of Zummurud and Nur ed Din shows that true love is able to flourish and overcome all obstacles — but not in European society.

Pasolini selected several tales from the one hundred in Giovanni Boccaccio's *Decameron*, written in the years before the author's death in 1375. Basically, like the original, Pasolini presents a series of conniving, unpleasant, lustful people who are nevertheless rendered somewhat sympathetic through humor, their unfortunate fates, and the down-to-earth way in which the actors play their parts. In Pasolini's Part One, the dominant tale of Ser Ciapelletto (day 1, tale 1) is told in three parts with the other stories set in between. An evil man who robs and kills, and "is a bit of a fairy," Ciapelletto is lauded as a saint on his deathbed. Here, he mocks the very notion of confession — although the populace is impressed by his apparent sincerity — by ignoring his heinous crimes and admitting only the most trivial of sins — that as a child he cursed his mother when she didn't give him some milk. Pasolini's second tale (day 2, tale 5) presents more vices: Andreuccio, on his way to buy horses, is seduced by a woman who steals his money and tricks him into falling into a pile of excrement. But then he is accidentally buried in a bishop's tomb he is trying to rob, scares off a second set of robbers who think he is a ghost, and emerges successfully from his grave-robbing venture with a valuable ruby ring. Pasolini's third choice (day 3, tale 1) depicts with erotic detail a man who pretends to be deaf and dumb in order to have sex with a convent's nuns: they are quite willing and are thrilled when a "miracle" occurs and he begins to speak. In the final story of Pasolini's part one (day 7, tale 2) a woman commits adultery while her husband cleans out a large jar for the buyer, who is her lover.

Pasolini brings himself into *Decameron* in part two. Boccaccio's story of the painter Giotto (day 6, tale 5) is the shortest of the entire book. Giotto is traveling with a lawyer in a storm who tells him no one would imagine he was the greatest painter in the world given his ragged appearance. For the only time in the film, Pasolini significantly departs from Boccaccio's text and invents an entire story for Giotto, the part the director himself plays. Giotto/Pasolini goes to town and prepares to paint a fresco on the church wall. He is a man obsessed: he gulps down his food and calls his assistants and apprentices, who are always at his beck and call, at odd times when inspiration strikes. At the film's conclusion, only two-thirds of the fresco is finished. Pasolini's assistants are mostly attractive boys — the most attractive of all does not wear a shirt and stays closest to him — yet there is no sign of any homosexual behavior.

I can only speculate why Pasolini plays this part and makes so much of Giotto. He seems to be hinting that a man such as Giotto, and by extension himself, is more devout than the clerics who eat, drink, and enjoy life when they are not flagrantly breaking the commandments. And by not yielding to the temptation posed by his apprentices he is symbolically calling attention to the fact that he did not generally use his films to deal with homosexual themes. With a white band around his head, Pasolini also looks remarkably like the French playwright Antonin Artaud — himself persecuted, and ultimately committed to spend over two decades in an insane asylum — for his outrageous art and behavior. The identification of Pasolini with his unfortunate predecessor can be taken two ways: the director may be implying that either both men have been comparably harassed, or else he is telling his critics that they have gone too far in comparing what he considered his genuinely religious works to Artaud's celebration of "the theatre of cruelty."

In contrast to the devout Giotto's story, the other tales in part two of the film, with one exception, plumb the depths of human perversity. The one bright spot is the second tale (day 5, tale 6) in which a young man secretly sleeps with his beloved; her father catches them, and offers a choice of death or marriage, the latter being a foregone conclusion as we observe the genial older man and his wife. But in the third tale (day 4, tale 5) a woman's brothers murder her lover. She then digs up his head and keeps it beside her in an act of necrophilia that emerges as tender yet horrifying. Bestiality appears in the fourth tale (day 9, tale 10), where a man — whom we first see kissing his horse — requests that his wife be turned into a mare. Finally, (day 7, tale 10) one of two men in love with the same woman dies, returns from the grave, and tells his friend that there is no punishment in hell or purgatory for that particular act, whereupon the living man hastens to the woman's bed. The film ends with Giotto staring at his incomplete work, a symbol of Pasolini's own unfinished, or perhaps misunderstood, project.

Pasolini films three of the *Canterbuty Tales* more or less as written: the Merchant's Tale, the Miller's Tale, and the Wife of Bath's Tale. But the director fleshes out the shortest story of all, the Cook's Tale, with a hilarious sketch in which one of his regular actors, Ninetto Davoli, plays the saucy apprentice. Pasolini gives him the hat and bearing of Charlie Chaplin's Little Tramp, the only notable anachronism in the film. Like the Tramp, the apprentice outwits his betters, and despite his poverty and lack of a job never loses his sense of humor. Even when he is placed in the stocks, he sings and comically turns his head, the only part of his body which is still mobile.

But it is the grim Friar's Tale which dominates the film. Pasolini takes two lines — "But he could boast/ That lechery was what he punished most"— and turns them into a powerful critique of homophobia.[11] Pasolini's summoner only spies on men making love: those who can pay him off escape death, but a poor man is condemned to be burned on the gridiron while the summoner gleefully goes about the crowd selling "griddle cakes." Much as Jarman repeatedly implied, Pasolini believes that homosexual desire, unable to be expressed freely in Christian and European society, underlies homosexual persecution. The summoner himself smiles knowingly at the young guardsman with whom the victim was caught in the act, suggesting the price of his freedom might well be a tryst with the summoner.

In his next appearance, the summoner meets the devil in the guise of a young man. Together they bilk a widow out of her most valuable possession — a silver pitcher — upon pain of denouncing her for heresy. But in the film's final scene the summoner is vouchsafed a glimpse of hell — a hell only hinted at by Chaucer, but sarcastically fleshed out by Pasolini. We not only see devils prodding the wicked with pitchforks, but immoral clergymen dwell in the lowest spot in hell — inside Satan's bottom. He farts them out to show the depraved clergyman the future that awaits him. The next-to-last tale, the Miller's, had also concluded with a prominently displayed posterior: that of Nicholas, who in the middle of the night prepares to break wind in Absalom's face only to be surprised with a red hot poker. Parodies of anal sex combined with well-deserved torments afflict those who persecute or mock true, as well as homosexual, love.

Chaucer, who is played by Pasolini himself, pens the words "the Last Judgment" as this scene ends. The director is here judging his critics, especially the sanctimonious contemporary church. This finale may be paired with one of the film's opening scenes, in which Chaucer/Pasolini exemplifies true but rarely found Christian behavior. When he enters the city gates, instead of jostling a man seeking to enter at the same time, he makes light of the incident and it ends with genial camaraderie. This male bonding, also appearing in the wrestling match which opens the film, contrasts with the ending: Chaucer/Pasolini is brought back to reality by a shrewish wife shouting "Geoffrey," a potent reminder not only of Pasolini's homosexuality, but of the everyday world in which thinkers who contemplate cosmic problems must live.

Pasolini does not appear in the *Arabian Nights*. In non–Western medieval culture, unlike European, same-sex love is tolerated and exists without tension alongside heterosexual activity. For instance, a wealthy old poet invites three boys to his house for food, drink, and "pleasure": they enjoy each other's company and he writes a poem for each of them. Other men, such as the two princes on the deserted island, enjoy each other's bodies while not indicating they are primarily homosexual. Pasolini does not need to invent here: all he has to do is remind his audience that the *Arabian Nights* are more than Sinbad and Ali Baba and the Forty Thieves, the tales usually taught the young. But the centerpiece of Pasolini's film is the story of Zummurud, a slave girl, and Nur ed Din, the young master she selects after mocking the sexual failings of a group of old men who would like to buy her. The lovers are betrayed by a "blue-eyed Christian," who abducts Zummurud and turns her over to thieves who plan to rape her. But she outwits them, disguises herself as a man, and becomes the king of a wealthy city. After crucifying her enemies, she and Nur ed Din are united.

The gender-bending in Zummurud's tale is mind-boggling. A woman can find happiness with a man, by pretending to be a man. She has had to do so to avoid rape by forty thieves. There is also the hint, at least, that she enjoys the company of the bride chosen for her. As so often in Pasolini's films (*Oedipus, Medea*, and the *Gospel According to St. Matthew* are other examples), people who portray kings and nobles, such as Zummurud in her official role as "king," wear masks to hide their faces and their true identity, and absurdly high hats to represent their authority, which Pasolini is simultaneously mocking. The masks and hats come off (usually along with the characters' clothes) when they present their human "faces" and make love or face personal tragedy, as in the case of Oedipus.

By presenting the *Arabian Nights* as the third part of a trilogy with roughly contemporaneous European-Christian tales, Pasolini points to the disjunction between European Christian thought and practice and suggests alternatives. Although Islam, which achieved its greatest cultural ascendance in the Middle Ages, is highlighted, Pasolini is careful to set some scenes in Christian, African Ethiopia and others in Buddhist Nepal. (Yemen and Iran are also used.) To be sure, he does not glorify other cultures uncritically: there are evil figures — such as the demon who chops up the woman who rejects his love — and thoughtless ones — a man who pursues an unknown woman, rejects his loving cousin who dies of grief, and is castrated as punishment. Such characters compare morally with the worst in Boccaccio and Chaucer. But same-sex love and casual sex in general are accepted; Pasolini makes both as attractive as possible, set in medieval Middle Eastern cities whose beauty will astonish those unfamiliar with non–Western societies that offered more possibilities for personal fulfillment than one uncritically accepted by his contemporaries — especially in conservative, Catholic Italy — as superior.

The Modern World

Perhaps the best place to approach Pasolini's critique of his own society is with *Love Meetings* (*Comizi D'Amore*), which he made in 1964. Here, he interviewed Italians from various social classes and regions to discover their attitudes toward sexuality. He begins with children who have no idea where babies come from, which sets the tone for the film. For the most part, people are afraid to talk frankly with him or to question the nuclear family. A few young women (mostly upper or middle class, in the more modernized North) claim they are as free as men and favor divorce (banned in Italy at the time), but in general men and women accept patriarchal society uncritically.

In the peasant culture of southern Italy, just beginning to modernize when Pasolini made the film, women as well as men accept the double standard. Men tolerate prostitutes and are angry that the bourgeois North has imposed a law banning the brothels in which young men acquire their sexual experiences, and older men find escape from wives who have internalized the church's dogma that sexual relations are a duty and a burden.

Pasolini urges the people of the South to join with the Marxist workers of the North to realize that the law against prostitution, like economic exploitation, stems from the bourgeoisie, which fears sexual liberation as a threat to its political domination. Perhaps the most repressed people in the film are not the women of the South, but upper-class men who regard sex as a duty, value the nuclear family primarily for its contribution to political stability, and condemn homosexuality as disgusting because it implies unrestrained pleasure and contempt for the duty of begetting a family. Whereas the southern peasants will cite the church and "the way it is" to justify sexual restraint, the educated bourgeoisie do not hesitate to tell Pasolini that preservation of state and society — which they assume benefit everyone rather than primarily the rich — requires heterosexual monogamy.

Love Meetings is a powerful call for sexual liberation. The viewer likes most of the people Pasolini presents, and feels sorry for the rest. Sexual repression on the one hand, denial on the other (no divorce, so millions of people live apart in unlawful relationships) is so universal in Italy that Pasolini's message that people need frankly to face up to the situation and enjoy their bodies in non-traditional ways comes through powerfully.

The Hawks and The Sparrows, released two years later in 1966, again points to the consequences of political and sexual repression. A man and his son are undertaking a long journey on foot — it pains the father to walk — to collect rent from a poor woman who cannot feed her family. "It's only business," the older man states as he threatens to take her house. In turn, he goes to his own creditor — a wealthy man who is hosting a conference on "Dentists for Dante" — who gives him the same reply to his own request for an extension. On the way, they encounter a raven, who claims to be "ideology," an intellectual, whose time has past. The bird tells the story of two priests (played by the same actors who play the father and the son) sent by St. Francis to preach to the hawks and the sparrows. The older man's great devotion finally brings Christ's message — which is "Love"— across, but it only works for the hawks among themselves.

He still cannot stop the hawks from devouring the sparrows. They may understand the word, but do not practice it. Similarly, the boy and his father eat the raven. Unlike the Communist workers who are shown at the film's end raising their fists in defiance at the funeral of their leader Togliatti, the two satisfy themselves with a prostitute and continue on their uncomprehending way. Juxtaposing scenes of great wealth and medieval ruins with the horrible housing projects of modern Italy, set up on the outskirts of cities without paved streets, trees, or anything except square buildings in the midst of dirt, Pasolini mourns that Italians have forsaken their radicalism, embracing instead a "progress" and individualism that cannot bring about the spiritual fulfillment, the solidarity, of a community of people united in a just cause. Pasolini contrasts two "real" Italies: the camaraderie of the poor and the workers against a repressive bourgeoisie determined to do away with traditional culture and landscape.

Jarman's and Pasolini's views of the modern world are similar and bleak. Pasolini consistently maintained that "all middle-class persons are, in fact, fascist, always, everywhere and to whatever party they belong."[12] Where tolerance, creativity, and liberty exist, it is because people struggled in the face of oppression: these were never gifts of the powers-that-be. Like Jarman in *The Last of England*, Pasolini puts Hitler himself on the screen in *Porcile* (*Pigsty*—1969) in the form of a Herr Hirdhitze who looks exactly like him. Formerly a fascist known as Hirt (ironically, shepherd), he loves beautiful music (as did Hitler)— he plays the harp — and has become an industrialist in modern Germany. The narrator tells us ironically that his factory only makes peacetime consumer goods — except, of course, for export. Hirdhitze and his chief competitor Klotz, however, become partners when they realize each has a terrible secret. Hirdhitze conducted deadly medical experiments on human beings. Klotz's secret, however, is that his son Julian is enamored of pigs, and is constantly driven to sexual intercourse with them. This young man with no direction in life is finally devoured by the animals in a pigsty.

Pasolini's intent is to shock us by making us rethink the way fascism and homosexuality are considered equivalent vices by a contemporary bourgeoisie that is protofascist itself (for instance, it supports politicians and budgets that guarantee unequal access to justice, health care, and education for the poor). Also appearing in the film are medieval cannibals, who are themselves staked out on the ground to be devoured by dogs — here, like the Nazi medical experiments, is a real crime, rather than what is merely the pursuit of sexual eccentricity. Neither Julian nor the other characters "dare speak the name" of his vice: it is too abominable to mention, although they attempt in vain to spurt it out, as was sodomy for much of Christian history. The manner in which respectable folks abhor his sexual abnormality, and the difficulty Julian has coming to terms with himself, parallel the plight of so many homosexuals in homophobic societies, especially young people who kill themselves at an incredible rate after suffering repeated gay-bashing.

Julian's death, where he is (off-screen) devoured, trampled, and torn apart by pigs is a none-too-subtle reference to the similar fate of Sebastian Venable in Tennessee Williams' play, and the film based upon it, *Suddenly Last Summer*. Here too homosexuality is implied almost ad infinitum without being actually mentioned: we see Sebastian chased and attacked by the young boys he cruises much as the pigs assault Julian. That the torture and murder associated with fascism carry no more stigma in the eyes of many than sexual self-expression proves for Pasolini that there is no line between bourgeois and fascist.

Salò, Or the One Hundred Twenty Days of Sodom (1975), Pasolini's last film, made in the year he was killed by one of the street boys he regularly solicited, renders this equation of fascism and its contemporary successors even more shocking. A group of fascists — not the sort who wear army uniforms, but respectable industrialists and intellectuals dressed in business suits — have retreated to a medieval fortress where they await their conquest by the Allies in the Second World War. They have taken with them a group of very attractive youths, upon whom they commit all sorts of tortures and indignities before they finally kill them. They justify their sadism by quotations from Nietzsche's *The Genealogy of Morals*, proving to their satisfaction that they are "superior" and thus entitled to do as they will with their inferiors. Irony abounds here, both because Nietzsche was a favorite philosopher of the Nazis (who atrociously misinterpreted him) and because these would-be "supermen" are the pathetic remnants of a "master race" having a last-ditch fling at perversity before they are annihilated. Just as Jarman shows that repressed homophobia leads to sexual abuse and violence, and presents several of his sadistic characters as cross-dressers to show their confusion, Pasolini argues forcefully in *Salò* that sadism, child abuse, and other forms of sexually-based violence arise out of a homophobic society that encourages and countenances repression. Fascism now appears respectable — our leaders do not rant and rave and wear military uniforms — but its essence remains unchanged.

Mamma Roma (1962) and *Accatone* (1961) — Fellini's first two major films — make the same point as *Salò*, although with respect to less nauseating behavior. Mamma Roma is a prostitute by night who works so that her ultra-respectable and uptight son can advance socially. She is the earthy life-force which her upright clients and the city and nation they embody require if they are to retain any joy and vitality beneath their facade of respectability. Ironically, she too yearns for this respectability and despises herself. Accatone is a poor pimp, a member of Rome's lumpen proletariat, whose undoing comes about not from his misdeeds, but results from his efforts to show kindness.

Pasolini does offer an alternative to these grim visions of the contemporary world. In *Teorema*, (*Theorem* — 1968) various members of a wealthy industrialist's household sleep with a beautiful yet mysterious young man played by Terence Stamp (a gay actor who came to fame for his role as Billy Budd in the film of that name based on Herman Melville's tale of repressed homosexuality, sadism, and masochism in the British navy.) Each of "the visitor's" partners is changed by the experience. The maid Emilia becomes a religious fanatic, prays constantly, performs miracles, eats nettles, and floats in the sky — a scene reminiscent of the "miracle" in Fellini's *La Dolce Vita* when a religious statue, transported by a helicopter that disappears in the clouds, is believed by those who see it to be floating on its own — before ordering a friend to bury her alive. The son Pietro, having enjoyed sex with the visitor, feels that the act places him outside of respectable society. He becomes an abstract artist who thinks his work is garbage, but invents intellectual justifications to give it the respectability he personally craves but thinks he can never deserve. The daughter Odetta, so devastated at losing the visitor, becomes catatonic: she is carted away to an insane asylum. On the other hand, the mother, Lucia, played by a voluptuous Sylvana Mangnano, finds resemblances to the visitor in various young men, and seduces them even though she feels guilty about it.

Finally, the pater familias, Paolo. In the middle of the film, he seems disturbed about the visitor's influence on the family, and wants to have a discussion with him to figure out what is going on. But the discussion does not occur: instead, they jocularly spar with each other before relaxing at the side of a lake. The film ends with Paolo having sex with another young man (implied, but not seen) and running off, screaming, naked into a barren landscape. This ending explains the film's beginning, where Paolo has made headlines by turning his factory over to his workers. The bourgeois life is shown to be sterile and meaningless.

But is there a way out? At the film's opening, journalists pepper the industrialist with questions. To be sure, he is a hero, but they ask — what will happen to the class struggle? Will he simply turn the workers into middle-class types, much as the Italian economic miracle was beginning to do? Pasolini leaves us with a troubling vision: sexual fulfillment is temporary, and granting people greater wealth and freedom will not solve their problems either.

Why did Pasolini make his films? He wanted to "reproduce reality," and in so doing "live according to my philosophy." The reality he found was "the obscene health of neo-capitalism," a continuation of Nazism "which defined the petite bourgeoisie as 'normal'" and which continues to practice "mass murder" in the Third World by suppressing revolutions.[13] "I cannot accept anything of the world in which I live: neither the apparatuses of state centralism — bureaucracy, legal system, army, school, and all the rest — nor its cultured minorities," Pasolini wrote.[14] *Salò* was his last full-length film, the year before Jarman began his career with *Sebastiane*. There is continuity in the two directors' denunciation of a world that dehumanized its people and its landscape. If Pasolini's more conservative culture could not brook the all-out defense of the homosexuality as did Jarman's a mere decade later, his films still provided themes and ideas that the younger director would develop into a fascinating series of variations.

Notes

Preface

1. Roy Grundmann, "History and the Gay Viewfinder: An Interview with Derek Jarman," *Cineaste* 18: 4 (1991): 26.
2. Derek Jarman, *Dancing Ledge*, ed. Shaun Allen (London: Quartet Books; Woodstock, New York: Overlook Press, 1984): 54; hereafter cited as DL.
3. I use "heterosexist" as Jarman used "heterosoc" to indicate the belief that heterosexual behavior is the only proper expression of human sexuality. It is quite possible to be heterosexual without being heterosexist.
4. Derek Jarman, *Modern Nature: The Journals of Derek Jarman*, (London: Century; Woodstock, New York: Overlook Press, 1991): 63; hereafter cited as MN.
5. Derek Jarman, *At Your Own Risk: A Saint's Testament*, ed. Michael Christie (London: Hutchinson; Woodstock, New York: Overlook Press, 1992): 83; hereafter cited as AYOR.
6. AYOR: 82.
7. AYOR: 29.
8. Derek Jarman, *Smiling in Slow Motion*, ed. Keith Collins (London: Vintage, 2001): 171, 77; hereafter cited as SISM.
9. SISM: 83.
10. SISM: 29.
11. See in particular Donald B. Redford, *Akhenaten: The Heretic King* (Princeton: Princeton University Press, 1984) and Cyril E. Aldred, *Akhenaten: King of Egypt* (London: Thames and Hudson, 1988). Jarman spells Akenaten without the "h," and for convenience I use his spelling in this book.
12. See, for example, Hugh Montefiore, *Sermons from Great Saint Mary's* (London: Fontana, 1968): 182; Morton Smith, *The Secret Gospel: The Discovery and Interpretation of the Secret Gospel According to Mark* (New York: Harper and Row, 1973), esp. 16-17, 114, 124-130; Tom Horner, *Jonathan Loved David: Homosexuality in Biblical Times* (Philadelphia: The Westminster Press, 1978), ch. 9, "Jesus and Sexuality."
13. See especially Peter R. L. Brown, *The Body and Society: Men, Women, and Sexual Renunciation in Early Christianity* (New York: Columbia University Press, 1988). See also Edith Scholl, "The Sweetness of the Lord; *Dulcis* and *Suavis*," *Cistercian Studies Quarterly*, 27 (1992): 359-366; Franz Posset, "*Christi Dulcedo*: The 'Sweetness of Christ' in Western Christian Spirituality," *Cistercian Studies Quarterly*, 30 (1995): 245-265, and numerous other articles in this journal.

14. For example, see Michel Foucault, *The History of Sexuality*, trans. Robert Hurley, 3 vols. (New York: Pantheon, 1978–1986); John Boswell, *Christianity, Social Tolerance, and Homosexuality: Gay People in Western Europe from the Beginning of the Christian Era to the Fourteenth Century* (Chicago: University of Chicago Press, 1980); idem., *Same-Sex Unions in Pre-Modern Europe* (New York: Villiard, 1994); John D'Emilio, *Sexual Politics, Sexual Communities: The Making of a Homosexual Minority in the United States* (Chicago: University of Chicago Press, 1983); idem., *Making Trouble: Essays on Gay History, Politics, and the University* (New York: Routledge, 1992); Jonathan Ned Katz, *The Invention of Heterosexuality* (New York: Dutton, 1995); Marc Stein, *City of Brotherly and Sisterly Love: Lesbian and Gay Philadelphia, 1945–1972* (Chicago: University of Chicago Press, 2000); George Chauncey, *Gay New York: Gender, Culture, and the Making of the Gay Male World* (New York: Basic Books, 1994).

15. (Minneapolis: University of Minnesota Press, 2001).

16. (Durham, N.C.: Duke University Press, 1994).

17. Derek Jarman, *Kicking the Pricks*, ed. David Hurst (London: Vintage, 2001): 69, 163, 197, 40; hereafter cited as KTP.

18. SISM: 246–47.

19. AYOR: 30.

20. Tony Peake, *Derek Jarman: A Biography* (London: Little, Brown; Woodstock, New York: Overlook Press, 2000): 419.

21. SISM: 10, 69.

22. AYOR: 31.

23. Judith Bennett, "Lesbian-like Behavior and the History of Lesbianism," *Journal of the History of Sexuality*, 11 (2000): 1–24.

24. Michael Warner, *The Trouble with Normal: Sex, Politics, and the Ethics of Queer Life* (Cambridge: Harvard University Press, 1999).

25. Nicholas Slonimsky, *Lexicon of Musical Invective* (Seattle: University of Washington Press, 1969); Peake's biography is a good source for those interested in the critical reception of Jarman's work.

26. SISM: 188, 203.

Introduction

1. James Cary Parks, "Et in Arcadia." Homo Sexuality and the Gay Sensibility in the Art of Derek Jarman," in Roger Wollen, ed., *Derek Jarman: A Portrait* (London: Thames and Hudson, 1996): 142.

2. SISM: 161–62; 175–76.

3. AYOR: 103.

4. Walter Benjamin, "Theses on the Philosophy of History," in *Illuminations*, ed. Hannah Arendt (New York: Schocken Books, 1968): 255. In 1940, trying to escape from Nazi-occupied France over the Pyrenees into Spain, Benjamin panicked when his party was denied entry and committed suicide. The group was allowed entry the next day.

5. DL: 220.

6. SISM: 43, 31

7. MN: 94.

8. KTP: 235.

9. Derek jarman, *Derek Jarman's Caravaggio* (London: Thames and Hudson): 15; hereafter referred to as C.

10. DL: 123.

11. Peake: 191.

12. KTP: 173.

13. AYOR: 85; Michael O'Pray, *Derek Jarman: Dreams of England* (London: British

Films Institute, 1996): 99, 155; Matt Cook, "'Words written without any stopping': Derek Jarman's Written Work," in Wollen: 110.
  14. SISM: 217.
  15. Chris Lippard, "Interview with Derek Jarman," in Chris Lippard, ed., *By Angels Driven: The Films of Derek Jarman* (Westport, Connecticut: Praeger, 1996): 166.
  16. SISM: 136, 217, 232, 356, 358, 369.
  17. O'Pray: 182.
  18. Derek Jarman, *War Requiem* (London: Faber and Faber, 1989): 35; hereafter cited as WR.
  19. SISM: 198.
  20. SISM: 252, 291, 308.
  21. Lippard: 164 (see note 15 above).
  22. AYOR: 46.
  23. Michel Foucault, "Nietzsche, Geneaology, and History," in Paul Rabinow, ed. *The Foucault Reader* (New York: Pantheon, 1984): 87–88.
  24. AYOR: 23, 32.
  25. AYOR: 60.
  26. DL: 246.
  27. Jonathan Ned Katz, *The Invention of Heterosexuality* (New York: Dutton, 1995); Michel Foucault, "The Subject and Power," Afterword to *Beyond Structuralism and Hermeneutics*, ed., Hubert Dreyfus and Paul Rabinow (Brighton: Harvester Press, 1982): 224–226.
  28. W. E. B. DuBois, *The Souls of Black Folk* (New York: New American Library, 1969, orig. pub. 1903).
  29. Lynn Hunt, "History as Gesture: Or, The Scandal of History," in Jonathan Arac and Barbara Johnson, ed., *Consequences of Theory* (Baltimore: Johns Hopkins University Press, 1991): 103.
  30. Gilles Deleuze and Felix Guattari, "Rhizome," in *On the Line* (New York: Semiotexte, 1983): 53.
  31. AYOR: 25.
  32. Roberta Kevelson, *Inlaws/Outlaws: A Semiotics of Systematic Interaction* (Lisse and Bloomington: Peter de Ridder Press and Research Center for Linguistic and Semiotic Studies, University of Indiana, 1977): 88.
  33. Michel Foucault, *Discipline and Punish* (English trans. of French, published 1975; Harmondsworth: Penguin, 1979).
  34. MN: 167.
  35. Michel Foucault, "Of Other Spaces," *Diacritics*, 16: 1 (Spring, 1986): 22–27.
  36. DL: 214.
  37. AYOR: 19; DL: 244.
  38. AYOR: 35.
  39. AYOR: 64; MN: 276.
  40. DL: 164.
  41. SISM: 223.
  42. DL: 203.
  43. SISM: 146.
  44. MN: 79.
  45. SISM: 32, 81, 204, 314.
  46. AYOR: 66.
  47. Derek Jarman, *Queer Edward II* (London: British Film Institute, 1992): 106; hereafter cited as QE2.
  48. MN: 163; SISM: 55.
  49. DL: 220.
  50. DL: 238–239.
  51. AYOR: 124.
  52. AYOR: 151–152.

Chapter 1

1. SISM: 276, 286.
2. UITA, 3.
3. The sources I have consulted by Redford and Aldred are cited in the preface. I refer to Aldred's work, since it appeared four years after Redford's, in the footnotes to indicate the consensus of scholarly wisdom c. 1988, which has not changed with respect to the issues considered here.
4. Aldred: 7.
5. Aldred: 134–141.
6. Aldred: 145, 151, 169.
7. Aldred: 132.
8. Aldred: 306.
9. Scenes 7, 8, and 14 from filmscript, UITA (Hereafter cited by scene in this chapter).
10. Scene 8.
11. Scene 16.
12. Aldred: 172.
13. Scenes 27, 44, 35. The texts of the poems, in a different translation, may be found in J. B. Pritchard, ed., *Ancient Near Eastern Texts Relating to the Old Testament* (Princeton: Princeton University Press, 1955).
14. Scene 57.
15. Aldred: 204.
16. Aldred: 295.
17. Scenes 51–53.
18. Aldred: 291, 257.
19. Scenes 22 and 40.
20. Scenes 57, 59, 71.
21. Scenes 10, 15.
22. Scene 72.
23. Scene 44.

Chapter 2

1. Derek Jarman, *derek jarman's garden* (London: Thames and Hudson; Woodstock, New York: Overlook Press, 1996): 7, 11, 105; hereafter cited as G.
2. G: 14.
3. MN: 18, 31.
4. G: 61, 63.
5. Quoted in O'Pray, Michael. *Derek Jarman: Dreams of England* (London: British Film Institute, 1996): 151, 152.
6. Michael B., Young, *King James and the History of Homosexuality* (New York: New York University Press, 2000): 44.
7. See Tom Horner, *Jonathan Loved David: Homosexuality in Biblical Times* (Philadelphia: The Westminster Press, 1978): 76–84, 133.

Chapter 3

1. AYOR: 83.
2. SISM: 254.
3. DL: 165; SISM: 255.
4. Gore Vidal "proposed the notion that the two [Ben Hur played by Charlton Heston and Messala played by Stephen Boyd] had been adolescent lovers and now Messala

returned from Rome wanting to revive the love affair but Ben Hur does not.... This is what's going on *underneath* the scene" in which they "*seem* to be talking about politics." Boyd was fascinated and played the scene that way to an unsuspecting Heston. Quoted in Vito Russo, *The Celluloid Closet: Homosexuality in the Movies* (New York: Harper and Row, 1981): 76–77.

5. Jarman's interest in alchemy, in which the four earthly elements are symbolically transformed into gold or transcendence, is discussed more fully in chapters 8, 9, and 14 of this book.

6. Brown, *The Body and Society*.

7. For a thorough discussion of this process, see Keith Thomas, *Religion and the Decline of Magic* (New York: Scribner's, 1971).

8. Peake: 223.

9. In some versions of Sebastian's legend, he is rescued from the arrows, revived, and martyred at a later date.

10. AYOR: 83–84.

Chapter 4

1. SISM: 90.
2. MN: 206, 211.
3. Christopher Marlowe, *Edward II*: Act 1, Scene 4 (all references to the play cited by act and scene as many editions exist.)
4. QE2: 84.
5. A. L. Rowse, *Christopher Marlowe: His Life and Work* (New York: Grosset and Dunlap, 1964): 33.
6. Claire Sponsler, "The King's Boyfriend: Froissart's Political Theater of 1326," in Glenn Burger and Steven F. Kruger, eds., *Queering the Middle Ages* (Minneapolis: University of Minnesota Press, 2001): 143–167, esp. 150.
7. Raphaell Holinshed, *The Chronicles of England* (first published 1586; London: J. Johnson, 1707) 2: 547.
8. Michael B. Young, *King James and the History of Homosexuality* (New York: New York University Press, 2000): esp. 51–54.
9. QE2: iii.
10. Young, *King James*: ch. 4.
11. Marlowe, *Edward II*: Act 1, Scene 4.
12. Jonathan Goldberg, *Sodometries: Renaissance Texts and Modern Sexualities* (Stanford: Stanford University Press, 1992).
13. David Mathew, *James I* (London: Eyre and Spottiswood, 1967): 34–44; David Bergeron, *Royal Family: Royal Lovers: King James I of England and Scotland* (Columbia: University of Missouri Press, 1991): 11, 27–36, 44–46.
14. Neville Williams, *All the Queen's Men: Elizabeth and Her Courtiers* (London: Macmillan, 1972): 182–184, 211–219.
15. Michael Manheim, *The Weak King Dilemma in the Shakespearean History Play* (Syracuse: Syracuse University Press, 1973).
16. J. S. Hamilton, *Piers Gaveston, Earl of Cornwall, 1307–1312: Politics and Patronage in the Reign of Edward II* (Detroit: Wayne State University Press, 1988); Harold F. Hutchinson, *Edward II* (New York: Stein and Day, 1971); Natalie Fryde, *The Tyranny and Fall of Edward II* (Cambridge: Cambridge University Press, 1979).
17. Teun Van Dijk, *Racism and the Press* (London: Routledge, 1991).
18. Philomena Essed, *Understanding Everyday Racism* (Newbury Park, California: Sage Publishers, 1991).
19. Marlowe, *Edward II*: Act 2, Scene 2.
20. QE2: 4.
21. Young, *James I*: ch. 5.
22. MN: 294.

Chapter 5

1. Henry Fuseli, *Lectures on Painting Delivered at the Royal Academy* (London: Johnson, 1801): 100.
2. DL: 13.
3. Walter Friedlaender, *Caravaggio Studies* (Princeton: Princeton University Press, 1955): plate 51.; hereafter cited as WF; C: 48.
4. These documents are printed in WF: 228–316; and Howard Hibbard, *Caravaggio* (New York: Harper and Row, rev. ed. 1985): 343–387; hereafter cited as HH.
5. DL: 13.
6. HH: 344.
7. HH: 374.
8. Peake: 273, 299.
9. Carl Becker, "Everyman His Own Historian," *American Historical Review*, 37 (1932): 221–236.
10. DL: 24.
11. HH: 112; WF, frontispiece; C: 7.
12. HH: 373.
13. WF: plates 41, 30, and 4, respectively.
14. C: 130–131.
15. WF: 120.
16. HH: vii.
17. Maurizio Calvesi, "Caravaggio o la ricerca della salvazione," *Storia dell'arte*, 9/10 (1971): 92–142.
18. HH: 355.
19. HH: 350, 357.
20. HH: 344.
21. HH: 371.
22. HH: 359.
23. WF: 7.
24. WF: 120.
25. HH: vii.
26. C: 21.
27. C: 113.
28. Bellori cited in HH: 371.
29. See Jason M. Kelly, "Turner's Golden Vision: Alchemy in the Works of J.M.W. Turner," *American Journal of Semiotics*, 11 (1995/98): 211–228; John Read, *The Alchemist: In Life, Literature, and Arts* (London: Thomas Nelson and Sons, 1947).
30. Luigi Spezzaferro, "La cultura del Cardinal Del Monte e il primo tempo di Caravaggio," *Storia dell'arte*, 9/10 (1971): 76–78.
31. HH: 226; G. Legman, *The Guilt of the Templars*, intro. by Jacques Barzun (New York: Basic Books, 1966).
32. Harry C. Schnur, *Mystic Rebels: Apollonius Tyraneus, Jan Van Leyden, Sabbatai Zevi, Cagliostro* (New York: The Beechurst Press, 1949): 248.
33. HH: 236.
34. Michelangelo, "Se nel volto per gli occhi il cor si vede," in George R. Kay, ed. and translator, *The Penguin Book of Italian Verse* (Baltimore: Penguin, 1958): 163.
35. Guido Cavalcanti, "Avete 'n voi li fiori e la verdura," ibid.: 55. See also poems ibid., on p. 177 by Gaspara Stampa, "By your arrows, Love, I swear, and by your mighty, sacred torch, that, although the one burn me and waste my heart, and the other wound, I do not mind," from "Per le saette tue, Amor, ti giuro" and Torquato Tasso, p. 185 "your soft smile is the sun" from "Giammai piu dolce raggio." I am deeply thankful to my colleagues Laura Giannetti and Guido Ruggiero for making this point, and to Guido for his encouraging reading of this chapter.

36. Derek Jarman, *Chroma: A Book of Colour* (London: Century; Woodstock, New York: Overlook Press, 1994): 75–77; hereafter cited as Ch; Derek Jarman, *Blue* (London: Basilisk Films with accompanying book, 1993): 5.
37. HH: 347.
38. HH: 372.
39. HH: 355.
40. HH: 379.
41. HH: 383, quoting Francesco Susinno's remark of 1724.
42. DL: 14.
43. C: 15.
44. WF: plates 32 and 13.
45. Edmund White cited by James Miller, *The Passion of Michel Foucault* (New York: Simon and Schuster, 1993): 56.
46. Michel Eqyem de Montaigne, *Essays* (1580), trans. Charles Cotton (Chicago: Encyclopedia Brittanica, 1952): 77, 68, 91–89; for a discussion of the problem of agreeing on acceptable Italian language, see Santa Casciani, "Ruzante: A Dissenting Voice in the Italian Renaissance," *American Journal of Semiotics*, 11 (1995/98): 185–209.
47. WF: plates 7, 32, 14.
48. HH: 371.
49. C: 54.
50. C: 114.
51. C: 118.
52. C: 120.
53. C: 132.
54. C: 94.
55. C: 21.
56. C: 90.
57. HH: 344, citing Van Mander.
58. C: 15.
59. HH: 344; WF: 284.
60. DL: 22.
61. QE2: iii.
62. C: 133.
63. C: 10.
64. C.: 131.

Chapter 6

1. The most thorough treatment of Dee, including a study of his mystical writings and practices, is I.R.F. Calder, "John Dee Studied as an English Neoplatonist," Ph.D. thesis, University of London, 1952. For my purposes, the most useful published work is Wayne Shumaker, *Renaissance Curiosa* (Binghamton, New York: Center for Medieval and Early Renaissance Studies, 1982), ch. 1.
2. *Queering the Renaissance* (Durham: Duke University Press, 1994).
3. SISM: 161.
4. KTP: 133, 134, 138.
5. S. J. Bradley, ed. *Anglo-Saxon Poetry* London: Dent, 1982): 322–325.
6. KTP: 133.
7. KTP: 134.
8. Peake: 336.

Chapter 7

1. DL: 163.

2. KTP: 68.
3. Peake: 266.
4. C: 45.
5. O'Pray: 112, citing Colin McCabe, "Edward II: Throne of Blood," *Sight and Sound*, vol. 1, no. 6 (1991).
6. DL: 189, 182.
7. DL: 183.
8. Peake: 267.
9. DL: 188.
10. On production practices in Shakespeare's time, see, for example, the Stephen Orgel's introduction to *The Tempest* (Oxford: Clarendon Press, 1987): 57–64.
11. Michel Foucault, "What is Enlightenment?" in Paul Rabinow, ed. *The Foucault Reader* (New York: Pantheon, 1984): 32–50.
12. DL: 196.
13. Howard Hibbard, *Caravaggio* (New York: Harper and Row, 2nd. ed., 1985): 371, citing 1672 remark of Giovanni Bellori.
14. DL: 128.
15. Alden T. Vaughan and Virginia Mason Vaughan, *Shakespeare's Caliban: A Cultural History* (Cambridge: Cambridge University Press, 1991).
16. DL: 198.
17. Peake: 267.
18. DP: 191.
19. DL: 122.

Chapter 8

1. W: 12.
2. W: 106, 112.
3. W: 65.
4. SISM: 134.
5. Ludwig Wittgenstein, *Remarks on Colour* (Oxford: Oxford University Press, 1977), hereafter cited by section and remark, viz.: *Remarks*, I: 54 in this case.
6. *Remarks*, I: 33; III: 100.
7. *Remarks*, III: 79.
8. Ch: 143.
9. W: 71.
10. Ray Monk, *Wittgenstein* (London: Jonathan Cape, 1990).
11. W: 74.
12. SISM: 236.
13. *Remarks*, III: 156.
14. *Remarks*, III: 10.
15. *Remarks*, III: 213.
16. *Remarks*, III: 216, 223.
17. *Remarks*, I: 36.
18. SISM: 133, 254.
19. Ch: 31.
20. Ch: 145–146.
21. W: 67.
22. W: 136.
23. W: 82.
24. W: 92, 130.
25. W: 82, 86.

26. W: 132.
27. W: 64.
28. *Remarks*, III: 112, 118, 330.
29. *Remarks*, III: 295.
30. W: 140.
31. W: 66; SISM: 235.
32. W: 76.
33. W: 143–144.
34. *Remarks*, III: 31.
35. W: 142.
36. W: 106.
37. W: 98.

Chapter 9

1. WR: 11.
2. WR: 35.
3. WR: 8, 13, 14.
4. WR: xi.
5. WR: 6.
6. WR: 34.
7. WR: 10.
8. WR: 12.
9. WR: 36.
10. WR: 6.
11. WR: 15.
12. WR: 29.
13. WR: 24.
14. WR: 29–30.
15. WR: 38.
16. WR: 28.

Chapter 10

1. Derek Jarman, *Up in the air: Collected Film Scripts* (London: Vintage, 1996): 43; hereafter cited as UITA.
2. Peake: 246.
3. DL: 170.
4. DL: 176.
5. Peake: 111.
6. Peake: 246.
7. Peake: 242.

Chapter 11

1. C: 114.
2. DL: 219.
3. KTP: 192–193.

Chapter 12

1. DL: 7.
2. Carl Gustav Jung, *Aion: Researches into the Phenomenology of the Self* (Princeton: Princeton University Press, 1959): 86. Volume 9 no. 2 of Jung's collected works, and volume 20 of the Bollingen series published by Princeton.

3. Peake: 111.
4. UITA: 55.
5. Peake: 293.
6. UITA: 132.
7. DL: 209.
8. UITA: 159–160.
9. UITA: 147.
10. KTP: 183.
11. KTP: 11.
12. MN: 150.
13. AYOR: 86.
14. KTP: 109.
15. AYOR: 134.
16. MN: 102.

Chapter 13

1. Hibbard, *Caravaggio* (New York: Harper & Row, 1985, rev. ed.): 371, Giovanni Bellori.
2. SISM: 205–208.
3. Edward Said, *Orientalism* (New York: Pantheon, 1978).
4. AYOR: 46.
5. SISM: 320.

Afterword

1. Information about *Imagining October*, including much of the script, appears in KTP: 78, 92–109.
2. See Alfred Kazin, ed. *The Portable Blake* (New York: Viking Press, 1946): 150–154. Blake used similar rhythms elsewhere, but this poem is the best-known of these.
3. See DL: 220, where Jarman notes how the film *Chariots of Fire* encouraged support for the Malvinas (Falklands) War as well as the rewriting of history by ignoring actor Ian Charleson's appearance in Jarman's film *Jubilee* before his appearance in the Oscar-winning production.
4. Kazin, ed., *Portable Blake*: 107.
5. KTP: 151–153.

Appendix

1. SISM: 155, 168.
2. My chief sources for Pasolini are: Sam Rohdie, *The Passion of Pier Paolo Pasolini* (Bloomington: Indiana University Press, 1995); Stephen Snyder, *Pier Paolo Pasolini* (Boston: Twayne, 1980), which includes chapter-length studies of his films; *Pasolini on Pasolini: Interviews with Oswald Stack* (Bloomington: Indiana University Press, 1969); and Pasolini's own collection of essays, *Heretical Empiricism* [hereafter HE], trans. Ben Lawton and Louise K. Barnet (Bloomington: Indiana University Press, 1988). I have been able to view all the films discussed below. For Pasolini's influence on Jarman, see David Gale, "Perverse Law: Jarman as Gay Criminal Hero," in Lippard: 44–51. For other influences on Jarman, which encompass much of the history of cinema, see Peake: 217, 292, 296, 337, 348–349, 424, 476–477, 543, 550, 556, 559; also James Park, *Learning to Dream: The New British*

Cinema (London: Faber and Faber, 1984), which stresses how following an uninspired tradition of epic, literary, and sentimental films, young film-makers such as Jarman, in the 1980s, reacting both to the repression of the Thatcher regime and the shortage of funds, created a lively, non-narrative, radical cinema.

    3. Pier Paolo Pasolini, *Oedipus Rex* (screenplay), trans. John Matthews (New York: Simon and Schuster, 1971): 101 [hereafter OR].

    4. Pasolini, *Heretical Empiricism*: xx.

    5. OR: 101.

    6. OR: 64.

    7. OR: 102.

    8. Euripides, *Medea and Other Plays*, trans. Philip Vellacott (Harmondsworth: Penguin, 1963): 31, 30, 23.

    9. See Snyder, *Pasolini*: 59–72.

    10. *Pasolini on Pasolini*: 63.

    11. Geoffrey Chaucer, *The Canterbury Tales*, trans. into modern English by Neville Coghill (Harmondsworth, 1977, rev. ed.): 311.

    12. HE: xxviii.

    13. HE: 132–139.

    14. HE: xvi.

Works Cited

Works by Jarman

AYOR—*At Your Own Risk: A Saint's Testament*, ed. Michael Christie (London: Hutchinson; Woodstock, New York: Overlook Press, 1992).
B—*Blue: Text of a Film by Derek Jarman* (London: Richard Salmon, limited ed.; Woodstock, New York: Overlook Press, 1993).
C—*Derek Jarman's Caravaggio* (London: Thames and Hudson, 1986).
Ch—*Chroma: A Book of Colour* (London: Century; Woodstock, New York: Overlook Press, 1994).
DL—*Dancing Ledge*, ed. Shaun Allen (London: Quartet Books; Woodstock, New York: Overlook Press, 1984).
G—*derek jarman's garden* (London: Thames and Hudson; Woodstock, New York: Overlook Press, 1996).
KTP—*Kicking the Pricks*, ed. David Hirst (London: Vintage, 1996; published in 1987 as *The Last of England*). Includes script for *Imagining October*.
MN—*Modern Nature: The Journals of Derek Jarman* (London: Century; Woodstock, New York: Overlook Press, 1991).
QE2—*Queer Edward II* (London: British Film Institute, 1992).
SISM—*Smiling in Slow Motion*, ed. Keith Collins (London: Vintage, 2001).
UITA—*Up in the Air: Collected Film Scripts* (London: Vintage, 1996). *Akenaten, Jubilee, Bob-Up-a-Down*; *B Movie: Little England/A Time of Hope*; *The Neutron*, and *Sod 'Em*.
W—*Wittgenstein: The Terry Eagleton Script, The Derek Jarman Film* (London: British Film Institute, 1993).
WR—*War Requiem* (London: Faber and Faber, 1989).

Works About Jarman

Lippard—Chris Lippard, ed., *By Angels Driven: The Films of Derek Jarman* (Westport, Connecticut: Praeger, 1996).
O'Pray—Michael O'Pray, *Derek Jarman: Dreams of England* (London: British Film Institute, 1996).
Peake—Tony Peake, *Derek Jarman: A Biography* (London: Little, Brown; Woodstock, New York: Overlook Press, 2000).
Wollen—Roger Wollen, ed., *Derek Jarman: A Portrait* (London: Thames and Hudson, 1996).

Other Works

HE—Pier Paolo Pasolini, *Heretical Empiricism*, trans. Ben Lawton and Louse K. Barnet (Blomington: Indiana University Press, 1998).
HH—Howard Hibbard, *Caravaggio* (New York: Harper and Row, rev. ed. 1985).
OR—Pier Paolo Pasolini, *Oedipus Rex* (screenplay), trans. John Matthews (New York: Simon and Schuster, 1971).
WF—Walter Friedlaender, *Carvaggio Studies* (Princeton: Princeton University Press, 1955).

Principal Films Discussed

1976 — *Sebastiane* — Cinevista

1977 — *Jubilee* — Whaley-Malin Productions [UITA]

1979 — *The Tempest* — Kendon Films [Shakespeare play]

1984 — *Imagining October* — super 8 (blown up to 16 and then 35 mm.) [KTP]

1985 — *The Angelic Conversation* — with the financial assistance of the British Film Institute [Shakespeare sonnets; see Chapter 6 below]

1986 — *Caravaggio* — Cinevista [C]

1987 — *The Last of England* — Anglo-International Films [KTP]

1989 — *War Requiem* — Anglo-International Films [WR]

1990 — *The Garden* — Basilisk Communications

1991 — *Edward II* — New Lane Video [QE2]

1993 — *Wittgenstein* — Channel 4 (Britain) [W]

1993 — *Blue* — Basilisk Communications and Uplink in association with Channel 4 [B]

Information in brackets indicates the published work in which a script is available; none of the films corresponds exactly to the script.

Index

Abraham 123, 125, 128–129
Accatone (film by Fellini) 183
Achilles 57
Aeldred 5
Afghanistan 122
Africa 103
Age of Aquarius 151–152
Age of Pisces 151–152
Agrippa, Cornelius (*Of Occult Philosophy*) 100
Agrippina 52
AIDS 9, 11, 13, 14, 18–20, 31, 32, 41, 45, 68, 122, 130, 148, 151, 157–166
Aion (book by Carl Gustav Jung) 151–152, 162
Akenaten (pharaoh and film script by Jarman) 3, 4, 11, 21–28
Alchemy 77, 85–87, 100–107, 151–152, 162
Alcibiades 58
Aldred, Cyril 185, 188
Alexander the Great 2, 57, 135, 162, 163
Amenhotep III (pharaoh) 21–24
America 103
Anachronism 15, 21, 28, 80–82, 172–173, 179
The Angelic Conversation (film by Jarman) 11, 85–99, 137
Anglo-Saxon era 87–90, 99
Anselm, St. 5

Ant, Adam 136, 138, 139, 140, 141
Anti-Christ 33–34, 151–153
Antigone 164
Antinous 2
Apollo 45, 49
Arabian Nights (film by Pasolini; work of literature) 176–180
Archbishop(s) of Canterbury 64, 140, 155
Aristotle 116
Art 18, 65, 70–84
Artaud, Antonin 178
At Your Own Risk: A Saint's Testament (book by Jarman) 15, 20
Athens, Athenians *see* Greece
Auden, W. H. 124
Augustus 57

B Movie: Little England / A Time of Hope (script by Jarman) 140–141
Bacchus 74, 79
Bach, choir 129–130
Bach, Johann Sebastian (*St. Matthew Passion*) 175
Bacon, Francis 12
Baglione, Giovanni 15, 73, 74, 81
Bank of England 129
Bannockburn, Battle of 63
Becker, Carl 73
Bellori, Giovanni 72, 78
Ben-Hur 48, 189

Benjamin, Walter 12
Bennett, Judith 6
Bible 37, 39
Bizet, Georges (*The Pearl Fishers*) 165
Blair, Tony 19
Blake, William 13, 168
Bloomsbury set 113
Blue (film and screenplay by Jarman) 77, 102, 157–166
Boccaccio, Giovanni 175–178
Bodicea 52
Bolshevik Revolution 167–170
Bosnia 158, 159
Botticelli 12
Bowie, David 152
Boy Scouts 6
Boyd, Stephen 48, 189
Brahms, Johannes 100
Branagh, Kevin 15
Britain *see* England, history of
Britannia (symbol) 121, 129
British Film Institute 14
Britten, Benjamin 11, 15, 21, 120–131
Bronzino, Agnolo 87
Brooker, Howard 155
Brown, Ford Madox (*The Last of England*, painting) 144
Brown, Peter 50, 185
Buckingham, George Villiers, Duke of 31

Index

Buddha, Buddhism 161
Burroughs, William S. 15, 19
Burton, Sir Richard 176
Byron, Lord (George Gordon) 155

Caesar, Julius 2
Cagliostro, Count 77
Callas, Maria 173–174
Calvesi, Maurizio 74
Cambodia 122
Cambridge (town and university) 108, 113, 114, 118
Camus, Albert 36
Canby, Vincent 73
Canterbury Tales (film by Pasolini; book by Chaucer) 176–179
Caravaggio (painter and film by Jarman) 12, 13, 15, 70–84, 102, 142, 143, 157, 169
Cardinale, Claudia 48
Causubon, Meric 85
Cavalcante, Guido 77, 191
Chariots of Fire (film) 12, 168
Charles, Prince of Wales 141, 146, 148
Charles I, King of England 62
Charleson, Ian 12
Chaucer, Geoffrey 176–180
Christ *see* Jesus
Christianity 2, 3, 16, 29–42, 62, 70–84, 102, 120–131, 134, 145, 147, 151–152, 160, 161, 174–180
Christmas 33–34, 37, 155
Chroma (book by Jarman) 110–117
Churchill, Winston 135, 136, 147
Cicero 57
Cocteau, Jean 15, 164–165
Coil 87
Collins, Keith 1, 69
Color *see* Art; *Chroma*; *Blue*
Conservative Party 19, 106, 127, 134; *see also* Heath, Edward; Thatcher, Margaret
Coppola, Francis Ford 15
Coventry Cathedral 120, 124
Critics and Criticism 15, 73, 155

Crusaid 18
Cupid 78, 79
Czechoslovakia 170

Dancing Ledge (place; book by Jarman) 90, 97, 144
Dante (Divine Comedy) 50, 79, 80, 144
Darenth Park Hospital 127
David, King of Israel 112, 135, 137
Decameron (film by Pasolini; work by Boccaccio) 175
Dee, John 85–87, 132–134, 140, 192
Deleuze, Gilles 8, 16
Del Monte, Cardinal Francesco 76–81, 84, 142
D'Emilio, John 4
DeMille, Cecil B. 48
Dench, Judi 87, 88, 90
Devereux, Robert (Earl of Essex) 62
Diana, Princess of Wales 146, 148
Dido 52
Diocletian (Roman Emperor) 45, 49
Diogenes 144
Doctor Faustus (play by Christopher Marlowe) 86–87
Doré, Gustav 144
Drysdale, Lee 152
DuBois, W. E. B. 16, 20
Dungeness 13, 18, 29–43, 136

Eagleton, Terry 4, 108–110, 113, 118
Ecology 29–31, 89, 127, 130, 132–156
Edward I: King of England 56
Edward II (play by Christopher Marlowe; film by Jarman) 11, 14, 15, 55–69, 83, 154–155, 171, 172
Edward II, King of England 3, 14, 55–69, 155
Edward III, King of England 56, 65
Edwardian Era (1900–10) 6
Egypt 2–4, 21–28

Eisenstein, Sergei 81, 167–170
Elgar, Edward ("Land of Hope and Glory") 146
Eliot, T. S. ("The Wasteland") 145
Elizabeth, Queen of Bohemia 100–101
Elizabeth I, Queen of England 11, 85, 100, 134, 136, 137, 140
Elizabeth II, Queen of England 61, 62, 132, 133, 134, 137, 155
Elizabethan Age 15, 55–69, 85–107, 134, 140–141
England, history of 1, 12, 13, 16–19, 42, 55–69, 87–90, 120–170; *see also* London
The Enlightenment 17, 102–104, 106
Environmental destruction *see* Ecology
Essed, Philomena 63

Faithfull, Marianne 149
Falkland Islands and War *see* Malvinas
Fascism 172, 175, 183–184
Fassbinder, Werner 81
Faust 86–87
Fellini, Federico (*Satyricon*; *La Dolce Vita*) 45, 47, 176, 184
Ficino, Marsilio 116
Fischer-Dieskau, Dietrich 120
Fitzgerald, F. Scott 111
Foucault, Michel 4, 8, 15, 78, 102, 103, 106, 110
Francesca, Piero della (*Resurrection*) 130
French Revolution 101, 136
Friedlaender, Walter 74, 75
Froissart, Jean 58
Fukuyama, Francis (*The End of History and the Last Man*) 141

Galas, Diamanda ("Mask of the Red Death") 148
The Garden (film by Jarman) 11, 22, 29–43, 45, 90, 138, 150, 159, 174
Gardens, Jarman's personal and other 13, 17, 18, 29–43, 136

Gaveston, Piers 11, 14, 56–59
Gay News 53
Gay rights, struggle for 4, 6, 7, 8, 18–20, 68, 151, 154–156
General Motors 129
Genet, Jean 15
George V, King of England 130
Gibbon, Edward 44
Ginsberg, Alan 15, 145
Ginsborg, Michael 137
Giotto 177–178
Goldberg, Jonathan 4, 87
Goliath 72, 74
The Gospel According to St. Matthew (film by Pasolini) 174–176
Greece, Greeks 6, 45, 47, 110, 160–161, 171–174
Greenaway, Peter 15
Guattari, Felix 8, 16
Gulf War 125

Hadrian 2
Halicarnassus 107
Hatshepsut 22
The Hawks and the Sparrows (film by Pasolini) 181–182
Heath, Edward 19
Hector 57
Hegel, G. W. F. 103
Henri III, King of France 62
Henry VII, King of England 62
Heston, Charlton 48, 189
Heterosexuality 5
Hibbard, Howard 74, 75
Hirohito, Emperor of Japan 145
Hitler, Adolf 111, 112, 135, 138, 146
Hockney, David 15
Holinshed, Raphael 58, 59, 61, 63, 68
Holocaust *see* Nazis, Nazism
Homer (*Iliad* and *Odyssey*) 160, 161
"Hora Staccato" (tune) 106
Hunt, Lynn 16
Huxley, Aldous (*Doors of Perception*) 162

Hylas 57
Hyphaestus 2, 57

Imagining October (script by Jarman) 11, 164, 167–170
Industrial Revolution 36, 101
Inquisition, Roman Catholic 39
Isaac 123, 128–129
Isabella, Queen of England 56, 58, 63, 65, 66
Isle of Dogs (in London) 140–141
Italy (Renaissance and Modern) 70–84, 100, 172, 174, 175, 180–184
Ivan IV, Czar of Russia 161

Jacobite Rebellion (1745) 149–150
Jagger, Charles Sargent 121
James I, King of England 3, 31, 59, 61, 62, 101, 102
Jerome, St. 79
"Jerusalem" (anthem by Hubert Parry) 138, 168
Jesus 3, 29–54, 74, 90, 110, 121, 124, 128–131, 138, 146, 153, 159–161, 174–176
Jews 13, 39, 42, 56, 110, 111, 112, 154, 174
John (disciple of Jesus) 31, 72, 74, 75, 77
John XXIII, Pope 174–175
Johnny (Wittgenstein's protégé) 115
Johnson, Karl 113
Journalism 13, 36, 137
Jubilee (film by Jarman) 11, 12, 13, 14, 106, 130–141, 142, 154
Judas 33–37, 82
Jung, Carl 103, 151–152, 162

Katz, Jonathan Ned 4, 16
Kelly, Edward 87
Kelly, Jason M. 77
Kevelson, Roberta 17
Keynes, John Maynard 113, 115, 118
King's College, London 1
Knights of Malta 70, 77

Labour Party 19, 141, 154

Language (debates over) 79, 192
Laski, Albert 87
The Last of England (film by Jarman) 5, 11, 14, 17, 85, 99, 142–150, 182
Leonardo da Vinci 12, 116
Leoni, Ottavio 73
Lippard, Chris 1
Lloyd, Christopher 31
Locke, John (*Essay Concerning Human Understanding*) 163
London 4, 13, 18, 34, 132–156
Lorre, Peter 33
Love Meetings (film by Pasolini) 180–181

Machiavelli (Machiavellian) (and works by him) 58, 102, 103
Magnano, Silvana 172–173, 184
Malvinas Islands and War 12, 125, 126, 146, 147, 149, 150, 168
Mamma Roma (film by Fellini) 175, 183
Mancini, Guilio 74, 78
Marat, Jean 81
Marlowe, Christopher 12, 15, 21, 55–69, 81, 82, 86, 87
Marxism 7, 108, 132, 145, 171, 173
Mary, Virgin (Madonna) 35, 36, 39, 78
Mary the Magdalen 37, 43
Mausolus 107
McKellen, Ian 19
Medea (film by Pasolini) 173–174
Medieval period *see* Middle Ages
Medusa 72, 74, 79
Melville, Herman (*Billy Budd*) 183
Messalina 52
Michelangelo 12, 77, 135
Middle Ages 4, 14, 55–68, 176–180
Monatigne, Michel de 79
Monk, Ray 111
Monotheism 21–28
Montreal Charter 20
More, Thomas 111

Index

Morrell, Ottoline 113
Moses 22
Murnau, Friedrich Wihelm 81
Mussolini, Benito 172

Napoleon 136
NATO 158
Nazis, Nazism 12, 13, 19, 35, 42, 110, 111, 146, 153, 154, 164, 182–184
Nefertiti 21, 25–28
Nero 53
Neutron (script by Jarman) 151–155
New York 4
New York Times 73
Newton, Isaac 116, 155
Nietzsche, Friedrich 15, 118, 183
Nomads, Nomadology 16
Norway 113
Nuclear power plant and catastrophe 31, 32
Nureyev, Rudolf 15

Octavious *see* Augustus
Oedipus Rex (film by Pasolini) 172–173
Olivier, Laurence 122–125, 131
Olympic Games 2
O'Pray, Michael 1
Orient, Orientalism 162–164
Orton, Joe 81
Orwell, George (*1984*) 168
OUTrage! 14, 68
Owen, Wilfred 11, 35, 120–131

Parks, James Cary 1
Parliament (English, British) 62, 68
Parsifal 34
Pasolini, Pier Paolo 8, 81, 171–184, 195–196
Patroclus 57
Peake, Tony, biographer of Jarman 1
Pears, Peter 131
Peter (disciple of Jesus) 35, 159
Philadelphia 4, 45
Piaf, Edith 163
Pilate, Pontius 39
Pink Floyd 19

Pirates 17
Plato 12, 96, 155
Polo, Marco 162–163
Pope(s) 36, 76, 78, 79, 80, 81
Porcile (*Pigsty*, film by Pasolini) 182–183
Porter, Cole *see* "Stormy Weather"
Post-modern, post-modernism 7, 37, 135
Prospect Cottage *see* Garden, Jarman's personal
Prospero 100–107
Punch, Miss 163, 166
Punk (movement) 18, 132–136, 135

Queer behavior and theory 6, 7, 16, 17, 20, 35, 87

Rachmaninoff, Sergei (*Isle of the Dead*) 165
Raleigh, Sir Walter 62
Ranuccio 15, 75, 80, 81, 82
Ravel, Maurice 110
Redford, Donald 21, 185, 188
Reed, John (*Ten days That Shook the World*) 170
Remarks on Colour (by Ludwig Wittgenstein) 110–117
Rembrandt 76, 111, 134
Revolution 170
Richard II, King of England 58
Richard III, King of England 136
Ricotta (film by Pasolini) 175–176
Robert Bruce, King of Scotland 63
Robespierre, Maximilien 101
Robin Hood 17
Robinson Crusoe 104
Romans, Roman Empire, Rome 12, 44–54, 70–84, 110
Rossini, Giacchino (*The Barber of Seville*) 106
Royal family 146
Royal Institute for the Blind 164
Russell, Bertrand 113, 114, 116, 127

Said, Edward 162
Sardinia 45
Savanarola, Girolamo 134
Scanelli, Francesco 74, 75
Scarlatti, Alessandro 176
Scotland 63, 66
Sebastian, Saint 44–54
Sebastiane (film by Derek Jarman) 2, 3, 11, 13, 22, 44–54, 171
Semiotics 7
Sex Pistols 134, 139
Shakespeare, William 11, 12, 85–107, 144, 154, 155
Shostakovitch, Dmitri 175
Sibelius, Jean 30
Sisyphus 36, 90
"Sky-Boat Song" 149–150
Slonimsky, Nicholas 7
Smenhkare (pharaoh) 25–28
Smiths (rock group) 147
Socrates 58, 110
Sod 'Em (script by Jarman) 154–156
Sonnets *see* Shakespeare
Soviet Union 113, 114, 126, 167–170
Speer, Albrecht 153
Sphinx 28
Stamp, Terence 183
Stampa, Gaspare 191
Stein, Marc 4
Stonewall 4
"Stormy Weather" (song by Cole Porter) 100–101, 106–107
Stuart, Esme 62
Sun worship 21–28, 44–54
Swinton, Tilda 32, 111, 122, 148, 157
Syberberg, Hans Jurgen 34

Taj Mahal 164
Tasso, Torquato 191
The Tempest (play by Shakespeare, film by Jarman) 11, 14, 73, 100–107, 172
Teorema (*Theorem*—film by Pasolini) 183
Terry, Nigel 71, 157
Thatcher, Margaret (and Thatcherism) 19, 42, 64, 65, 104, 140, 142–143, 146, 148, 149, 151, 154–156, 168–169

Index

Theater 2, 60–64
Titanic (ship) 126
Trotsky, Leon 170
Tully *see* Cicero
Turner, J. M. W. 77
Tutankahmen (pharoah) 25–28
Tutu, Bishop Desmond 148

UB-40 (rock group) 148
United States 167–170
Unknown Soldier (World War I) 122–131
Utopia 105, 111

Van Dijk, Teun 63
Van Mander, Carel 72, 74, 75, 81
Van Sandrart, Joachim 77
Velasquez, Jorge (*Las Meninas*) 105–106

Verdi, Giuseppe 39, 176
Vestal Virgins 52
Vidal, Gore 189
Vietnam 123, 126
Vikings 87
Visconti, Luchino 155
Vishnevskaya, Galina 121

Wagner, Richard 34
"The Wanderer" (Anglo-Saxon poem) 87–90
War Requiem (music by Benjamin Britten, film by Jarman) 11, 13, 14, 15, 17, 35, 111, 120–131
Warhol, Andy 15
Welch, Elisabeth (picture) 101, 106–107
Welles, Orson 175–176
White, Edmund 78
Whitehouse, Mary 52

Wilde, Oscar 154–155
Williams, Heathcote 101
Williams, Tennessee (*Suddenly Last Summer*) 183
Wittgenstein (philosopher Ludwig and film by Jarman) 5, 14, 21, 108–|119
Wittgenstein, family 110–111
Wollen, Roger 1
World War I 11, 14, 17, 111, 113, 115, 120–131, 147, 164
World War II 14, 31, 158, 164, 175

Yugoslavia 157

Zamfir 106

www.ingramcontent.com/pod-product-compliance
Lightning Source LLC
Chambersburg PA
CBHW032058300426
44116CB00007B/797